The Science Fiction
Mythmakers

CRITICAL EXPLORATIONS IN SCIENCE FICTION AND FANTASY
(a series edited by Donald E. Palumbo and C.W. Sullivan III)

1 *Worlds Apart? Dualism and Transgression
in Contemporary Female Dystopias* (Dunja M. Mohr, 2005)

2 *Tolkien and Shakespeare: Essays on Shared Themes and Language*
(ed. Janet Brennan Croft, 2007)

3 *Culture, Identities and Technology in the* Star Wars *Films: Essays on
the Two Trilogies* (ed. Carl Silvio, Tony M. Vinci, 2007)

4 *The Influence of* Star Trek *on Television, Film and Culture* (ed. Lincoln Geraghty, 2008)

5 *Hugo Gernsback and the Century of Science Fiction* (Gary Westfahl, 2007)

6 *One Earth, One People: The Mythopoeic Fantasy Series of Ursula K. Le Guin,
Lloyd Alexander, Madeleine L'Engle and Orson Scott Card* (Marek Oziewicz, 2008)

7 *The Evolution of Tolkien's Mythology: A Study
of the History of Middle-earth* (Elizabeth A. Whittingham, 2008)

8 *H. Beam Piper: A Biography* (John F. Carr, 2008)

9 *Dreams and Nightmares: Science and Technology in Myth and Fiction*
(Mordecai Roshwald, 2008)

10 Lilith *in a New Light: Essays on the George MacDonald Fantasy Novel*
(ed. Lucas H. Harriman, 2008)

11 *Feminist Narrative and the Supernatural: The Function of
Fantastic Devices in Seven Recent Novels* (Katherine J. Weese, 2008)

12 *The Science of Fiction and the Fiction of Science: Collected Essays on SF Storytelling
and the Gnostic Imagination* (Frank McConnell, ed. Gary Westfahl, 2009)

13 *Kim Stanley Robinson Maps the Unimaginable: Critical Essays* (ed. William J. Burling, 2009)

14 *The Inter-Galactic Playground: A Critical Study
of Children's and Teens' Science Fiction* (Farah Mendlesohn, 2009)

15 *Science Fiction from Québec: A Postcolonial Study* (Amy J. Ransom, 2009)

16 *Science Fiction and the Two Cultures: Essays on Bridging the Gap Between
the Sciences and the Humanities* (ed. Gary Westfahl, George Slusser, 2009)

17 *Stephen R. Donaldson and the Modern Epic Vision: A Critical Study
of the "Chronicles of Thomas Covenant" Novels* (Christine Barkley, 2009)

18 *Ursula K. Le Guin's Journey to Post-Feminism* (Amy M. Clarke, 2010)

19 *Portals of Power: Magical Agency and Transformation in Literary Fantasy*
(Lori M. Campbell, 2010)

20 *The Animal Fable in Science Fiction and Fantasy* (Bruce Shaw, 2010)

21 *Illuminating* Torchwood: *Essays on Narrative, Character and Sexuality
in the BBC Series* (ed. Andrew Ireland, 2010)

22 *Comics as a Nexus of Cultures: Essays on the Interplay of Media, Disciplines
and International Perspectives* (ed. Mark Berninger, Jochen Ecke, Gideon Haberkorn, 2010)

23 *The Anatomy of Utopia: Narration, Estrangement and Ambiguity in
More, Wells, Huxley and Clarke* (Károly Pintér, 2010)

24 *The Anticipation Novelists of 1950s French Science Fiction:
Stepchildren of Voltaire* (Bradford Lyau, 2010)

25 *The* Twilight *Mystique: Critical Essays
on the Novels and Films* (ed. Amy M. Clarke, Marijane Osborn, 2010)

26 *The Mythic Fantasy of Robert Holdstock: Critical Essays
on the Fiction* (ed. Donald E. Morse, Kálmán Matolcsy, 2011)

27 *Science Fiction and the Prediction of the Future: Essays on Foresight
and Fallacy* (ed. Gary Westfahl, Wong Kin Yuen, Amy Kit-sze Chan, 2011)

28 *Apocalypse in Australian Fiction and Film: A Critical Study* (Roslyn Weaver, 2011)

29 *British Science Fiction Film and Television: Critical Essays* (ed. Tobias Hochscherf, James Leggott, 2011)

30 *Cult Telefantasy Series: A Critical Analysis of* The Prisoner, Twin Peaks, The X-Files, Buffy the Vampire Slayer, Lost, Heroes, Doctor Who *and* Star Trek (Sue Short, 2011)

31 *The Postnational Fantasy: Essays on Postcolonialism, Cosmopolitics and Science Fiction* (ed. Masood Ashraf Raja, Jason W. Ellis and Swaralipi Nandi, 2011)

32 *Heinlein's Juvenile Novels: A Cultural Dictionary* (C.W. Sullivan III, 2011)

33 *Welsh Mythology and Folklore in Popular Culture: Essays on Adaptations in Literature, Film, Television and Digital Media* (ed. Audrey L. Becker and Kristin Noone, 2011)

34 *I See You: The Shifting Paradigms of James Cameron's* Avatar (Ellen Grabiner, 2012)

35 *Of Bread, Blood and* The Hunger Games: *Critical Essays on the Suzanne Collins Trilogy* (ed. Mary F. Pharr and Leisa A. Clark, 2012)

36 *The Sex Is Out of This World: Essays on the Carnal Side of Science Fiction* (ed. Sherry Ginn and Michael G. Cornelius, 2012)

37 *Lois McMaster Bujold: Essays on a Modern Master of Science Fiction and Fantasy* (ed. Janet Brennan Croft, 2013)

38 *Girls Transforming: Invisibility and Age-Shifting in Children's Fantasy Fiction Since the 1970s* (Sanna Lehtonen, 2013)

39 Doctor Who *in Time and Space: Essays on Themes, Characters, History and Fandom, 1963–2012* (ed. Gillian I. Leitch, 2013)

40 *The Worlds of* Farscape: *Essays on the Groundbreaking Television Series* (ed. Sherry Ginn, 2013)

41 *Orbiting Ray Bradbury's Mars: Biographical, Anthropological, Literary, Scientific and Other Perspectives* (ed. Gloria McMillan, 2013)

42 *The Heritage of Heinlein: A Critical Reading of the Fiction Television Series* (Thomas D. Clareson and Joe Sanders, 2014)

43 *The Past That Might Have Been, the Future That May Come: Women Writing Fantastic Fiction, 1960s to the Present* (Lauren J. Lacey, 2014)

44 *Environments in Science Fiction: Essays on Alternative Spaces* (ed. Susan M. Bernardo, 2014)

45 *Discworld and the Disciplines: Critical Approaches to the Terry Pratchett Works* (ed. Anne Hiebert Alton and William C. Spruiell, 2014)

46 *Nature and the Numinous in Mythopoeic Fantasy Literature* (Christopher Straw Brawley, 2014)

47 *J.R.R. Tolkien, Robert E. Howard and the Birth of Modern Fantasy* (Deke Parsons, 2014)

48 *The Monomyth in American Science Fiction Films: 28 Visions of the Hero's Journey* (Donald E. Palumbo, 2014)

49 *The Fantastic in Holocaust Literature and Film: Critical Perspectives* (ed. Judith B. Kerman and John Edgar Browning, 2014)

50 Star Wars *in the Public Square:* The Clone Wars *as Political Dialogue* (Derek R. Sweet, 2016)

51 *An Asimov Companion: Characters, Places and Terms in the Robot/Empire/Foundation Metaseries* (Donald E. Palumbo, 2016)

52 *Michael Moorcock: Fiction, Fantasy and the World's Pain* (Mark Scroggins, 2016)

53 *The Last Midnight: Essays on Apocalyptic Narratives in Millennial Media* (ed. Leisa A. Clark, Amanda Firestone and Mary F. Pharr, 2016)

54 *The Science Fiction Mythmakers: Religion, Science and Philosophy in Wells, Clarke, Dick and Herbert* (Jennifer Simkins, 2016)

55 *Gender and the Quest in British Science Fiction Television: An Analysis of* Doctor Who, Blake's 7, Red Dwarf *and* Torchwood (Tom Powers, 2016)

The Science Fiction Mythmakers

Religion, Science and Philosophy in Wells, Clarke, Dick and Herbert

Jennifer Simkins

CRITICAL EXPLORATIONS IN
SCIENCE FICTION AND FANTASY, 54
Series Editors Donald E. Palumbo *and* C.W. Sullivan III

McFarland & Company, Inc., Publishers
Jefferson, North Carolina

LIBRARY OF CONGRESS CATALOGUING-IN-PUBLICATION DATA

Names: Simkins, Jennifer, 1986– author.
Title: The science fiction mythmakers : religion, science and
    philosophy in Wells, Clarke, Dick and Herbert / Jennifer
    Simkins.
Description: Jefferson, North Carolina : McFarland & Company,
    Inc., Publishers, 2016. | Series: Critical explorations in science
    fiction and fantasy ; 54 | Includes bibliographical references and
    index.
Identifiers: LCCN 2016034276 | ISBN 9781476668093 (softcover :
    acid free paper) ∞
Subjects: LCSH: Science fiction, American—History and criticism.
    | Science fiction, English—History and criticism. | Myth in
    literature. | Religion in literature.
Classification: LCC PS374.S35 S55 2016 | DDC 813/.0876209—
    dc23
LC record available at https://lccn.loc.gov/2016034276

BRITISH LIBRARY CATALOGUING DATA ARE AVAILABLE

ISBN (print) 978-1-4766-6809-3
ISBN (ebook) 978-1-4766-2725-0

© 2016 Jennifer Simkins. All rights reserved

No part of this book may be reproduced or transmitted in any form
or by any means, electronic or mechanical, including photocopying
or recording, or by any information storage and retrieval system,
without permission in writing from the publisher.

Front cover images © 2016 iStock

Printed in the United States of America

McFarland & Company, Inc., Publishers
  Box 611, Jefferson, North Carolina 28640
     www.mcfarlandpub.com

Contents

Acknowledgments ix
Preface 1
Introduction 3

CHAPTER 1
Evolution, Morality and Religion
in H. G. Wells 19

CHAPTER 2
Materialism and Mystery: Mixed Myths
in Arthur C. Clarke 53

CHAPTER 3
Science Fiction as Truth: Sociology, Philosophy
and Theology in Philip K. Dick 86

CHAPTER 4
Resisting Tradition: The Messiah Myth
and Authentic Dasein
in Frank Herbert's *Dune* Series 121

Conclusion 153
Chapter Notes 159
Works Cited 175
Index 187

Acknowledgments

I am greatly indebted to Professor Van Ikin. Without his advice and support this work would not have been published. His words of wisdom and his insights into academic publishing have been essential to the production of this book. I must also thank him for his astute feedback on my original thesis.

I am also grateful to my PhD supervisor, Associate Professor Paul Sheehan. My development as a researcher and writer can be attributed to his demands for precision of language, rigorous investigation and critical thinking. His patience in providing feedback and advice has been greatly appreciated. I must also thank my associate supervisor, Professor Tony Cousins, for sharing his wisdom and insight, particularly during the developmental stages of the project. I am also grateful to Macquarie University for granting me the Australian Postgraduate Award, which allowed me to complete this work.

Thanks are also due to the staff of the Macquarie University Library. In particular, I am very grateful to Rebecca Simkins, my sister and favorite librarian, for her constant assistance in collecting and returning books, especially interlibrary loans.

I would also like to thank my friends and family for their understanding and encouragement. I am particularly grateful to Nathan Finger, a fellow writer, for providing support and understanding during the writing process. I must also thank my sister, Sarah Simkins, for offering advice at a crucial moment.

I am tremendously grateful for the support I have received from my parents, Luke and Julie Simkins. I must thank them for always encouraging me in my endeavors. The patience, generosity and love they have always shown me has been incredible and inspired me to persevere with my writing and to, finally, produce this book. I would also like to extend a special thanks to my mother for first encouraging my love of literature.

Finally, I must thank my fiancé, James Robinson. His constant kindness and understanding has been greatly appreciated. As a science fiction aficionado, he provided me with a great deal of expert advice and information. I am deeply grateful for his unflagging faith in me and for his encouragement and love.

Preface

Science fiction (SF) produces living myths that offer statements about humanity's place in the universe and represent the intersection of science, religion and philosophy in modern society. While the blending of these discourses in SF has been noted by scholars, there has been little consideration of the thematic significance of the coexistence of discordant philosophies in a literary genre that has become so pervasive in contemporary culture. The present study addresses this issue through an examination of the myths produced in the works of four of the most influential SF writers: H. G. Wells, Arthur C. Clarke, Philip K. Dick and Frank Herbert. Furthermore, this study provides a much needed examination of the specific cultural discourses that influence the writings of these key authors.

Chapter 1 examines the intersection of traditional religion and evolutionary science in the early works of H. G. Wells. Well's SF denigrates traditional Christianity. However, in responding to debates in science and philosophy over the future of human society, his works tend to reinscribe spiritual myths. Chapter 2 illustrates that conflicting vitalist and materialist discourses in the writings of biologist J. B. S. Haldane inform the mixed myths produced in Arthur C. Clarke's early novels, particularly *Childhood's End* and the *Space Odyssey* series. In contrast to the scientifically motivated perpetuation of spiritual myths in the early works of Clarke, Chapter 3 examines the deliberate engagement in religious mythmaking in Philip K. Dick's SF. It is argued that Dick's SF draws explicitly from a vast range of philosophical and religious works, ranging from the Presocratics to Herbert Marcuse, to resist capitalist ideologies and construct myths of divine intervention. Finally, Chapter 4 examines the extirpation of the messiah myth in Frank Herbert's *Dune* series, which draws on the works of Martin Heidegger and Karl Jaspers to advocate an authentic understanding of being-in-the-world and promote democratic cooperation.

In examining the myths produced in the works of these pivotal SF authors, this study engages with a range of the scientific, religious and philosophical discourses that have contributed to the construction of human reality since the Presocratics. The mythic narratives of contemporary SF are thus revealed to reflect the contemporary blending of the myriad discourses that inform human society.

Introduction

Science fiction (SF) emerged in the rapidly changing world of the nineteenth century. The development of the mode in a period that saw the popularization of science and the destabilization of traditional religion led to the association of SF with scientific worldviews that eschew religion in favor of the material. However, in engaging with new developments in knowledge, including scientific discoveries, SF inevitably reflects on established modes of thought and, in so doing, incorporates traditional, spiritual ideas into its purview. Indeed, some of the most influential SF works incorporate both scientific and religious notions. Therefore, rather than being a solely materialist mode, SF functions as a vehicle for exploring the myriad discourses that constitute modern reality.

Through the use of estranged, albeit plausible, settings, SF examines pre-existing systems of thought in relation to contemporary changes in knowledge. SF adopts, appraises and reshapes the ideas, religious, scientific and otherwise, that are fundamental to humankind's understanding of the universe. In formulating narratives that express contemporary ideas about the nature of existence, SF thus constructs relevant living myths that articulate the intersection of science, religion and philosophy in modern society. These myths often reaffirm spiritual conceptions of the universe by blending materialist and spiritual notions. The incorporation of discordant philosophies in SF reflects the diversity of beliefs extant in modern culture so that SF simultaneously mirrors and contributes to the store of narratives that form contemporary understanding. We can, therefore, regard SF as a mode that examines the dominant discourses of its time, provides social commentary and generates new myths.

The inclusion of spiritual notions alongside materialist science in SF has been noted by critics. However, there are few works that examine the specific cultural conditions that lead to the combination of seemingly contradictory philosophies in the works of individual SF authors. Instead, studies tend to argue that the social conditions prevalent at the inception of the genre determine the thematic orientation of all subsequent SF.[1] While the historical development of the mode is important, it is vital to recognize that SF texts are also shaped by the cultural discourses prevalent at the time of their composition.[2] I therefore examine some of the contextual factors that inform the coexistence of science, philosophy and religion in the works of four specific SF authors. This work thus demonstrates that the generation of new myths in SF does not only occur because the genre developed during a time of ideological turmoil but also because each SF text responds to the diverse philosophies at work in its historical milieu.

This work explores the myths presented in the novels of four of the most influential SF writers of the twentieth century: H. G. Wells, Arthur C. Clarke, Philip K. Dick and Frank Herbert. By examining the intersection of religion, science and philosophy in the mythic narratives conveyed in the SF of these key authors, this study explores the conflicting discourses that construct modern conceptions of humanity's place in the universe.[3] Given the major influence of Wells, Clarke, Dick and Herbert on SF, this study also illuminates the narrative tropes that have contributed to the persistent blending of materialist and spiritual notions in so much twentieth-century SF. Furthermore, a particular emphasis is placed on examining the cultural factors that have contributed to the tendency for SF narratives to reaffirm spiritual myths. In closely examining the seminal works of these four SF authors, this work thus identifies the mythic narratives that SF has contributed to modern understanding through its engagement with the myriad discourses that construct contemporary reality.

Defining SF

While it is essential to define SF in order to delineate the area for study, there has been a distinct lack of consensus among scholars when it comes to classifying the genre. Indeed, protracted debates over the definition and origin of the mode have hampered the development of scholarly works that engage deeply with specific SF texts. There is, instead, a tendency in SF criticism to propose a definition and then apply it broadly to a range of SF texts, which are analyzed in terms of their correlation with an overarching hypothesis about the genre. Alternately, writers present chronological surveys that assign SF works to particular historical periods.

Given that many SF writers are productive over a number of decades,[4] categorizing them chronologically can limit analysis by inaccurately associating a writer with one particular era. This is especially problematic in the case of an author such as Arthur C. Clarke, whose SF articulates different myths over the course of his career. While broad studies have done much to highlight the importance of SF as a distinct mode, I offer a different approach to studying the genre. By examining works in relation to the specific intellectual context of their author, I present a detailed analysis of pivotal SF works while also illustrating one of the wider functions of the mode. It is shown here that SF is primarily concerned with examining contemporary systems of thought and producing new living myths.

It is necessary, however, to first situate this thesis in relation to existing arguments about the parameters of the genre. Though there has been much scholarly debate over the definition of SF, most literary critics agree that SF explores the impact of science on human society. For instance, the critic Frank McConnell writes that SF "seriously examines the implications of scientific and technological development ... for our lives" (4).[5] SF writers themselves have also stressed the connection between SF and science. Isaac Asimov describes SF as "that branch of literature that deals with human responses to changes in the level of science and technology" (*Asimov* 22). Likewise, Robert A. Heinlein notes that SF is a form of literature in which "the author shows awareness of the nature and importance of ... the scientific method, shows equal awareness of the great body of human knowledge already collected through that activity, and takes into account ... the effects [of science] ... on human beings" ("Science" 4).

It is important to note that these definitions do not regard SF as merely illustrating scientific fact. Rather, they acknowledge an extrapolative function of the genre whereby writers employ SF to consider how science influences existing social structures. Critic Roger Luckhurst also notes this aspect of the genre, describing SF as concerned with "the historical interaction of scientific knowledge and cultural forms" ("Pseudoscience" 404). Given, then, that SF engages with scientific theory to consider the interaction of science with established norms, it is surprising that few studies of the genre focus on the intermingling of science and other social discourses, such as religion and philosophy, in SF. It is this intersection that is charted here in the works of Wells, Clarke, Dick and Herbert.

Essential to this study is the notion that the relationship between science and other discourses in SF is not one in which SF texts represent universal scientific "truths" and dismiss other philosophies. As Luckhurst states:

> The genre need not be subsumed under the strict protocols of scientific truth, or texts be discarded if they generate fantasmatic versions of science.... [because SF] is ... a hybrid form that loops together the material of science with mass cultural narrative, making it a fascinating social locus of conflict, cross-fertilization, and negotiation ["Pseudoscience" 407–08].[6]

Furthermore, modern science itself constitutes an ever-evolving body of knowledge, so it is misleading to assert that any author can represent static scientific truth. Rather, SF authors write narratives that draw on theories that may later be dismissed and replaced by new hypotheses. Therefore, SF does not propound enduring scientific fact but incorporates the changing theories of contemporary science alongside other dominant discourses.[7] As Luckhurst observes, SF is a "historically situated [form] that constantly change[s] shape and boundary as scientific and technological possibilities emerge" ("Pseudoscience" 404).[8] Since science shifts and changes over time as new discoveries are made, the relationship between science and existing systems of thought is constantly evolving.

In engaging with various, and often contradictory, social discourses, SF explores the whole breadth of human knowledge. It is thus a fictional medium that is uniquely placed to explore the nature of human society and humanity's place in the universe. Critics Robert Scholes and Eric S. Rabkin argue that "The history of science fiction is also the history of humanity's changing attitudes toward space and time. It is the history of our growing understanding of the universe and the position of our species in that universe" (3).[9] While I hesitate to subscribe to the sense of linear progression that this definition implies, I agree that SF examines and expands the cultural narratives that inform human understanding. This position aligns with that of Aldiss and Wingrove who state, in their influential history of the genre, that "*Science fiction is the search for a definition of mankind and his status in the universe which will stand in our advanced but confused state of knowledge*" (25).

When defining humankind in relation to the universe, SF must draw on scientific, religious and philosophical modes of thought. These systems of thought all seek to examine the nature of existence and continue to influence the popular consciousness of contemporary society. It is therefore inevitable that religious, philosophical and scientific modes of thought intersect in a genre that seeks to examine existential questions. As Tom Woodman states, "Metaphysics and theology have arisen naturally out of [SF's] common themes, the limits and ethics of science, time, eternity, [and] creation" (126). Thus, while SF is concerned with the impact of science on human society, it must also, by extension, deal with the contemporary discourses that interact with science.[10]

In examining, criticizing and interweaving established modes of thought, SF uses estranged, yet plausible, settings in a way that distinguishes the genre from other fictional modes. Darko Suvin describes SF as the *"literature of cognitive estrangement"* (*Metamorphoses* 4) in which the *"main formal device is an imaginative framework alternative to the author's empirical environment"* (8). In describing SF as cognitive, Suvin is differentiating it from fantasy and fairy tale by indicating that SF is based on the rational, rather than the magical. Asimov makes a similar distinction between fantasy and SF. He writes that, while both genres are surrealistic in that they depict social backgrounds that do not exist, SF offers plausible worlds derived from science and technology (*Asimov* 17–18).[11] Similarly, Scholes classifies SF as "Fabulation" (47), which he defines as "fiction that offers us a world clearly and radically discontinuous from the one we know, yet returns to confront the known world in a cognitive way" (47). I concur that SF uses rational, albeit estranged, settings to subtly engage with the realities of modern social life.

SF is particularly concerned with the coexistence of religious and materialist conceptions of the world in contemporary society. The blending of spiritual and material discourses can be witnessed in some of the most influential SF narratives of the twentieth century. David Seed notes in *Science Fiction: A Very Short Introduction* (2011) that "religion has remained an important focus throughout the development of science fiction" (123) but has been ignored by critics in favor of more materialist themes (123). However, there have been some recent exceptions to this rule. Chief among them is Adam Roberts' 2006 work *The History of Science Fiction*. Roberts' valuable chronological survey of the genre identifies and examines a vast range of SF texts that incorporate both religious and materialist notions. In charting the intersection of materialism and spiritualism in SF, Roberts' study asserts that the most influential SF texts articulate a "religious dialectic" (3). Additionally, Woodman's 1979 article notes that much SF takes religion as a central theme and becomes a "vehicle for metaphysical and even theistic speculations" (110).

Other SF critics have made passing observations about the prevalence of religious ideas in SF. For instance, David N. Samuelson writes that "sf judged both aesthetically and commercially successful often mixes hard science with mysticism" (496) and, in a 2005 work, Stephen R. L. Clarke similarly notes that "science fiction is often 'religious' in a wider sense" (95). Thus, as James F. McGrath observes in *Religion and Science Fiction* (2011), the connection between religion and SF has become a fairly regular subject for discussion in recent years; however, it has been treated in a fragmentary way (1). Although critics have acknowledged the centrality of religion in SF, most note the trait in passing without considering why spiritual themes have been a persistent element in SF narratives since the genre's inception. When scholars do posit a rationale for the prevalence of religious notions in SF, they tend to point to the origins of the genre, a subject that has been controversial in itself.

Broadly speaking, there are three distinct contexts that have been put forward by critics as having originated SF. These are Greek Antiquity, seventeenth-century Europe and nineteenth-century Europe. Luckhurst observes that assertions regarding the inception of the genre are often influenced by each critic's conceptualization of the mode (*Science* 15). For example, he comments that, where critics stress the scientific aspects of SF, the scientific revolution of the seventeenth century is proposed as the site of the genre's emergence whereas when others emphasize the "sublime imagination of SF" (16) the genre tends to be traced back from the Gothic and Romantic toward classical mythology (16). The understanding of SF upon which this thesis rests is that, although the seventeenth century saw the emergence of stories that, retrospectively, can be seen to display some of the hallmarks of SF, the genre did not fully develop or flourish until the nineteenth century. The rapid social change that characterized the nineteenth century in Europe led writers, including H. G. Wells, to experiment with SF as a form that could be used to articulate new myths for the modern world.

Difficulties arise when SF histories place the origins of the genre in Ancient Greece because there is then an onus on the writer to propose a connection between ancient texts and contemporary SF.[12] Aldiss and Wingrove argue that attempts by SF critics to identify ancient and illustrious forerunners to modern SF lead to "the error of spurious continuity—of perceiving a connection or influence where none exists" (28). Indeed, critic Robert Conquest flatly denies that there is any connection between Ancient Greek narratives, seventeenth century stories of interplanetary flight, and contemporary SF (36). Additionally, on a thematic level, we cannot regard Ancient Greek texts as embodying the characteristic consciousness of the influence of science on society that we expect from SF. As Stephen R. L. Clarke observes, Greek myth articulates no awareness of science or technology (96). Seed goes so far as to also dismiss seventeenth-century narratives of space flight, such as Cyrano de Bergerac's *The Comical History of the States and Empires of the Moon* (1657),[13] as fantasy because they make no attempt to explain the technology used for the journey (*Science* 6).

Roberts charts the development of SF from late sixteenth- and early seventeenth-century works such as Johannes Kepler's *Somnium* (1634), Cyrano de Bergerac's writings and Francis Godwin's *The Man in the Moone: or, A Discourse of a Voyage Thither by Domingo Gonsales, the Speedy Messenger* (1638) (*The History* ix). According to Roberts' historicized definition, SF is a form of fantastic romance in which the implausible magic of fantasy is displaced by the materialist discourse of science (xi). For Roberts, magical and spiritual fantasies are linked with Catholicism, and materialism corresponds with Protestant humanism. However, he argues that "a distinctive Catholic strand ... is present in the vast majority of ... SF" (xi) so that "science fiction is determined ... by the dialectic between 'Protestant' and 'Catholic' ... that emerges out of the seventeenth century" (xi–xii).

Although Roberts comments that the fantastic voyages of the Ancient Greek novel can be regarded as the roots of SF, the main thrust of his thesis relies on the assumption that the genre truly emerged and flourished following the Protestant Reformation (*The History* vii). This later point of origin allows Roberts to single out a specific context and propose a historically determined hypothesis about the thematic concerns of SF. He argues that "the genre ... still bears the imprint of the cultural crisis that gave it birth, and that this crisis ... [was] a European religious one" (3).[14] Roberts' history is particularly valuable for its recognition of the centrality of the interaction of materialist and spiritual discourses in SF. Of course, the Reformation was not the only site of ideological change in Europe preceding the ascendance of SF as a popular genre. Stephen R. L. Clarke also argues that SF has "taken its start from religion, or at least from a religious revolution" (96) but cites the Enlightenment of the seventeenth and eighteenth centuries as the source of this religious catalyst.

Importantly, the short history model, which suggests that SF did not take shape until the nineteenth century, also regards SF as having developed during a time of rapid scientific development and religious upheaval. It is with the short history that this thesis will align.[15] Peter Nicholls, in his entry "History of SF" in *The Encyclopedia of Science Fiction*, also argues in favor of the short history:

> Sf ... requires a consciousness of the scientific outlook, and ... a sense of the possibilities of change, whether social or technological. A cognitive, scientific way of viewing the world did not emerge until the seventeenth century, and did not percolate into society at large ... until the ... nineteenth ... [and] a sense of the fragility of social structures and their potential for change did not ... become widespread until the political revolutions of the late eighteenth century.

Aldiss and Wingrove make a similar observation, explaining that "The evolutionary revolution and the Industrial Revolution occurred in the same period of time" (29) so that living conditions, social structures and worldviews were changing rapidly and simultaneously in the nineteenth century.[16] Tatiana Chernyshova, in her article "Science Fiction and Myth Creation in our Age" (1976), also writes that the popularization of science in the nineteenth century meant that the popular consciousness was no longer being exclusively informed by religious doctrines and began to be influenced by science (351). This development, facilitated by technological change, illuminated the power of science to impact established systems of thought and behavior. Subsequently, SF began to flourish as a mode that examines the influence of science on traditional social structures and offers unitary myths that articulate the intersection of science and religion in the modern world.

Thus SF developed as a response to the changing world of the nineteenth century and engages with the wide range of discourses that inform contemporary society. This means that the estranged settings of SF narratives are built on the reality that we know and, therefore, incorporate the myriad philosophies that exist in the modern world. Rather than producing an exclusively materialist outlook, SF embodies the intersection of spiritual, philosophical and materialist discourses. For this reason, we often see scientifically plausible scenarios depicted alongside spiritual entities in twentieth-century SF so that the myths propounded by SF tend to reflect the contemporary blending of discordant philosophies.

Myth

It is necessary to clarify here what is meant by "myth." When I propose that SF generates modern myths, I am suggesting that it creates narratives that are significant to humankind in that they articulate powerful statements about the universe and humanity's place in it. Under this conception, myth is not regarded as a fictional or out-dated mode that presents stories about ancient gods but as a narrative form that is vital to human society because it provides ways of understanding the nature of existence. SF, as a genre that incorporates diverse systems of thought, is well situated to produce combinatory narratives that position humanity in relation to the universe. We see that SF critically examines, integrates and reworks existing systems of thought and, in doing so, provides myths that reflect contemporary concerns and beliefs.

In regarding SF myth as articulating true reflections on the nature of the universe, this study is fundamentally different from other works that explore the connection between SF and myth. Chernyshova describes SF as a site of modern myth creation but regards myth as constituting "a false image of reality" ("Science" 347). She argues that SF is a mode in which the exact knowledge of science is transformed into the kind of "everyday thought" (352) that the mass consciousness can adopt (353).[17] For Chernyshova, SF plays a vital role in the popularization of science and can be said to mythologize science in that it presents a false version of science that is communicable to the masses (353). This conception of SF differs from that propounded in this study, which argues that SF incorporates contemporary discourses, including science, not to simply communicate scientific theories to the masses, but to critically reflect on the influence of such discourses on human society and to articulate new truths about the universe.

Other works that examine the link between SF and myth tend to take a Jungian approach. C. G. Jung describes myths as "revelations of the preconscious psyche" ("The Psychology" 154) that metaphorically express archetypal content (221). This definition regards myth as reflecting inner reality, or psychological needs, rather than articulating ideas about external reality. Thomas C. Sutton and Marilyn Sutton argue that SF acts as myth in this sense. They assert in their 1969 article "Science Fiction and Mythology" that "myth attempts to project inner reality ... in the metaphor of outer reality" (232). Similarly, Kenneth L. Golden adopts this view in *Science Fiction, Myth, and Jungian Psychology* (1995), writing that "Myth ... relate[s] to the universe within" (8). Myth, then, for Jungian critics, is a metaphorical, or fictional, representation of the human psyche, whereas science, by comparison, attempts to represent humanity's understanding of "objective reality" (Sutton and Sutton 232).

For Golden, SF texts produce a "new mythology" (21) to replace traditional worldviews, which Jung believes have lost validity in the modern world, with technological fantasies (Jung, *Flying* 22–23; Golden 10). Jung argues that, in the twentieth century, "rationalist enlightenment predominates" (*Flying* 22), and that, subsequently, "archetype[s] ... take the form of ... technological construction[s]" (23). In *Flying Saucers: A Modern Myth of Things Seen in the Sky* (1959), Jung argues that stories of UFO encounters are "psychic projections" (147) that constitute a modern revision of myths of metaphysical intervention (23). Thus, studies that view SF myth in the Jungian sense regard SF as reflecting an inner world of psychological needs and desires.

This study resists such a view of myth and instead argues that SF produces myths that seek to comment on and reflect external reality. I regard myth as a term to describe the narratives that inform humankind's understanding of all facets of existence, including human sociology and the nature of the universe. In this sense, myth is not distinct from science but, rather, incorporates it.

I suggest that contemporary society is informed by a range of mythic types, including scientific theories, religious doctrines, political ideologies and SF, which produces new myths that incorporate and rework all other mythic forms. This is not to suggest that the individual stories in SF are presented as true narratives. However, some SF narratives, particularly those written by the most renowned SF authors of the twentieth century, use fiction to comment on the real world and to present serious ideas about the nature of the universe. These illustrations of the universe become mythic in that they examine existing worldviews and suggest certain truths about existence.

This definition of myths as socially important narratives aligns with contemporary scholarship. In particular, I take the view of myth articulated by William G. Doty in his comprehensive study *Mythography: The Study of Myths and Rituals* (2000). In it, he writes that a mythological corpus consists of a "complex network of myths that are ... culturally important ... stories" (33), which use metaphoric and symbolic language to describe "aspects of the real, experienced world and ... humankind's roles and relative statuses within it" (33). Doty argues that myths convey "the political and moral values of a culture and ... provide systems of interpreting ... individual experience within a universal perspective" (33). He notes that myths may involve the intervention of "suprahuman entities" (33) and include "aspects of the natural and cultural orders" (33) known to humanity. Thus, according to Doty's definition, while myth may include supernatural beings, it is also informed by other cultural discourses, including science. It should not, then, be seen as a mode that opposes empirical science.[18]

There has, however, been a lingering suggestion in scholarship that myth is the primitive equivalent of modern science and will eventually be subsumed by empirical thought.[19] To account for the ongoing association of myth with falsehood and illusion, Doty points to the linguistic development of the term *myth*. He writes that *myth* derives from the Greek *mythos*, meaning "word" or "story," and that "*mythos* came into Latin as *fabula*, the basis of both 'fable' and 'fabulous'" (6; 7). Thus, myth became associated with fictional invention. The conception of myth as falsehood has tended, particularly in nineteenth-century scholarship, to cast myth in a pejorative light. However, twentieth-century thinkers, including Alan

Watts, declare that "'myth' is not to be used ... as meaning 'untrue' or 'unhistorical'" (*Myth* 7). Rather, as Watts argues, "Myth is ... a complex of stories—some no doubt fact, and some fantasy—which, for various reasons, human beings regard as demonstrations of the ... meaning of the universe and human life" (7).

Similarly, Laurence Coupe writes that "'mythology'—the body of inherited myths in any culture" (4) articulates "narratives which human beings take to be crucial to their understanding of the world" (4). Thus, while modern humanity may regard ancient myths as archaic fictions that bear no relevance to reality, our society is still engaged in the practice of myth creation and transmission. As Doty writes, "Myths vary in *cultural viability* across [a] society's history" (18) so that certain myths become outmoded and others develop to take their place. It is the "*Living myths*" (Doty 38; Eliade, *Myth* 2) that give meaning to modern life, that are the subject of this work.

Living myths pervade contemporary society and act to articulate a model of reality that incorporates, but is not limited to, contemporary knowledge and beliefs. Coupe identifies literature as an important means of extending mythology. He writes, "literary works may be regarded as 'mythopoeic,' tending to create or re-create certain narratives" (4). SF acts as such a mythopoeic mode and is particularly concerned with exploring religious and scientific myths. While SF does generate new amalgamative myths for the modern world, it also perpetuates existing religious myths. Coupe notes the tendency for each new age to reinvigorate existing myths, saying: "The religious beliefs, social customs and linguistic commonplaces of each age are reaffirmations of, and elaborations upon, primitive mythic patterns" (112). This tendency can be observed in the SF of Wells, Clarke and Dick. Although twentieth-century SF incorporates materialist notions there is a frequent recourse to spiritual cosmologies in SF narratives. Clearly this can be seen as a reflection of the continued coexistence of material and spiritual myths in twentieth-century society. However, I posit that the intersection of religious and scientific myths in SF is also due to the fact that the disciplines of science and religion are less adversarial than has been popularly suggested.

Science and Religion

There is a tendency in contemporary society for science and religion to be viewed as mutually exclusive disciplines. However, historically, the relationship between science and religion has been far more complex than such a view suggests. We may regard religion as those belief systems that adhere to an externally generated, relatively concrete set of tenets that guide behavior; that present certain ideas about the universe; and that represent a particular element, or figure, as divine.[20] If science is defined as a discourse that excludes the spiritual and accepts only experimentally verifiable facts, a clear binary emerges between religion and science. Roberts, for instance, defines science as a "discipline which seeks to understand and explain the cosmos in materialist (rather than spiritual or supernatural) terms" (*The History* 4). However, I suggest that, while science differs from religion by being a far more flexible discourse in terms of its ability to shift and change in response to new data, science does not necessarily preclude the paranormal.

John Hedley Brooke argues, in his study of the historical interaction between science and religion, that there exists an "extraordinarily rich and complex ... relationship between science and religion" (5). As he asserts: "The popular antithesis between science, conceived as a body of unassailable facts, and religion, conceived as a set of unverifiable beliefs, is assuredly simplistic" (6). Definitions that regard science as a strictly materialist discourse fail to account for the vast number of scientific thinkers, mathematicians and natural philosophers who have incorporated spiritual notions into their hypotheses. For instance, René Descartes (1596–1650) argues that, although the human body functions like a machine, it contains a divine soul and is created by God ("Discourse" 65; 73; 76). Similarly, nineteenth- and early-twentieth-century biologists, including Alfred Russel Wallace and Lawrence J. Henderson, suggest that a divine, coordinating force controls life on Earth (Wallace vi; Henderson 276). Indeed, science writer Margaret Wertheim argues that physics originated as a religiously inspired enterprise and that a preoccupation with a divine principle continues to preoccupy scientists in the twentieth century (7; 12).[21]

Thus, scientists have, historically, incorporated spiritual notions within the purview of science. This is not entirely surprising if we regard science as a discipline that seeks to examine all data impartially and to employ empirical methods, when possible, to determine the plausibility of each hypothesis. Chernyshova defines science in this way, arguing that scientists incorporate unverified theories into working hypotheses and discard them only when they are proven false by experimentation ("Science" 351). Philosopher of science Paul Feyerabend goes so far as to argue that science ought not to be hampered by methodological limitations but should incorporate all theories. He writes, "*Science is an essentially anar-*

chic enterprise" (9) and asserts that "The history of science ... does not just consist of facts and conclusions drawn from facts. It also contains ideas, interpretations ... mistakes, and so on" (11). For Feyerabend, the conception of science as an objective discourse, governed by strict rules, is inaccurate and unhelpful (11).

If we therefore acknowledge that science incorporates the spiritual and paranormal within its scope, it is unsurprising that even the most scientifically minded SF writers include religious notions in their works. Chapter 2 illustrates this point in relation to the writings of Arthur C. Clarke, which draw on biological theories that speculate about the existence of a divine being in the universe. There is also, of course, an intertextual dimension that comes into play here whereby the works written by Clarke inform other SF texts and the coexistence of science and religion is perpetuated. A similar cycle is observed in society at large by Chernyshova who argues that, even when scientific theories are proven false in a laboratory, they can gain a wider social acceptance that the scientist never intended ("Science" 351). Furthermore, Brooke argues that scientists "[experience] difficulty ... when experimental criteria fail[s] to discriminate decisively between two or more theories" (26–27) and that the process of theory selection is influenced by "religious (and antireligious) preferences" (28). In other words, established myths can influence the production of new theories. Therefore, science and religion cannot be regarded as mutually exclusive, independent disciplines. Rather, they coexist and intermingle within the matrix of human thought. In engaging with these complex systems of thought, SF inevitably incorporates both science and religion into new modern myths. Interestingly though, spiritual myths tend to be reaffirmed in SF, even when authors seek to dismiss established religion.[22]

This book closely examines the way the myriad social discourses of contemporary society intersect and produce new modern myths in the works of some of the most influential SF authors. Chapter 1 examines H. G. Wells' early novels in relation to their engagement with dominant religious, scientific and philosophical modes of thought. The late nineteenth century saw the emergence of Darwin's theory of evolution as a new way of conceptualizing humankind. Wells openly blames religious institutions for having perpetuated social inequalities and advocates Darwinian science as destabilizing entrenched religious systems. However, while there is a sharp criticism of traditional Christianity in Wells' SF, his early novels are also skeptical of the worldviews that emerged in the wake of Darwin's theory, including social Darwinism.

Wells' SF echoes the concerns of scientists, including Thomas. H. Huxley, who feared that the destabilization of religious myth would result in the moral degeneration of human society. Chapter 1 charts an increasing recourse to religious modes of thought, as a means of instilling humane values, in Wells' SF. This study of Wells' early works, including *The Time Machine* (1895), *The Island of Doctor Moreau* (1896), *A Modern Utopia* (1905) and *In the Days of the Comet* (1906), illustrates Wells' deliberate use of SF as a means of sociological critique and mythic speculation. We observe that Wells' SF produces myths that depict modern humanity as reliant on both science and religion, and that increasingly reinscribe traditional myths of a deity guiding humankind.

Chapter 2 demonstrates a similar trend in Arthur C. Clarke's SF. Through an examination of the scientific theories that underlie Clarke's novels, we see that vitalist notions inform the representations of paranormal events in Clarke's early works, including *Childhood's End* (1953), *The City and the Stars* (1956) and *2001: A Space Odyssey* (1968). This chapter charts the influence of the long-standing conflict between vitalism and materialism on Clarke's SF and explores the tendency for his early novels to represent human evolution as being guided by all-powerful alien intelligences. Importantly, this chapter also traces the increasingly materialist orientation of Clarke's later novels, especially the sequels to *2001*. A comparison of the changing conceptualization of biology in Clarke's *Space Odyssey* series demonstrates that SF authors shape and reshape their SF myths in accordance with changes in scientific knowledge and developments in their own personal beliefs.

Chapter 3 examines the way that Philip K. Dick's SF draws on classical and religious thought to develop ever-evolving myths that resist the ideological frameworks of consumer capitalist America and examine the nature of reality. Like Wells' fictions, Dick's SF deliberately offers a sociological critique of modern society. His works also demonstrate the breadth of human knowledge that is incorporated into SF narratives. Dick utilizes the contemporary writings of Herbert Marcuse to comment on his ideological environment and also engages with diverse philosophical writings, ranging from the Presocratics to Martin Heidegger. This chapter explores the progressive development of a new cosmogonic myth in Dick's SF between 1964 and 1981 and examines the correlations between Gnosticism, Presocratic writings, modern philosophy, Dick's personal revelations, and the myths developed in his SF.

Frank Herbert's SF also engages with Heidegger's philosophy but for a very different purpose than that pursued in Dick's writing. Chapter 4 examines the philosophical discourses that inform Herbert's conscious rejection of prevalent spiritual myths in both SF and society at large. Herbert's *Dune* series acknowledges the tendency for humans to rely on religious myths, particularly those that depict a savior or hero figure guiding human life. By charting the influence of such beliefs on a fictional culture, the *Dune* series seeks to reject messianic myths in favor of narratives of human self-determination. Herbert's SF depicts those who subscribe to savior myths as existing in a state of passive ignorance and advocates a state of being that is conscious of the artificiality of the ideologies that shape human society. Herbert's novels demonstrate the self-reflective potential of SF by acknowledging the tendency for twentieth-century SF to reaffirm traditional myths and calling for a shift in focus.

It must be noted that, although these chapters arrange the authors for discussion in a relatively chronological fashion, I am not suggesting that this structure reflects a thematic progression within the genre. Rather, this work represents some of the different ways that SF texts have engaged with contemporary discourses and acted mythopoeically. I argue that the works of these four seminal authors have established some of the key myths that continue to be represented in SF. As Seed observes, "the intertextual dimension to SF is particularly strong" (*Science* 118) so that SF writers tend to recycle the tropes developed by successful writers. Likewise, Roberts writes that SF "tak[es] as its 'standing reserve' not only discourses of science and technology, but also the whole backlist of SF itself" (18).[23] We can see clear evidence of the intertextual dimension of SF in the continued influence of the SF of Wells, Clarke, Dick and Herbert on the genre. Indeed, Clarke was still producing fictions until his death in 2008 and the twenty-first century has already seen television and filmic remakes of works by Wells, Herbert and Dick, while Brian Herbert and Kevin J. Anderson continue to publish additions to the *Dune* series. Of course, Wells, Clarke, Dick and Herbert have also had a major impact on the thematic orientation of the genre. The tendency to explore spiritual themes and to incorporate both science and religion into new myths about humanity's place in the universe can be charted throughout contemporary SF. It is the scientific, religious and philosophical basis of these myths that are charted herein so as to illuminate the specific discourses that have informed the major concerns of the genre.

Chapter 1

Evolution, Morality and Religion in H. G. Wells

For H. G. Wells (1866–1946), the novel provides a vehicle for the critical examination of the whole breadth of human life. He describes the novelist as "the most potent of artists" ("The Contemporary" 154) and believes that fiction writers are uniquely placed to consider the social, political and religious systems that control conduct (155). Importantly, Wells believes that the novel should not only be used for the artistic representation of reality. He argues that writers should use fiction to reconsider, resist and reshape established modes of conduct and the systems of thought that underlie them (154). Of course, social behaviors can only be changed if the mythic systems that inform them are altered. Wells' SF displays a particular eagerness to dismiss the conceptions of the universe articulated by the Church, which he regards as having perpetuated social inequality. To replace established social systems, Wells' SF works to articulate mythic narratives that incorporate Darwinian science and instill moral values. However, in attempting to encourage desirable social behaviors, Wells' works tend to reinscribe religious frameworks by producing new spiritual myths.

Wells' writings have been described as "mythopoeic" by critics including Bernard Bergonzi and Roger Bowen. However, these critics use *myth* to refer to the archetypal and classical narratives that Wells appropriates and reshapes in his fiction. For instance, Bowen suggests literary antecedents for *The Island of Doctor Moreau* (1896), including Homer's *The Odyssey*, and argues that "there are two basic myths which lay the foundation for the ... story of Dr. Moreau: the myth of the island ... and the myth of creation or metamorphosis" (320). Bergonzi similarly notes the correlation between Greek myth and *The Island of Doctor Moreau* (104), which he describes as an "island myth" (111).[1] In a somewhat inconsistent treatment of myth, Bergonzi also draws on the Jungian view of myth as articulating inner needs and "pattern[s] of human experience" (19) in his interpretation of *The War of the Worlds* (20). These approaches to myth are not relevant to this study, which presents Wells as a maker of living myths that illuminate the nature of the universe and posit new guidelines for understanding human civilization.

As critics have noted, Wells' sociological and scientific views reflect those expressed by biologist Thomas H. Huxley (1825–1895), who was a staunch supporter of Charles Darwin. Having studied biology under Huxley at the Normal School of Science, South Kensington in 1884, Wells embraces Darwinian science as a means of dismissing the theological doctrines upon which Christianity rests.[2] Importantly, Wells also draws from Huxley the fear that the destabilization of religion by evolutionary theory will jeopardize the church-sanctioned moral laws upon which civilization rests. Echoing Huxley's ideas, including those expressed in the 1893 lecture "Evolution and Ethics," Wells' SF makes a clear distinction between natural processes, governed by biology, and civilization, which is based on human beliefs and moral laws.[3] As critic John Huntington observes in *The Logic of Fantasy: H. G. Wells and Science Fiction* (1982), "Wells follows Huxley in distinguishing between nature and civilization" (16) and the "conflict between evolutionary and ethical imperatives" (8) forms a "fundamental structural element in all of Wells's early fiction" (21).[4]

Critics tend to regard the juxtaposition of nature and civilization in Wells' SF as an unresolved and ongoing dialectic. Huntington argues that Wells' early novels, including *The Time Machine* (1895) and *The Island of Doctor Moreau*, exhibit a "two world structure" (*The Logic* 21), in which nature and civilization are contrasted. Huntington asserts that these novels set up an opposition between differing states of existence but are "free from moral suggestions" (22). He writes: "in these ... novels Wells does not set out to defend a specific point of view ... instead, he constructs contradictions and then explores their structures and possibilities" ("The Science" 34). Similarly, David Y. Hughes asserts that "in the scientific romances [Wells] is never an explicit moralizer" (66) and Roger Luckhurst describes *The Time Machine* and *The Island of Doctor Moreau* as "ambivalent texts" (*Science* 40) in which there are no consistent lines of argument.

However, I argue that, in his early SF works, Wells examines nineteenth-century religious, moral, political and scientific discourses, challenges established beliefs, and ultimately suggests moral modes of conduct through the construction of new spiritual myths. As critic Ingvald Raknem asserts, "From the outset, social problems were Wells's main concern" (425). Indeed, Huntington concedes that *The Time Machine* encourages the reader to reconsider their world (*The Logic* 55) and Luckhurst notes that Wells' early-twentieth-century works become committed to a concrete sociological stance (*Science* 41). This chapter posits that Wells' earliest, seminal novels, including *The Time Machine* and *The Island of Doctor Moreau*, investigate the elements, both natural and artificial, that inform human society. It will be shown that these novels offer critiques of prevailing behaviors and beliefs and dismiss a range of established discourses. This chapter then examines the presentation of a clear design for the refashioning of human civilization in novels including *In the Days of the Comet* (1906) and *A Modern Utopia* (1905).[5]

It will be shown that Wells seeks, in his SF, to denounce the mythic systems that he regards as perpetuating inequality. He is especially dedicated to dismantling orthodox Christianity. In *The Island of Doctor Moreau* Wells draws on evolutionary science to highlight the incongruities between the biblical account of creation and the findings of nineteenth-century biology, while *In the Days of the Comet* represents institutional religion as responsible for producing thought patterns that sanction inequality. Importantly, Wells' SF does not seek to supplant traditional religion with social schemes based on evolutionary science. Instead, these works suggest that social systems based solely on natural processes will lead to the moral degeneration and ultimate destruction of society. This belief is a response to Herbert Spencer's misapplication of Darwinian science in his social Darwinist model. Spencer suggests that human society be organized according to the principle of the survival of the fittest, a phrase Spencer himself originated in response to Darwin's theory. Social Darwinism asserts that social inequalities are a natural product of biological evolution whereby the strongest exert authority over the weaker (Spencer 307).[6]

Social Darwinism is strongly repudiated in *The Time Machine*, which envisions a horrifying future for humankind, should social stratification be allowed to persist. Wells' rejection of social Darwinism correlates with Huxley's philosophy. Huxley argues that social evolution is a process entirely distinct from that which brought about the biological evolution of the species ("Prolegomena" 37). In "Evolution and Ethics" he states that the development of a morally sound social system depends on combating the laws of nature and safeguarding the rights of all human citizens (81). This approach, drawn from the writings of Plato and Jean-Jacques Rousseau, is also adopted in Wells' SF.

Wells' attempts to represent a humane society in his SF are complicated, however, by the fact that such a civilization requires a system of morality to curtail the natural individualism of its citizens. Given that morals had traditionally been prescribed by institutional religion, Wells recognizes that the dismissal of the Church imperils moral law. This is also an issue considered by Huxley and other thinkers in Wells' context, including Matthew Arnold. For instance, Arnold writes in his 1869 work *Culture and Anarchy* that Christianity is particularly occupied with "the moral side of man" (106).[7] In light of Spencer's misapplication of evolutionary theory in propounding a harsh individualist worldview, Wells and Huxley conclude that science is not an appropriate medium for the communication of moral precepts.[8] However, while Huxley and Wells both advocate a society governed by humane ideals and dismiss traditional religion as unscientific, they struggle to imagine a secular means of transmitting moral values to the populace.

This chapter illustrates that the creation of myths that articulate an awareness of science, reject dogmatic beliefs and convey moral values is the core goal of Wells' SF and leads to the ultimate reinscribing of religious sentiments in his works. His novels tend to suggest that a coordinating, benevolent force is at work in the universe and is guiding humankind toward a better future. Indeed, *A Modern Utopia* explicitly describes a new religion based on this idea. Wells' non-fiction treatise *God the Invisible King* (1917), which outlines Wells' personal religion, complete with Godhead and moral code, is thus a reflection of the ideas conceived in his early SF. Although Wells repudiated his theology in later life and *God the Invisible King* is sometimes regarded as an uncharacteristic aberration within his corpus, I argue that it highlights that the search for a morally desirable myth dominated Wells' career.[9] Furthermore, Wells' formulation of a religious system that differs from traditional Christianity reflects the intellectual orientation of his society. As Herbert Schlossberg explains in his 2009 study of Victorian religion, the early twentieth century saw the rise of new theological doctrines, reshaped to suit modern attitudes (2).

As Adam Roberts argues, "the turn ... in ... [Wells'] late writings towards the religious-mythical and theological fable can be thought of as merely making manifest a core dialectic present in his writings from the earliest" (*The History* 144). Roberts describes this dialectic as "between ... a *scientific* and ... a *mystical* perspective on the cosmos" (144). However, I suggest that the incorporation of religion and science in Wells' works stems from the fundamental connection of science and religion as social discourses that attempt to explain the nature of the universe and humankind's place in it. By engaging with emerging scientific theories, Wells inevitably deals with the religious myths that he regards science as destabilizing. We see in Wells' SF a deliberate attempt to use literature to articulate social commentary and examine the myriad discourses of modern society. His works also illustrate the inability of late-nineteenth-century science to provide the moral values required by civilized society, thus explaining the continued appeal of religious systems of thought in Well's context.

By utilizing the fledgling SF genre to examine and reconstruct the mythic underpinnings of human society, Wells sets the agenda for future SF. In examining the way that Wells' SF rejects entrenched systems of thought and produces myths that reflect new developments in knowledge, this chapter illustrates one of the key functions of SF: the production of amalgamative myths for contemporary humanity. In particular, the failure of scientific theories to satisfy the social needs serviced by religion is a persistent thematic in twentieth-century SF, which seeks to produce ways of understanding the universe that will ensure the positive development of human civilization.

Wells' Views on the Novel

In contemporary literary criticism, Wells is considered one of the most important figures in SF, his early works being regarded as having a seminal influence on the genre.[10] However, the popular and critical reception of Wells' SF has varied over time and Wells' status as a controversial public figure undermined the literary status of SF in the early twentieth century. Critics Patrick Parrinder and Christopher Rolfe note that, after his death in 1946, it took decades for Wells' reputation to be rebuilt in the realm of critical study (9). Indeed, Frank McConnell observes in 1981 that SF had not yet been entirely accepted as a valid area of study in literary circles (vii). I argue that academic ambivalence toward SF can be linked to the mixed reception of Wells' works. Responses to Wells' SF have been negatively influenced by Wells' personal beliefs about fiction and his public disagreement with successful artists, including Henry James, over the purpose of the novel. Wells' belief that novelists should use their craft to enact change and articulate social criticisms led to friction between him and James, who regarded the novel as an Art form that should be primarily occupied with aesthetic concerns.

James and Wells carried on a written correspondence between 1898 and 1915. Wells sent James copies of his works and the renowned writer responded with criticism couched in generous praise and expressed genuine pleasure in Wells' success. In a 1905 letter responding to *A Modern Utopia*, among other works, James tells Wells: "you are, for me ... the most interesting 'literary man' of your generation.... I am lost in amazement at the diversity of your genius" (James and Wells 103). James similarly admires the "extraordinary force and sincerity" (111) of Wells' *In the Days of the Comet*. However, James expresses concerns over the artistic cohesion and realism of Wells' writings. He writes of Wells' non-fiction *Anticipations of the Reactions of Mechanical and Scientific Progress upon Human Life* (1902): "I think your reader asks himself too much 'Where is *life* in all this, life as I feel it and know it?'" (76). Similarly, of Wells' non–SF novel *Love and Mr. Lewisham* (1900), James comments: "I have found in it a great charm and a great deal of the real ... if not *all* of it" (67).

James also publicly expresses his concerns over the artistic quality of early-twentieth-century novels in a 1914 article titled "The Younger Generation." In the article, James singles Wells out, stating that Wells over-represents his personal opinions in his fiction. James writes: "It is literally ... Wells's own mind, and the experience of his own mind, incessant, and extraordinarily various, ... that forms the reservoir tapped by him [in his fiction]" (189–90). Virginia Woolf makes a similar observation in her 1924 essay "Mr. Bennet and Mrs. Brown." She argues that Edwardian novelists "[are] never interested in character in itself; or in the book in itself" (12) but are, instead, "interested in something outside" (12). Woolf is noting here a degree of social commentary in Edwardian novels and the attempt in such works to inspire action and social change.

Woolf writes that the somewhat propagandist novels produced by writers such as Wells and his contemporaries, including Arnold Bennett, "leave [the reader] with ... a feeling of incompleteness and dissatisfaction [so that in] order to complete them it seems necessary to do something—to join a society" (12).[11] Woolf argues that, while novels can be invested in the artistic representation of character or in considerations of the form itself, in Wells' novels the focus is on the external world of society. James makes a similar observation in a private letter to Wells about *In the Days of the Comet*. He writes that he yearns to find refuge in literature but attains no such repose in Wells' novels because "reading [Wells] is really being 'acted upon' in a manner that is akin to conscience and anguish" (James and Wells 111).

Wells willingly admits that his novels aim to inspire philosophical and behavioral change in the reader. While James and Woolf regard the novel as an artistic medium that expresses ideas through complex characters,

Wells firmly believes the novel should be used as a discursive tool, rather than an aesthetic form. In a 1914 article based on his 1911 speech to the Times Book Club, Wells, as he puts it, "[makes] a ... pronouncement against the 'character' obsession" (*Experiment* 2: 495) and advocates a novelistic style focused on social issues rather than characterization and other aesthetic concerns. He further writes: "There is ... the theory that the novel is wholly and solely a means of relaxation" ("The Contemporary" 132) but that he, as a writer, is not content to merely serve as a producer of entertainment for the prosperous few (133).

Wells' 1905 "Note to the Reader" in *A Modern Utopia* clearly represents his beliefs about the novel and his attitude toward his readership. He writes: "I have done my best to make ... this book as ... entertaining as its matter permits ... I do not promise anything but rage and confusion to him who proposes ... to read without a constantly alert attention" (*A Modern* xxxi–xxxii). He further adds: "If you are not already ... interested and open-minded with regard to social and political questions, and ... exercised in self-examination, you will find neither interest nor pleasure here" (xxxii). For Wells, then, the novel is a medium for the discussion of serious social matters, with the entertainment of the reader a secondary objective. Wells refuses to have his intellectual agenda hampered by the artistic expectations of readers or critics. He believes literature to be a means of "get[ting] [his] point over to the reader" (*Experiment* 2: 497), rather than an artistic form or mode of entertainment.[12]

Wells claims that the novel "is to be the social mediator, the vehicle of understanding, the instrument of self-examination, the parade of morals and the exchange of manners, the factory of customs, the criticism of laws and institutions and of social dogmas and ideas" ("The Contemporary" 154). He further declares that the novel "is to be the ... initiator of knowledge, [and] the seed of fruitful self-questioning" (154). Thus, for Wells, the novel is inherently concerned with sociological critique and the production of new ideas and behaviours.[13] Wells writes that he and James were, therefore, "at cross purposes" (*Experiment* 2: 488) because "[James] had no idea of the possible use of the novel as a help to conduct. ... [and] thought of [the novel] as an Art Form" (488–89) while Wells saw it as a vehicle for questioning and reshaping human behavior and beliefs.

Of writers in his school, Wells declares "We are going to write ... about the whole of human life. We are going to deal with political questions and religious questions and social questions" ("The Contemporary" 155). He asks:

> What is the good of telling stories about people's lives if one may not deal freely with the religious beliefs and organisations that have controlled or failed to control them?... We [writers] mean to deal with all these things.... We are going to write about business and finance and politics and precedence and pretentiousness and decorum and indecorum, until a thousand pretences and ten thousand impostures shrivel in the cold, clear air of our elucidations.... We are going to appeal to the young and the hopeful and the curious, against the established, the dignified, and defensive. Before we have done, we will have all life within the scope of the novel ["The Contemporary" 155–56].

Furthermore, in response to James' public criticisms, Wells, writing under a pseudonym, articulates a scathing attack on James in his 1915 novel *Boon, The Mind of the Race, The Wild Asses of the Devil, and The Last Trump*. He states that James' "vast paragraphs sweat and struggle.... And all for tales of nothingness" (108). In a later letter to James, Wells sums up the basis of their conflict saying: "To you literature like painting is an end, to me literature like architecture is a means, it has a use. Your view was ... altogether too dominant in the world of criticism, and I assailed it in tones of harsh antagonism" (James and Wells 264).[14]

Wells' belief that the novel is a vehicle for the exposition of social commentary, in conflict with James' view of the novel as a form of art has, of course, tainted popular and critical responses to Wells' works and, indeed, to SF more generally. James was already a respected artist when Wells emerged on the literary scene and James' works became a stark counterpoint to Wells' own corpus and ideas. Wells himself writes that "[James] was the most ... artistic and refined human being I ever encountered, and I swam in the common thought and feeling of my period, with an irregular abundance of rude knowledge [and] aggressive judgements" (*Experiment* 2: 537). Wells' antagonistic response to James in *Boon* contributed to negative public appraisals of Wells, compared with the older artist. Given Wells' seminal influence on the emerging SF genre, this association of Wells with popular and didactic fiction undermined the way SF was initially conceptualized in the public mind and in literary circles.

Wells' insistence that the novel be used to critically examine current systems and overtly encourage social resistance has also influenced SF by delineating one the genre's primary objectives. I suggest that Wells' endeavors have meant that SF has become fundamentally concerned with the social discourses of its time and with suggesting new myths to encourage changes in human conduct. In his fiction, Wells openly seeks alternative systems to replace those that inform his society. As he declares in his autobiography, *Experiment in Autobiography: Discoveries and Conclusions of a Very Ordinary Brain (Since 1866)*: "if one does not accept the general ideas upon which the existing world of men is based, one is bound to set about replanning and reconstructing the world on the ideas one finds acceptable" (1: 167). This attitude underlies the SF myths presented in Wells' fictions, in which we see the dismissal of traditional religion, the utilization of scientific theory and the construction of new spiritual narratives.

Evolution and the Church

Wells was born in 1866, between the publication of Darwin's *On the Origin of Species by Means of Natural Selection, or the Preservation of Favoured Races in the Struggle for Life* (1859) and *The Descent of Man and Selection in Relation to Sex* (1871). For Wells, these works undermine the validity of Christian doctrines and destabilize traditional conceptions of humankind's status in the universe. In his autobiography, Wells writes that, as an adolescent, he felt that is was "of primary importance to find out if there was ... a God" (*Experiment* 1: 161). The fundamental question that occupied Wells' young mind was "In the absence of a God what [is] the universe and how [is] it run?" (1: 161). Wells is quite eager to dismiss Christianity, regarding it as the system that informed the disorderly nineteenth-century society that he disliked so much. This rejection of traditional religion, and the social system it informs, acts as a catalyst for Wells' search for social reform and for new myths to explain the nature of the universe.

Other nineteenth-century thinkers were also dissatisfied with the living conditions and belief systems extant in their world. In 1890 Huxley writes: "there is an immense amount of remediable misery among us ... which is the result of individual ignorance ... and ... faulty social arrangements" ("Letters" 238). Similarly, Thomas Carlyle, whose writings Wells read as a young adult, also describes the nineteenth century as a time of "endless calamity, disruption, dislocation, [and] confusion" (1).[15] Having been raised in a lower-middle-class family, Wells witnessed the oppressive conditions under which the lower classes struggled for existence in late-nineteenth-century Britain. Indeed, Wells describes his childhood home in Bromley, Kent as a "dismal insanitary hole" (*Experiment* 1: 59).

Wells' early SF also incorporates vivid images of lower-class poverty. Echoing Huxley, William Leadford, the protagonist of *In the Days of the Comet*, describes his nineteenth-century milieu as "a dark word ... full of preventable disorder, preventable diseases, and preventable pain" (12). He explains that this miserable society is the product of systems of thought that are informed by "old-fashioned narrow ... religious formulae" (13) that do not reflect the needs of the populace. He regrets that life is controlled by "rules of conduct ... [and] conceptions of social and political order, that [have] no ... relevance to the realities ... of everyday contemporary life" (13). In Wells' SF, the institution responsible for this "Age of Confusion" (Wells, *Men* 248) is the Church.

For Leadford, social life in Britain consists of "a clear case of robbery" (20) whereby the "Landlord and the Capitalist ... with [their] cheat the Priest" (20) victimize the working classes, who are "herded together" (20) into a life of servitude and toil. Leadford describes his mother's worldviews as completely dominated by the predominantly religious systems that keep her subservient to the upper class, observing: "Hers [is] the accepted religion, her only social ideas [are] blind submissions to the accepted order ... and all ... persons in authority" (25–26). This account correlates with Wells' description of the influence of traditional religion on his own mother's conception of her place in the world. He writes, "the real link between my mother and the godhead, was the Dear Queen, ruling by divine right, and beneath this again, the nobility and gentry, who ... commanded the rest of mankind" (*Experiment* 1: 47). Wells further observes that "On every Sunday of the year, one went to church and refreshed one's sense of this hierarchy between the communion table and the Free Seats" (1: 47). This correlation between institutional religion and class inequality is the basis for Wells' desire to dismantle traditional spiritual myths.

Wells claims that, as a child, he "heartily destest[ed]" (*Experiment* 1: 67) the religious education his mother attempted to convey to him. It was not until his adolescence, however, that he began to understand the power religion held over society. In his autobiography Wells describes a moment of revelation in his youth when "A real fear of Christianity assailed [him]" (*Experiment* 1: 164) and he recognized that he had to "Either ... submit, or, ... declare the Catholic Church, the core and substance of Christendom ... wrong" (1: 165). Wells recognizes that to denounce Christianity is "to assert that error [has] ruled the world so far" (1: 165) but still declares the Church a "disseminator ... [of] fear and submission" (1: 166). He writes that, early in his youth, he realized that "The world would still turn on its axis, if all [current social systems] were replaced by different structures and arrangements" (1: 177).[16]

With the emergence of Darwin's theory in the late nineteenth century, science began to assert itself as a system of thought that could provide alternative, secular myths.[17] At the Normal School of Science Wells' teacher, Huxley, "put the fact of organic evolution upon an impregnable base of proof and demonstration" (Wells, *Experiment* 1: 203). Wells describes his studies under Huxley as "the most educational year of [his] life" (1: 201), a year in which he learned the importance of the pursuit of knowledge as a means of formulating a coherent understanding of reality. Significantly, Wells regards evolutionary science as contradicting the theological narratives that inform nineteenth-century social life.

In *The Outline of History* (1925), Wells writes that "the geological record [does] not correspond to the acts of the six days of creation; and ... [Darwin's theory] point[s] away from the Bib[lical] assertion of a separate creation of each species ... [and] towards a genetic relation between all forms of life" (616). Wells further states that, if humankind evolved from a simple life form, "there [were] no first parents, no Eden, and no Fall" (616). Given that the theological fabric of Christianity rests on the Fall of humanity and the subsequent need for divine grace, the contradictions between the Biblical creation myth and Darwin's theory meant, for Wells, that "the entire ... fabric of Christianity ... collapsed like a house of cards" (616). Wells makes a similar observation in *Anticipations*, stating that Darwin's theory "destroyed the dogma of the Fall upon which ... Christianity rests" (290). Instead of a unique species, created in the image of God, humans become, for Darwinian thinkers, highly evolved animals. For Wells, this means that the belief systems upon which his society is based are not only unfair but are also untrue and need to be reshaped in light of scientific evidence.

Huxley also recognizes that biological science offers an entirely new way of understanding what it means to be human. He writes, "our whole theory of life [is] ... influenced ... by the ... conceptions of the universe ... forced upon us by physical science" ("Science" 149). Through a scientific study of the anatomical affinity of humans and apes Huxley further concludes that "the structural differences which separate Man from the Gorilla ... are not so great as those which separate the Gorilla from the lower apes" ("On the Relations" 144). This assertion that humanity is separated from the animals by no greater structural barrier than that which separates animal species from one another, demands a fundamental readjustment of the mythic systems that had previously elevated humankind above all other life forms. An attempt is made in Wells' *The Island of Doctor Moreau* to repudiate Christian doctrines by illustrating the physical similarities between humans and beasts and articulating a myth that conceives of human beings as tamed animals.

In the novel, Doctor Moreau believes he can surgically transform animals into humans via vivisection. When protagonist Edward Prendick encounters one of Moreau's creations, a humanoid constructed from a bovine specimen, he cannot see "how [it] differ[s] from some ... human yokel" (115). Further, when he returns to London from Moreau's island, Prendick cannot convince himself that the men and women he meets are not "Beast People, animals half-wrought into the outward image of human souls" (183). Indeed, the physiological correlation between Moreau's creations and human beings is so marked that, before learning of Moreau's methods, Prendick initially imagines that the creatures are humans upon whom Moreau has performed a cruel experiment (79–80). In this novel, we thus see the presentation of a new worldview that recognizes the anatomical similarity of humans and beasts in accordance with Darwin's theory.[18]

Huxley's conception of reality also incorporates modern science as a means of understanding humanity's place in nature. He states in 1876 that, in contrast to the traditional understanding of humanity as distinct from beasts, "man ... is a living creature" ("On the Study" 270) and must, therefore, be included within the purview of biological science. He argues that "psychology, politics, and political economy [should] be absorbed into the province of Biology" (270). He further posits that, by understanding the biological origins of the species, it may be possible to gauge our evolutionary potential and adjust our social orientation to ensure the positive development of humanity ("On the Relations" 77–78). Interestingly, however, the social models that emerged in the late nineteenth century in response to evolutionary theory were, according to both Wells and Huxley, just as damaging as the traditional, religious alternatives.

The Social Contract in a Darwinian World

Social Darwinism, as propounded by Spencer, seeks to apply natural law to human social behavior. It advocates individualism and laissez-faire capitalism as manifestations of the evolutionary process, in which, according to Spencer, only the strongest survive. However, thinkers such as Wells and Huxley regard social Darwinism as supporting the social inequalities established by traditional systems. Wells' SF, particularly *The Time Machine*, illustrates that mass subscription to individualist doctrines may lead to the evolutionary decline of the species because natural law does not accommodate the moral principles essential to the successful functioning of human civilization. In opposition to Spencer, Huxley and Wells argue that humankind can only achieve positive evolution if natural law is resisted and the species works collaboratively to create a moral society where science is used to control the forces of nature.[19] Huxley's metaphorical description of human society as a cultivated garden is reflected in Wells' early SF, including *A Modern Utopia*, which also looks to Plato's writings for pre–Christian morals with which to replace religious laws.

In his 1862 work *First Principles*, Spencer argues that the same laws that Darwin outlined to explain the evolution of species can be applied to human social life. For Spencer, the separation of nineteenth-century humanity into distinct social classes is evidence of the evolutionary process at work. Spencer states that evolution involves a change from "the homogeneous to the heterogeneous" (307) so that "The authority of the strongest and cunningest makes itself felt among savages, as in the herd of animals or a posse of schoolboys" (307). He thus regards class inequality as a naturally occurring inevitability, declaring that "in the course of social evolution, we find an incipient differentiation between the governing and the governed" (307). He further observes that the role of ruler eventually becomes hereditary (308) and the community is finally "segregated into distinct classes" (310). Thus, according to Spencer, the inequality of nineteenth-century society is a natural result of evolution. Indeed, he argues that "A civilized society is made unlike a savage tribe by the establishment of regulative classes" (283).

However, as we have already established, Wells "deep[ly] resent[s] ... social inequality" (*Experiment* 1: 160). He hopefully observes in his autobiography that, throughout the seventeenth, eighteenth and nineteenth centuries, "World forces were at work [that tended] to disperse the aristocratic estate system in Europe, ... necessitate new and better informed classes ... and bring all men into one planetary community" (1: 242). Wells' desire for an egalitarian, cooperative society is entirely at odds with the social Darwinism propounded by Spencer. This is not to say that Wells disagrees with Darwin's theory. Rather, he believes it dangerous to apply blind natural law to human civilization and recognizes that Darwin never intended for his theory to be used as a social model. However, as Wells observes, by the end of the nineteenth century, Spencer's "crude misunderstanding of Darwinism had become the fundamental mindstuff of ... the 'educated' everywhere" (*The Outline* 617). This meant that the successful believed that "they prevailed by virtue of the Struggle for Existence, in which the strong and cunning get the better of the weak and ... [have] to be strong ... [and] ruthless" (Wells, *The Outline* 617) to maintain their dominance.

The manipulation of biological theories by individualist doctrines troubles Wells and his SF strongly critiques social Darwinist notions. *The Time Machine* offers a disturbing representation of the future of an individualist culture. The novel's protagonist travels from his nineteenth-century society to the year AD 802,701. He expects to encounter a more highly evolved form of humanity and is devastated to discover that the human race has evolved into two inferior species: the Eloi, descended from the ruling elite, and the Morlocks, a race that developed from the working class. The Time Traveller describes the Eloi as a childlike race of indolent fools (31) and learns that the Morlocks are a monstrous nocturnal species that lives in subterranean mines and hunts the Eloi for food.[20] The Time Traveller proposes several different theories to explain this evolution but, finally, social Darwinist doctrines are blamed for the evolutionary divergence of humanity along class lines in *The Time Machine*.[21] The Time Traveller concludes that "the gradual widening of the ... [nineteenth-century] social difference between the Capitalist and the Labourer" (64) led to the development of two new species.[22]

A similar prediction is presented in Wells' *The Sleeper Awakes* (1899)[23] in which the nineteenth-century protagonist, Graham, wakes from a two-hundred-year sleep to encounter a beleaguered society where "luxury, waste, and sensuality on the one hand and abject poverty on the other still prevails" (458). Graham reflects that his nineteenth-century society was "making the future ... [but] hardly [anyone had] troubled to think what future [they] were making" (458). In Wells' SF, however, we see a recurrent consideration of the long-term evolutionary implications of contemporary worldviews. In *The Time Machine* it is shown that, under the guidance of social Darwinism, the evolution of humanity will not involve any "triumph of moral education and general co-operation" (66) but will instead result in the destruction of both the working class and the aristocracy that seeks to exploit them.

The evolutionary decline that *The Time Machine* forecasts for any individualist society highlights the flawed logic of social Darwinist theory. Spencer asserts that "Evolution ... is a change from a less coherent to a more coherent form" (291). It is this assumption that underlies social Darwinism and implies that, in nature, evolution always involves a movement from a weaker state to a fitter one. According to this view, by following the laws of nature, humans will ascend toward a stronger form. However, this interpretation of Darwin's theory is incorrect. As Wells points out in his 1891 article "Zoological Retrogression," the evolutionary path of any given species does not always progress in a positive direction so that "There is ... no guarantee in scientific knowledge of man's permanence or permanent ascendancy" (168).²⁴ Hence, the social Darwinist deferral to nature imperils the ascendency of humankind by preventing humanity from controlling its own evolutionary development. We see the negative impact of such a philosophy in *The Time Machine*, in which there has been an evolutionary "sliding down" (77) of humanity because the species failed to consider how social stratification would hamper its future development.

Ironically, in *The Time Machine* it is the fitter class, by Spencer's standards, that becomes the prey of the formerly downtrodden, working-class Morlocks. The aristocracy, having established its supremacy through a rigid class system loses the vital ability to adapt to change and thus precipitates its own decline. In seeking "security and permanency" (Wells, *The Time* 104) the upper class metaphorically "commit[s] suicide" (104) by creating a social system that leads it toward indolence and intellectual stagnation. The Time Traveller observes that "It is a law of nature we overlook, that intellectual versatility is the compensation for change, danger, and trouble.... There is no intelligence where there is no change" (105). Hence, the aristocracy, in its perfect dominance of a static social system, loses the need for innovation and evolves into the feeble-minded Eloi. Further, because nature "lack[s] ... absolute permanency" (Wells, *The Time* 105), when environmental change eventually occurs, the Eloi lack the mental faculties to adapt and fall victim to the more enterprising Morlocks, who, as a result of their struggle for survival as underprivileged citizens, have retained a degree of intelligence. Thus, the concretized class inequalities that social Darwinism presents as humanity's evolutionary destiny are depicted, in Wells' SF as imperiling the very survival of the species.²⁵

The dangers of individualism are also commented on by Huxley, who argues in the 1893 lecture "Evolution and Ethics" that civilization requires each citizen to exercise self-restraint, rather than their natural self-assertion, to ensure that "no act of his weakens the [social] fabric in which he has been permitted to live" (82). This sentiment is clearly drawn from Rousseau's *The Social Contract* (1762). Rousseau states that "The founder of nations must ... replace the ... independent existence we ... received from nature with a moral and communal existence" (84–85) in which all citizens relinquish their instinctual desire for dominance and work toward social cooperation. Rousseau further argues that the union of the multitude in a single social body allows for the survival of each individual so that "Duty and self-interest ... equally oblige ... [humankind] to give each other mutual aid" (63). However, Huxley is concerned that this social contract is being imperiled by "the fanatical individual[ists] of [his] time [who attempt] to apply the analogy of cosmic nature to society" ("Evolution" 82).

Wells echoes Huxley's statements, arguing that "In a measurable time mankind has to constitute itself into one state and one brotherhood, or it will certainly be swept down cataracts of disaster to an ultimate destruction" (*Experiment* 2: 752). This is not to say that Wells advocates a socialist state. In his twenties, Wells became a member of the Fabian Society, a socialist group chaired by playwright George Bernard Shaw, but he later dismissed the movement as unscientific. Wells describes the Fabian Society, and socialism more generally, in his autobiography, stating, "We denounced individualism ... [and] *laissez-faire*" (*Experiment* 1: 250) but "Socialism ... resisted any attempt to scheme or even sketch what the world was to be" (1: 262–63).[26] Wells declares that Karl Marx was an "uninventive man" (1: 263) who "lacked the imaginative power necessary to synthesize a project" (1:263) so sought, through the incitement of class warfare, to "reconstruct the world on a basis of mere resentment and destruction" (1: 180).

Wells' SF stresses that any successful social reform must involve careful planning and the communal striving of humanity as a collective.[27] After being transported to a parallel, utopian Earth, the protagonist of *A Modern Utopia* reflects that "If we are to have any Utopia at all, we must have a clear and common purpose, and a great steadfast movement of will to override ... egotistical dissentients" (90). Furthermore, the novel claims that "Utopia cannot come about ... but by co-ordinated effort ... a community of design ... and wise social arrangements" (90). Wells states in his autobiography that, from *Anticipations* onward, "the cardinal reality of [his] thought and work" (*Experiment* 2:652) was to search for such a social arrangement.

Wells' SF dismisses any social system based solely on natural law but represents scientific thinking as crucial to ensuring humanity's positive evolution. In Wells' novel *In the Days of the Comet*, Leadford's friend declares that "science is more important than socialism. ... [because] Socialism's a theory ... [while] science is something more" (30). Wells elaborates on this point in his autobiography, stating that the Fabian Society was ineffectual because it lacked "an experimental and analytical spirit" (*Experiment* 1: 251) and exhibited a "disposition to finality of statement which it is the task of experimental science to dispel" (1: 251). For Wells, then, the scientific spirit is characterized by a flexibility of mind that allows for the readjustment of one's worldview and conduct in response to changes in knowledge and situation.[28] Wells regrets that positive social change is hampered by what he regards as a general refusal to adopt this scientific point of view.

In the 1904 novel *The Food of the Gods,* Wells criticizes Edwardians for being locked into traditional patterns and for refusing to recognize that they live in a changing world. In the novel, British scientists discover an edible substance that promotes gigantic growth, producing a race of giant humans that will ultimately inherit the Earth. However, the unevolved citizens of Britain fight against this development. In the face of sudden human evolution, a staid country vicar refuses to even acknowledge the change. He declares: "We live in an atmosphere of simple and permanent things.... Things change ... but Humanity—*aere perennius*" (106). Furthermore, Wells has the protagonist of *In the Days of the Comet* lament "the infinite want of adjustment in the old order of things" (33). For Wells, Darwinian science reveals the ever-changing nature of the universe and thus offers a view of reality that will produce myths that accommodate for the constant adaptation needed to thrive in a changing world.

The importance of adaptability is clearly conveyed in *A Modern Utopia*, in which the protagonist reflects that "The [Modern] Utopia ... must ... differ ... from the ... Utopias men planned before Darwin. Those were all perfect and static States. ... the Modern Utopia must not be static but kinetic, must shape not as a permanent state but as a ... stage leading to a long ascent of stages" (11). Wells thus suggests that social models adopt a scientific recognition of the dynamic nature of the universe. His SF advocates cultural systems based on myths that change over time to accommodate the evolving needs of humankind.

Although Wells recognizes the potential application of science as a means of intervening directly in the physical evolution of humankind, his SF tends to present myths that adopt the scientific outlook as a means of formulating new social attitudes rather than forcing radical biological change.[29] In his 1895 article "The Limits of Individual Plasticity," Wells acknowledges that "a living thing might be ... so moulded and modified that ... it would retain scarcely anything of its inherent form and disposition" (36). He adds that the "shape and mental superstructure" (36) of a creature could be so extensively recast as to render an entirely new species. Wells thus recognizes that the future could involve "operators, armed with antiseptic surgery ... and ... knowledge of the laws of growth, taking living creatures and moulding them into the most amazing forms" (38–39). However, in *The Island of Doctor Moreau* such use of applied science is represented as horrific, inhumane and, ultimately, unsuccessful.

Moreau's cruel experiments are based on a perversion of the logic presented by Wells' himself in his article "The Province of Pain" (1895).

In the article Wells argues that pain is a protective mechanism that warns the sufferer against the stimulus that causes the painful sensation (195). Wells posits that, the more evolved a creature, the less they will need pain because "higher animals, like man, look before they act" (198) and are "less automatic and more intelligent" (198). Thus, the more intelligent a species, the less they will rely on physical sensations, like pain, for an understanding of their environment. Wells goes so far as to assert that "the province of pain is ... a phase through which life must pass on its evolution from the automatic to the spiritual" (198–99). Moreau echoes this sentiment, arguing that, "with men, the more intelligent they become the more intelligently they will see after their own welfare, and the less they will need [pain as a] goad to keep them out of danger" (100).

Moreau takes Wells' belief that evolution involves a movement beyond the need for pain to a ghastly extreme. He declares that "The study of Nature makes man at last as remorseless as Nature" (101) and sets himself the task of surgically forcing his experimental subjects beyond the province of pain, toward a higher evolutionary form. He claims, "Each time I dip a living creature into a bath of burning pain, I say, This time I will burn out all the animal, this time I will make a rational creature" (106). This approach is represented as horrendously inhumane in the novel and even Moreau admits that his methods meet with continual failure (106).[30]

Importantly, "The Province of Pain" suggests an entirely different approach to encouraging positive evolution. Wells suggests that the adoption of the scientific outlook will allow humankind to grow beyond the limitations of entrenched systems and achieve the intellectual capacity needed to progress toward a higher form of evolution. He writes: "May [humanity] not so grow morally and intellectually as to get at last beyond the need of corporeal chastisement, and foresight take the place of pain, as science ousts instinct?" (197). Wells thus suggests that the development of modes of conduct based on scientific and moral notions will allow the species to positively evolve without the need of surgical manipulation.

Huxley also argues that the positive evolution of the species requires the formulation of a morally oriented society that uses scientific principles to resist the harsh laws of nature. He asserts that "the ethical progress of society depends, not on imitating the cosmic process ... but in combating it" ("Evolution" 83).[31] Huxley thus envisions civilization as a way for humankind to manipulate natural law in favor of a system that will allow for the collective improvement of the species. Likening civilization to a cultivated garden, Huxley writes: "The garden is in the same position as every other work of man's art; it is the result of the cosmic process working through and by human energy and intelligence" ("Prolegomena" 12). In other words, human society, like a garden, is the result of human intervention in natural processes. Huxley calls this interference "the horticultural process" (11) and argues that it is necessary to adjust the natural world to suit the aims of humanity.

The horticultural process is thus antithetical to natural law, which is characterized by "the intense and unceasing ... struggle for existence" (Huxley, "Prolegomena" 13). Huxley writes that the horticultural process seeks the "elimination of that struggle, by the removal of the conditions which give rise to it" (13). Huxley believes that, by devising a civilization in which all individuals are assured of their basic needs, humankind will grow in intelligence and power, protected from the inhumane compulsions required for survival in the natural world. Thus, for Huxley, the positive evolution of human society is an entirely different process to that which brought about the evolution of the species ("Prolegomena" 37). It is a process that relies on humankind's manipulation of the social systems that guide human behavior and the myths that underlie them.

Huxley's statement that civilization is based on the rejection of natural law opposes the individualist doctrines being espoused in his context. He argues that "no society composed of human beings ... will, come to much, unless their code of conduct [is] governed and guided by the love of some ethical ideal" ("The School" 396). This sentiment correlates with representations of utopian societies in Wells' SF. It is observed in *A Modern Utopia* that "the way of Nature ... is to kill the weaker.... But man is the unnatural animal, the rebel child of Nature, and more and more does he turn himself against the harsh and fitful hand that reared him" (96). In this novel the utopian society has rejected, on moral grounds, the law of natural selection. Having recognized "with a growing resentment the multitude of suffering ineffectual lives over which [the] species tramples in its ascent" (96) the Utopians conclude that "order and justice do not come by Nature" (118). They therefore set about fashioning their own, morally-oriented laws. They seek to ensure that every human being, regardless of status or talent, "live[s] in a state of reasonable physical and mental comfort" (96) thus rejecting natural law in favor of a humane system of human devising.

However, in *A Modern Utopia* it is also stated that a successful society must consist of citizens willing to compromise their individual desires for the needs of the social body (28–30). Thus, while each citizen is afforded a life of comfort, their freedoms are curtailed to the extent necessary to ensure the preservation of the civilization and the positive evolution of the species. This means that not all citizens in the Modern Utopia have equal influence or liberty. Such a notion correlates with Huxley's philosophy, which opposes democratic equality. Huxley suggests that the governance of society "should be in the hands of those ... with the largest share of energy ... industry ... intellectual capacity ... tenacity of purpose ... [and] sympathetic humanity" ("Prolegomena" 42).

Such a ruling class is also depicted in *A Modern Utopia* in which a voluntary elite, referred to as the samurai, govern society. It is explained that "Any intelligent adult in a ... healthy and efficient state may ... become one of the samurai, and take a hand in the universal control" (187) of society. Importantly, Wells' samurai are expected to use their superior powers to serve the weaker members of the human race, rather than to achieve social dominance. However, it is also stated that utopian governance "demands a more powerful and efficient method of control than electoral methods can give" (174).[32] This dismissal of democracy in Wells' SF also correlates with Carlyle's belief that the electoral method fails to promote the fittest politicians to office. Carlyle asserts that "there [is] no Nation that [can] subsist upon Democracy" (19) and adds, "the few Wise will have ... to take command of the innumerable foolish" (30).[33]

Despite the fascist overtones of Wells' samurai, *A Modern Utopia* draws more from Plato's philosophy than from contemporary politics. This is not surprising given Wells' disenchantment with the political, religious and social systems of his time. Wells writes: "*A Modern Utopia* ... derives frankly from [Plato's] *Republic*" (*Experiment* 2: 658) and admits that "the ... notion of the Samurai, marks [his] debt to Plato" (2: 658). Furthermore, the protagonist of *A Modern Utopia* notes the similarities between the samurai and the Guardians of Plato's Republic (174–75). Wells' samurai, like Plato's Guardians, are expected to use their powers to serve the human race rather than to amass personal wealth. Plato also notes that a level of compulsion should underlie the appointment of intellectually superior individuals to the ruling class. He acknowledges that good men avoid power because they recognize that a true ruler sacrifices his own desires to pursue the interests of his subjects (*Republic* 29). Carlyle similarly states that "He that is fittest [to govern], is ... the unwillingest unless constrained" (20).

In spite of their disinclination, Plato declares that the best minds must be compelled to attain the highest form of knowledge and share their wisdom with the rest of society (*Republic* 246). It is acknowledged that this life of public service will "[force] them to live a poorer life than they might [otherwise] live" (Plato, *Republic* 246) but Plato asserts that compelling the most intelligent to lead is the best way to ensure the successful development of society as a whole. The citizens of Wells' Modern Utopia are described as having reached a level of universal superiority sufficient to prevent the need for compulsion and to allow a voluntary elite to be formed. However, it is made clear that the samurai live under a set of rules that "forbid a good deal" (191) to ensure that they are not distracted from governance by self-indulgent pleasures. The laws of Wells' utopia follow the tenets described by Plato, who states that, in his Republic, "the object of ... legislation ... is not the special welfare of any particular class ... but of the society as a whole" (*Republic* 246–47). For Plato, and subsequently for Wells, social organization should "unite all citizens and make them share together the benefits which each individually can confer on the community" (Plato, *Republic* 247).

Of course, this expectation that citizens will relinquish their personal needs for the good of the collective also extends to the less able members of society in Wells' Modern Utopia. Wells' utopia consists of highly evolved individuals because of a strictly enforced breeding program that aims to manipulate the genetic development of the species. It is argued in *A Modern Utopia* that "in the civilized State it is ... possible to make the conditions of life tolerable for every living creature, provided the inferiors can be prevented from increasing and multiplying" (125). This attitude is also reflected in Huxley's writings, which comment that the humane preservation of every life may be ruinous to society ("Prolegomena" 31–32). Plato also suggests a breeding program, stating: "We must ... if we're to have a real pedigree herd, mate the best of our men with the best of our women as often as possible, and the inferior men with the inferior women as seldom as possible" (*Republic* 171). Drawing on Plato's theory and Darwinian science, *A Modern Utopia* similarly suggests that "before you may add children to the community ... you must be above a certain minimum of personal efficiency ... and a certain minimum of physical development" (126).

This representation of a social system in which a degree of self-sacrifice is required of all citizens and humane precepts are tempered by scientific knowledge is echoed throughout Wells' early SF. In *The Food of the Gods*, the scientists who discover the substance that will transform humankind into giants are described in terms reminiscent of those used by Plato to describe the gifted few who attain knowledge to serve the masses (Plato, *Republic* 244–47). We are told in Wells' novel that the knowledge scientists build "is so wonderful, so portentous, so full of mysterious half-shapen promises for the mighty future of man" (4) that "the splendour has blinded [the scientists]. ... so that for the rest of their lives they can hold the light of knowledge in comfort ... that [everybody else] may see" (4).

Furthermore, these scientists ultimately usher themselves out of the world altogether, relinquishing Earth to the new society they have helped create. At the conclusion of *The Food of the Gods*, Redwood, a professor of physiology, declares, "We have made the new world, and it isn't ours" (202). His friend, Cossar, a civil-engineer, similarly states, "We do our job and go.... That is what Death is for. We work out all our little brains ... and then [the next generation] begins afresh" (203). This representation of positive evolution as the result of successive generations submitting to a higher purpose is also articulated by nineteenth-century writer Winwood Reade who argues: "In each generation the human race has been tortured that their children might profit by their woes. Our own prosperity is founded on the agonies of the past" (447).

This sacrificial attitude whereby each generation contributes to the next stage in humankind's evolutionary journey is cast in a Biblical light in *The Sleeper Awakes*.[34] The protagonist realizes that his nineteenth-century society spawned the undesirable future in which he awakes and therefore feels duty bound to sacrifice his life to redirect the evolutionary path of humanity. He reflects that "It is expedient for us that one man should die for the people" (463).[35] Thus, in this novel, the individual who is willing to subordinate his life to the greater good of humanity becomes a Christ-like figure, saving the masses from themselves. Plato suggests that "persuasion or compulsion" (*Republic* 247) be used to ensure each individual submits to their social duty. However, as we have seen, individuals voluntarily sacrifice themselves for the good of the species in Wells' early SF.

Thus Wells' SF represents a moral system whereby self-sacrificing martyrs willingly relinquish their individual desires for the general welfare of the community. However, Wells recognizes that the dissemination of moral sentiments in his context is problematized by the destabilization of traditional Christianity, which had previously been responsible for the communication of moral law. In Wells' works, there is therefore a question as to how humane myths of social harmony and cooperation will be re-established in his increasingly individualist world. This is a dilemma that is grappled with in Wells' early SF, which seeks to reconcile myths that represent the bestial origins of humanity with grand designs for moral future societies.

Religious Myth as a Vehicle for the Inculcation of Moral Values

As we have seen, Wells' SF closely examines existing social systems and, drawing on Platonic philosophy and the ideas of contemporary writers, attempts to imagine how society can be reshaped to ensure the positive evolution of the species. Such social change naturally involves reshaping the mythic systems that inform our understanding of the world and guide our conduct. Wells is acutely aware of the contrast between the natural human, descended from self-assertive savages, and the civilized human, whose conduct is shaped by social ideologies. He is thus aware that a firm system of ideas is required to instill desired beliefs and behaviors into humankind. Both Huxley and Wells recognize that religion is an effective means of moderating human behavior.

Wells goes so far as to create his own religion in *God the Invisible King* (1917) as a means of conveying the moral system that he believes necessary for the achievement of a modern utopia. Whilst Wells later repudiates this religion, there is evidence of a recourse to religious phraseology in his earlier SF novels, in which characters often seek for, or believe in, a divine, higher purpose. Wells is determined, in his writing, to reject entrenched social systems and represent new modes of conduct. However, he struggles to imagine a way that moral values can be inculcated without religion. This illustrates a core dilemma in SF, whereby, in engaging with and attempting to resist the dominant myths of their time, writers recognize the major role of religious discourse in the formulation of human worldviews and ways of behaving.

Wells' SF acknowledges that, as an intelligent animal, humankind requires mythic narratives to conceptualize its role in the world and inform its behavior within the construct of civilized society. Although the physiological correlation of humans and beasts is emphasized in *The Island of Doctor Moreau*, it is also made clear that there is a vast intellectual disparity between humans and other terrestrial species that allows for positive social evolution. Huxley too notes that, despite the structural affinity shared by human beings and chimpanzees, a "great gulf intervenes between the lowest man and the highest ape in intellectual power" ("On the Relations" 140–42). Huxley regards the power of speech as instrumental to the social and intellectual development of humanity. He states that, without the capability for complex communication, humankind "would be little ... removed from the brutes" ("On Our" 474). Huxley explains that, without language, humans would be unable to organize their experience over successive generations and formulate social plans (474). This notion is echoed by Moreau, who argues that "the great difference between man and monkey is in the larynx ... in the incapacity to frame ... sound-symbols by which thought [can] be sustained" (98).[36]

Wells recognizes that the nature of humankind is generated by the interaction of inherent nature, or instinct, and socially determined behavioral norms. In the 1896 article "Human Evolution" he explains that "in civilised man we have ... an inherited factor, the natural man, who is the product of natural selection ... and a type of animal ... and ... an acquired factor, the artificial man, the highly plastic creature of tradition, suggestion, and reasoned thought" (217). By this, Wells means that, in biological terms, humanity is simply a highly evolved animal but that physiology is only part of what determines the nature of humankind. Tradition, in the form of mythic narratives, constructs what Wells describes as the "artificial man." By terming the enculturated human "artificial," Wells is signaling that civilized humanity is a social construct, created and manipulated by man-made ideological systems and the narratives that inform human understanding.

Wells thus draws a sharp distinction between Darwinian evolution and social evolution. He writes that "the evolutionary process ... operating in the social body is one essentially different from that which has differentiated species in the past and raised men to his ascendency among the animals" ("Human" 211). Wells further explains that "man ... is still mentally ... and physically, what he was during the later Palæolithic period" (211) and will remain so for the foreseeable future. Wells credits the development of civilization not to biological evolution but to an "evolution of suggestions and ideas" (211), stating that "Morality [is] the padding of suggested emotional habits necessary to keep the round Palæolithic savage in the square hole of the civilised state" (217).

In *A Modern Utopia* the protagonist is told that "civilization is an artificial arrangement, and ... the physical and emotional instincts of man are too strong, and his natural instinct of restraint too weak, for him to live easily in the civilized State" (196). Furthermore, it is a failure to recognize the power of instinctual impulses that thwarts Moreau's experiments in *The Island of Doctor Moreau*. Moreau focuses primarily on physiological modification and thus fails to instill in his creations a system of moral laws sufficient to ensure that they behave as civilized humans. He eventually realizes that his surgical procedures cannot alter "the seat of the emotions" (106), which holds "Cravings, instincts, [and] desires that harm humanity" (106).

Moreau recognizes that "moral education is ... an artificial modification and perversion of instinct" (98) and attempts to civilize his creatures by pronouncing himself their god and enforcing a crude set of moral prohibitions. However, Moreau's Beast People always revert back to animalism. Moreau notes that "As soon as my hand is taken from them the beast begins to creep back" (106) as "First one animal trait, then another, creeps to the surface" (106). Thus, while under the direct influence of their god, the creatures obey Moreau's orders but, when left to their own devices, they soon neglect his commandments. As Prendick observes, "A series of propositions called Law ... battle[s] in their minds with the deep-seated, ever rebellious cravings of their animal natures" (110). It therefore becomes clear that instincts are not dulled by biological evolution but by the civilizing influence of moral laws, which must be continually reinforced. Moreau's Beast People are thus representative of humankind. They highlight the biological correlation between humans and beasts while simultaneously signaling the ideological gulf that raises civilized humanity above the animals.[37]

By outlining the fundamental importance of universal codes of thought and behavior in human civilization, *The Island of Doctor Moreau* illuminates the dilemma faced by Wells' society. Nineteenth-century science had presented a new vision of life on Earth and, in dismissing traditional religion, created the need for new, socially beneficial mythic systems. The effectiveness of religion in enforcing moral codes of behavior is noted in *The Island of Doctor Moreau* when the Beast People revert more swiftly to animalism after the death of their god. Upon Moreau's demise, the creatures ask, "Is there a Law now?" (144) and declare, "We have no Master.... [but] We love the Law, and will keep it" (167). However, with the death of Moreau and the subsequent destabilization of the system that engendered moral behavior, the tenuous island civilization collapses.

There is a correlation between the death of god on Moreau's island and Friedrich Nietzsche's 1882 declaration that "God is dead" (*The Gay* 109).[38] Nietzsche argues that "the Christian God has become unbelievable. ... now that this faith has been undermined ... much must collapse because it was built on this faith ... for example, our entire European morality" (199). Nietzsche is invigorated by the prospect of a "new dawn" (199) in which "the lover of knowledge" (199) will be free to formulate new social ideas, unhampered by entrenched patterns.[39] We know that Wells detested social inequality and held the Church responsible for the wretched conditions faced by the working class in Britain. However, in *The Island of Doctor Moreau*, there is an acknowledgment that the destabilization of established religion could have a devastating impact on human civilization.

Arnold regards religion as fundamentally concerned with morality (32), describing it as "the greatest and most important of the efforts by which the human race has manifested its impulse to perfect itself" (32). Writing in 1869, Arnold recognizes the danger of discarding traditional systems. He writes that now that traditional social, political and religious systems have been destabilized, the danger for his society is

> not that people should obstinately refuse to allow anything but their old routine to pass for reason and the will of God, but either that they should allow some novelty or other to pass for these too easily, or else that they should underrate the importance of them altogether, and think it enough to follow action for its own sake, without troubling themselves to make reason and the will of God prevail therein [31–32].

Arnold hopes that traditional routines will be replaced by a new set of moral sentiments. He speaks of a culture in which love will promote beneficent action and a common desire to "leave the world [a] better and happier [place]" (30–31) by "stopping human error, clearing human confusion, and diminishing the sum of human misery" (30).

Like Arnold, Wells also hopes that a universal set of morals will emerge in modern culture. He comments in his 1897 article "Morals and Civilisation" that "the future of our civilisation depends upon the possibility of constructing a rational code of morality to meet the complex requirements of modern life" (227). However, Wells also recognizes that his society, which had previously been ordered by the political, social and moral tenets espoused by the Church, is in turmoil at the close of the nineteenth century, searching for a set of myths to redefine human existence in light of new scientific discoveries. In *A Modern Utopia*, the protagonist observes of the early twentieth century, "The old ... order has been broken up.... The old orthodoxies of behaviour ... [and] the old ritual of thought ... are smashed up and scattered ... and no worldwide culture of toleration ... has yet replaced them" (33–34).

The pivotal role of religion in shaping such behavioral codes is recognized by Arnold, Huxley and Wells. Arnold argues that the impulse toward moral behavior has been nowhere so powerfully manifested as within religious organizations (38). Similarly, despite his personal antipathy toward the Church, Wells recognizes the value of Christ's teachings for instilling desirable morals. He describes Christianity as containing a quality that "compels men to ... realize their own responsibility for the world" (*The Outline* 607). He also writes that "the teaching of Jesus of Nazareth had in it something profoundly new and creative.... There was nothing in [it] ... to ... interfere with any discovery or expansion of the history of the world and mankind" (615). However, Wells asserts that "St. Paul and his successors ... substituted another doctrine for ... the plain and ... revolutionary teachings of Jesus, by expounding a subtle and complex theory of salvation ... attained ... by belief and formalities" (615). Wells thus acknowledges the potential of religion to produce positive modes of conduct when it is unhampered by undesirable, formulaic theology.

Thus, although Wells celebrates the destabilization of the Church, he regards the teachings of Christ as having established valuable myths of communal love. Wells is therefore concerned that the dismissal of traditional theology in his context will precipitate the loss of Christian morals. Indeed, Wells writes that he regrets that, after the publication of Darwin's theory in 1859, "There was a real loss of faith. ... [and the] true gold of religion was ... thrown away with the worn-out purse that had contained it ... and ... was not recovered" (*The Outline* 617). Wells argues that "The new biological science [brought] nothing constructive ... to replace the old moral stand-bys" (616). Wells' recognition that no system of thought had emerged to sufficiently replace religion echoes Auguste Comte's 1848 statement that "although theology is ... palpably on the decline, ... it will retain ... some legitimate claims to the direction of society so long as ... new philosophy fails to occupy this important vantage-ground" (13).[40]

Acutely aware of the traditional correlation between the Church and morality, Wells notes in 1897 that moral ideas are "inseparably interwoven ... with the development of theological ideas" ("Morals" 227). Huxley also confesses that, although he is "in favour of secular education, in the sense of education without theology" ("The School" 397), he is "seriously perplexed to know ... [how] the religious feeling, which is the essential basis of conduct, [is] to be kept up ... without the use of the Bible" (397). Like Arnold, Huxley regards religious feeling as that which inspires moral conduct in humankind and, therefore, believes that the cultivation of religious feeling is an essential part of human socialization (Huxley 397; Arnold 32). Indeed, Huxley declares that, given the choice between schools in which religious instruction is given and secular education, he prefers the former because he believes that, although theology dulls the beneficial effect of religion, it cannot entirely destroy the positive morals espoused by religious discourse ("The School" 396).

Wells hopes that humankind will formulate a mythic system that produces moral values sans theology. In his article "Morals and Civilisation" (1897) Wells asks, "Are we not, at the present time, on the level of intellectual and moral attainment sufficiently high to permit of the formulation of a moral code, without irrelevant reference, upon which ... people can agree?" (228). It is this question that occupies much of Wells' early SF. Interestingly, a distinction between the religious attitude, taught by Christ, and limiting, orthodox theology is made clear in Wells' 1923 novel *Men Like Gods*. In this later novel, protagonist Mr. Barnstaple is transported to a utopian world in a parallel universe. Among Barnstaple's travelling companions is a narrow-minded priest whom Barnstaple eventually denounces with the declaration: "What you call Christianity is a black and ugly outrage upon Christ" (280). The Utopians in *Men Like Gods* have achieved a moral society that is devoid of theology by accepting Christ's teachings without worshipping him (251). Such an elegant solution is not, however, posited by Huxley or by Wells' early, seminal works. Wells' early novels fail to find an effective method by which a cooperative, moral civilization can be established without recourse to religion.

The society of *In the Days of the Comet* only achieves a utopian world state after green vapors emitted from a comet cause a profound and lasting change in the minds of all humankind. With the arrival of the comet, all humanity is liberated from old ways of thinking so that the "old muddle of ... traditions ... [and the] teaching of the Churches ... [become] nothing but a curious and ... faded memory" (154–55). While Leadford explains that the "Change" (165) did not alter his "essential nature" (165), he acknowledges that his "power of thought and restraint had been wonderfully increased and new interests had been forced upon [him]" (165) by the vapors. These new interests revolve around the reconstruction of human society on humane grounds, a task that seems easy once humankind is liberated from limiting dogma. However, while the novel presents a critique of nineteenth-century society it suggests no practical method by which social change can be enacted in Wells' world. Indeed, the novel ends with the statement that the comet caused "a change of heart and mind. ... [that] dehumanized the world" (200), suggesting that a united, moral civilization can only be achieved through the fundamental transformation of human nature.

Wells presents a more plausible moral society in *A Modern Utopia* by drawing on Plato's pre–Christian model for an ideal state. Like the Philosopher Rulers of Plato's Republic, the ruling elite of Wells' Modern Utopia draw morals from literature. In Plato's Greece, there was no Bible from which to draw modes of conduct, instead it was through poetry that religion and moral values were conveyed (Lee 67). It is thus suggested by Plato that poetical works be regulated to prevent the dissemination of undesirable myths and ensure the communication of beneficial morals (*Republic* 85). Such a notion must have been particularly appealing to Wells, given his belief in the power of literature to convey modes of conduct and create mythic narratives.

Indeed, in Wells' Modern Utopia, the founders of the society construct the Book of the Samurai, an anthology containing "a compilation of articles and extracts, poems and prose pieces, which ... embody the idea of the order" (189–90). We are told that this book "play[s] the part for the samurai that the Bible did for the ancient Hebrews" (190). Under constant revision, this evolving canon expresses "The whole range of noble emotions ... and all the guiding ideas of [the] Modern State" (190). More than just a guide for the ruling elite, "The Canon pervades [the] whole world" (191) and is taught to children in school.

However, the Utopia's Canon is regarded as insufficient as a behavioral guide. A lengthy set of rules, which restrict the physical pleasures indulged by the samurai, are also instated. Furthermore, the mythic structure of the Modern Utopia is not generated solely through law and literature. In fact, the society is far from secular, the samurai themselves following a religious belief system involving a "transcendental and mystical God" (202). The novel asserts that "[man] is religious; religion is ... natural to him" (200) but can be "turned to evil" (200) when hampered by "creeds and formulae" (201). It is therefore made clear that the religion of the samurai is not Christianity, or any other established religion. Rather, the Utopians "hold God to be complex and of an endless variety of aspects ... expressed by no universal formula nor approved in any uniform manner" (201). According to Wells' novel, the promotion of a private, personal religious life allows the Modern Utopia to "[escape] the delusive simplification of God that vitiates all terrestrial theology" (201).

The conceptualization of religion in *A Modern Utopia* as a private relationship between humanity and the divine correlates with the ideas espoused by William James in *The Varieties of Religious Experience* (1902). James writes, "Religion ... [is] *the feelings, acts, and experiences of individual men in their solitude, so far as they apprehend themselves to stand in relation to whatever they may consider the divine*" (31).[41] We see this view echoed in *A Modern Utopia*, which states that "religion must ... exist in human solitude, between man and God alone" (201). Such a definition of religion allows for the construction of spiritual myths and the inculcation of morals but rejects institutionalized systems of regulation and control.

In the Days of the Comet also advocates the deregulation of religion.

Leadford observes that "all men live by faith, but in the old time every one confused ... Faith and a forced ... Belief in certain pseudo-concrete statements" (89). In contrast, the belief systems depicted in *A Modern Utopia* and *In the Days of the Comet* have no organized or institutional aspects. A non-denominational, deistic religion is also outlined in Wells' nonfiction work *Anticipations*. In this work Wells argues that, in the future, civilization will consist of "religious men" (281) who "have no positive definition of God at all" (281). However, despite Wells' suggestion that these spiritual systems are entirely personal and private, his early works represent religious beliefs in a fairly consistent manner and describe a deity that actively seeks the positive evolution of humankind. For Leadford, God is "a Master Artificer, the unseen captain of all who go about the building of the world" (179). His utopian society is thus guided by a divine force, working through a transformed body of humanity.

A purposeful God who guides the development of humankind is also presented in *The Food of the Gods*, in which the new species of giants declares: "We fight ... for growth.... That is the law of the spirit for evermore. To grow according to the will of God!" (209). In the same way, the samurai in *A Modern Utopia* make pilgrimages into the wilderness to contemplate "God's purpose" (205). Similarly, in *Anticipations,* Wells' imagines the citizens of future Earth "know[ing] God ... under the semblance of a pervading purpose, of which [their] own individual freedom of will is a part" (283). Thus, we see Wells' early writings depict a religion in which humankind must foster the values necessary for their active participation in God's plan for the upward evolution of humanity.

However, religion is not solely regarded as a pragmatic means of engendering desirable conduct in Wells' writing. In *Anticipations*, Wells presents a genuine rationale for the existence of God and assumes humankind will "inevitably" (281) retain religious beliefs, of one kind or another. He writes:

> Either one must believe the Universe to be one and systematic, and held together by some omnipresent quality, or one must believe it to be ... an incoherent accumulation with no unity whatsoever.... All science and most modern religious systems presuppose the former, and to believe the former is ... to believe in God [281].

This logic underlies Wells' early SF in which a divinity is presumed to coordinate and guide the universe. Such a viewpoint coincides with the spiritual notions articulated by many of Wells' contemporaries.

Livingston explains in his 2006 study of Victorian religion that, although ecclesiastical theology was on the decline by the end of the nineteenth century, the intellectual discussion of religion flourished and new ways of understanding God and God's relation to the world were conceived (2).[42] Indeed, even Spencer, who seeks to apply biological science to human social life, believes in a divine creative force. He asserts that scientific knowledge can never explain everything in the universe (12; 53) and declares, "A Power of which the nature remains for ever inconceivable, and to which no limits in Time or Space can be imagined, works in us certain effects" (497). Spencer describes the "recognition of this supreme verity" (84) as the vital element of religion, which seeks to engage with the divine power that guides our lives. For Spencer, religion and science are reconciled in their mutual examination of "the Power which the Universe manifests to us" (37) as "an Absolute that transcends ... human knowledge" (xv).[43]

Thus, both Spencer and Wells regard science and religion as united in contemplation of a divine organizing principle in the universe. Given the continued recognition of religion as both an aid to conduct and a way of understanding the true nature of the universe in Wells' context, it is hardly surprising that Wells' early SF incorporates spiritual myths. Indeed in 1917 Wells even develops his own religion, which he outlines in the non-fiction treatise *God the Invisible King*. In this work Wells professes a "profound belief in a personal and intimate God" (Preface) that bears a strong resemblance to the active God depicted in Wells' early SF. This God is deliberately differentiated from the triune Christian God as "a single spirit and a single person" (9) who, like Leadford's God, is the "leader of mankind" (9). For Wells, this religion provides "salvation from the purposelessness of life" (9) by drawing the individual believer into "THE IMMORTAL PURPOSE OF GOD" (50). As in Wells' early SF, the purpose of this God is "[the] peaceful and co-ordinated activity of all mankind upon certain divine ends" (*God* 57).

The religion outlined in *God the Invisible King* regards God as desiring that humankind work toward the moral development of civilization and the positive evolution of the species. Wells therefore asserts that "the first purpose of God is the attainment of ... knowledge ... as a means to power" (52). Each believer is to "increase [their] knowledge and powers" (56) while guarding themselves against "baser motives" (56) and instincts so that "God may work through a continually better body of humanity and through better and better equipped minds" (57). The ultimate goal of this coordinated activity between God and humankind is that "[God] and [the human] race ... increase for ever, working unendingly upon ... the mastery of the blind forces of matter" (57). This purpose safeguards the future evolution of humanity and encourages the self-surrender necessary for a moral, cooperative community.

In contrast with *In the Days of the Comet*, in which mysterious vapors are required for the transformation of humankind's moral orientation, *God the Invisible King* declares that the adoption of Wells' religion will precipitate the "Self-transformation" (58) of the believer. Wells argues that "It is AFTER the moment of religion that we become concerned about our state and the manner in which we use ourselves" (72). He further asserts that the "self-surrender and the ending of the self" (74) that his religion inspires will generate the moral community dreamed of in his early SF. *God the Invisible King* thus clearly identifies and utilizes religion as an effective disseminator of moral values.

As previously noted, both Huxley and Wells struggle to envision a secular society that engenders moral conduct. In *God the Invisible King*, Wells goes so far as to deny the vitality of atheistic morals. He writes that "the benevolent atheist stands alone upon his own good will, without a reference, without a standard, trusting to his own impulse to goodness, relying on his own moral strength" (44). Wells regards this position as tending toward self-righteousness and lacking external coordination. He asserts that "[the atheist] is ... a masterless man. ... self-centred ... unrestrained by any exterior obligation" (44) and, therefore, subject to caprice. In contrast, the believer in Wells' Invisible King experiences "a complete turning away from self" (44) and is "filled with the desire to serve [God]" (56). Wells thus designs a religion to unite humankind in an ever-improving moral community.

Furthermore, Wells differentiates his religious myth from the interventionist doctrines that had, according to James Frazer, made the Christian God incompatible with science. In *The Golden Bough*, Frazer asserts that science will subsume religion as a means of understanding the universe (712). He makes a sharp distinction between religion and science, viewing them as mutually exclusive disciplines. He argues that religion involves a belief that the divinities that control nature can be persuaded to "deflect, for our benefit, the current of events from the channel in which they would otherwise flow" (51) while science is defined by the assumption that nature is controlled by "immutable laws acting mechanically" (51).[44] However, Wells strives to construct a theology that does not contradict science, writing that "no talisman, no God, can help you.... But God will be with you nevertheless.... God will be your courage" (*God* 19–20).

Wells thus asserts that his new religion is compatible with modern science and that, by amalgamating scientific principles and spiritual beliefs, it articulates the spirit of his generation. He recognizes the interest in alternative spiritual conceptions of the world in his context, writing that "the fog of obsolete theology has cleared" (84) and that "Men are beginning to speak of religion without the bluster of the Christian formulae" (81). In *God the Invisible King*, Wells asserts that "All mankind is seeking God" (82) and therefore regards himself as addressing, in his writing, the key concerns of his society.

However, Wells later seeks to repudiate the pronouncements he makes in *God the Invisible King*. In his 1934 autobiography, he represents his religious proselytizing as confined to a brief period during World War I and describes *God the Invisible King* as his attempt to personify and animate a god for the "God-needing people" (*Experiment* 2: 673) of his context. He writes that, during World War I, he became "aware of the numbers of fine-minded people who were still clinging ... to the comfort of religious habits and phrases" (2: 673) and sought to accommodate their beliefs in his writing. He denigrates this reliance on religious faith as "Some lingering quality of childish dependence" (2: 673) and as a "falling back ... towards immaturity under the stress ... and anxiety" (2: 673) of the war. Wells thus attempts to cast *God the Invisible King* as a regrettable lapse in an otherwise atheistic career.

Wells' adamant denouncement of *God the Invisible King* in his autobiography has led critics to regard Wells' religious writings during World War I as an aberration, uncharacteristic of the rest of his corpus. Critic Martha S. Vogeler comments that "The war ... made something of a religious mystic of Wells" (186). She writes that Wells was shocked by the horror of World War I and that, "Despairing over ... Europe's future, and no longer confident that scientific rationalism could produce social progress, [Wells] surprised ... his admirers with a series of novels presenting religious ideas" (186–87).[45] This is certainly the perspective Wells wishes to convey in his autobiography, which, as Vogeler notes, asserts that he returned firmly to atheism after this period (Vogeler 187; Wells, *Experiment* 2: 676–77).

However, as we have seen, there is a consistent recourse to a divine figure, similar to the God described in *God the Invisible King*, in Wells' earlier novels, indicating an ongoing engagement with spiritual myth in Wells' SF. *The Island of Doctor Moreau* and *The Time Machine* explore the impact of social systems, religious and otherwise, on the evolution of humankind and *A Modern Utopia*, *In the Days of the Comet* and *The Food of the Gods* all describe a divine being guiding humankind. Critic Ivor Brown also observes the correlation between *God the Invisible King* and the theology represented in Wells' *A Modern Utopia* (90).⁴⁶ I argue, therefore, that the religious ideas expressed in Wells' later writings are simply an extension of the spiritual notions explored in his early SF.

The ongoing inclusion of religious notions in Wells' SF indicates that, just as in twentieth-century society, scientific and religious discourses intermingle in SF conceptions of the universe. Wells describes civilization as a "fabric of ideas and habits" ("Morals" 221) that are not material but, rather, change over time in accordance with alterations in human conduct and beliefs. SF, in constructing combinatory myths out of the sum of knowledge available to modern humanity, both critiques and reflects the often contradictory ideas that prevail in human society. We see in Wells' SF both an attempt to produce revolutionary myths that articulate new ideas and resist traditional patterns, and a return to entrenched patterns of belief. This paradoxical blending of the old and the new is seen in much twentieth-century SF.

Arthur C. Clarke's SF, in particular, is shown to embody an amalgamation of spiritual and scientific ideas. However, Chapter 2 demonstrates that the spiritual myths articulated in Clarke's early novels are the result of the blending of mystical and materialist notions in early-twentieth-century science. We see in Clarke's works a deliberate attempt to adhere to scientific ideas, which results in the production of a variety of contradictory SF myths over the course of his career. In contrast, Philip K. Dick's SF invokes Presocratic notions, modern philosophy and ancient religious beliefs to reject consumer capitalist discourses and formulate new spiritual myths. Finally, we see that Frank Herbert resists traditional hero myths and spiritual conceptions of the world in a deliberate attempt to reshape the mythic orientation of SF. It is shown, though, that each of these authors utilizes SF as a vehicle for the examination of human systems and the construction of new myths for contemporary society.

Of humankind, Wells reflects: "We are ... caught in an irreversible process. No real going back to the old, comparatively stable condition of things is possible.... We are therefore impelled to reconstruct the social ... organization.... The sooner all men realize that impulsion, the briefer our stresses and the better for the race" (*Experiment* 1: 243). It will be shown that SF writers are particularly aware of this imperative and use their fictions to articulate new ways of understanding the world in the hope of influencing human conduct and ensuring the positive evolution of the species.

Chapter 2

Materialism and Mystery: Mixed Myths in Arthur C. Clarke

In the novels of Arthur C. Clarke (1917–2008) we see the Jules Vernian school of hard SF united with the fantastical tropes usually associated with soft SF.[1] Clarke's novels thus represent a paradoxical blending of materialist and paranormal philosophies. Peter Nicholls and John Clute describe this duality as the "Clarke paradox." They comment that, although "of all sf writers in his generation [Clarke is] most closely identified with knowledgeable, technological Hard SF," he is also "strongly attracted to the metaphysical, [and] even ... the mystical." Importantly, this dialectic is not unique to Clarke's fiction. Rather the blending of materialist and spiritual discourses can be observed in the writings of early-twentieth-century scientists, including J. B. S. Haldane. Therefore, I posit that the contradictory discourses in Clarke's fiction reflect a wider debate within the field of biology and illustrate Clarke's use of SF to produce myths that reflect the complex, and often contradictory, theories about life extant in his society.

Early-twentieth-century biology is characterized by a conflict between vitalist conceptions of life and more mechanistic, materialist philosophies. The latter are based on the assumption that all phenomena are subject to the laws of matter and that life is, therefore, the result of mechanical interactions in nature. Vitalism, by contrast, asserts that living organisms are fundamentally different from inorganic substances in that they manifest a vital influence that is not subject to physical and chemical conditions. (J. S. Haldane 22).[2] In *Creative Evolution* (1907) philosopher Henri Bergson explains that vitalist and mechanist theories continue to coexist in his context because science lacks sufficient advancement to confirm or discount either theory (24). Thus, in the early twentieth century, thinkers were torn between attributing life to automatic chemical processes and regarding consciousness as evidence of something mystical at work in the universe.

In *The Fitness of the Environment: An Inquiry into the Biological Significance of the Properties of Matter* (1913) physiologist Lawrence J. Henderson offers a historical analysis of this debate. He writes: "Since the early seventeenth century the conflict between vitalism and mechanism has ranged over the whole field of biology" (284).[3] Early-twentieth-century scientists and philosophers including Haldane, Bergson, J. D. Bernal, Alan Turing, S. Alexander and Alfred Russel Wallace all engage with questions about the nature of life that stem from the dialectic between vitalism and mechanism created by René Descartes' seventeenth-century declaration: "I suppose the body to be just a ... machine ... which God forms" ("Treatise" 99).

This conflict between mechanism and vitalism is evident in Clarke's early novels and the increasing prevalence of materialism in twentieth-century science is reflected in Clarke's later fictions. In contrasting the evolving theories of scientists, such as Haldane, with the ideas presented in Clarke's novels, it will become apparent that SF is fundamentally concerned with examining the discourses that inform modern knowledge and constructs new combinatory myths. It will also be shown that, while Clarke's later works incorporate more materialistic notions, the vitalist images of transcendent evolution and mystical forces in his most successful novels reinscribe traditional, spiritual myths.

The seemingly paradoxical inclusion of materialist and mystical philosophies in Clarke's fiction has been noted by SF scholars. While critics frequently observe the blending of discordant discourses in Clarke's SF, they tend not to speculate on the contextual factors and rationales that led Clarke to include such philosophies in his work.[4] However, Adam Roberts and Eric S. Rabkin both attempt to explain the paradox and describe Clarke's philosophical outlook. In a 1990 interview with Clarke's biographer, Neil McAleer, Rabkin argues that for Clarke, "Hard SF seems to be [a] stylistic trope ... rather than the heart of the matter" (McAleer 383). Rabkin explains the Clarke paradox as a conflict between the author's conscious and unconscious leanings. He declares: "There's [the] conscious mind that appreciates classical mechanics.... Then, on a lower level ... Clarke seems to want the ability to dissolve himself into something great and powerful" (McAleer 384).

Unlike Rabkin, Roberts describes Clarke as a "rationalist, atheist, Enlightenment writer" (*The History* 213). However, he also asserts that, on an unconscious level, Clarke is "drawn to fundamentally religious tropes of transcendence" (213). Roberts uses this observation as evidence that an opposition between "technology ... and ... magic is radically constitutive of science fiction" (xiv). He argues that "Clarke's particular mediation of the original determining dialectic of SF seems to bias the 'materialist'" (214) even though the "mystic/Fantastic ... strand is strongly present in subconscious form" (214).[5]

I suggest that the Clarke paradox is the result of Clarke's specific intellectual context. The coexistence of the mystical and the material in Clarke's fiction is a reflection of the same dialectic in early-twentieth-century biology. Likewise, the increasingly materialistic plotlines of Clarke's later novels, including the sequels to *2001: A Space Odyssey* (1968), are a result of Clarke's ever-evolving philosophy, which changes in accordance with scientific advancements. Indeed, in a 1986 interview for *Playboy*, Clarke himself declares his adherence to scientific notions, stating: "I write science fiction only about things I know are reasonably true, even though the extrapolations may not be known" ("Playboy" 57). Further, Clarke explains the inclusion of mystical ideas in his early novels in the 1989 Afterword of *Childhood's End* (1953), stating: "When this book was written in the early 1950s, I was still quite impressed by the evidence for what is generally called the paranormal" (239–40). Thus, Clarke's engagement with the mystical and the material represents his consideration of the breadth of ideas canvassed by twentieth-century science.

The works of Haldane (1892–1964) are particularly relevant when examining the notions that underpin Clarke's worldview. Haldane argues that it is essential that the public be made aware of contemporary scientific developments (*Possible* v). He hopes that the "scientific point of view" (v) will permeate society and be "applied ... to politics and religion" (v). For Haldane, the scientific standpoint is one that attempts to be "truthful and, therefore, impartial" (*The Inequality* 2). It judges established ideas and new scientific discoveries objectively and is infinitely plastic. The scientific point of view continually experiments and evaluates new evidence to produce, at each given moment, the most plausible set of theories about the nature of the universe. Thus, according to Haldane, science should incorporate contemporary discourses, canvassing all hypotheses until experimentation or new evidence establishes the dominance of a particular theory.

Haldane thus includes both materialist and vitalist notions in his early writing, but notes that neither theory is able to account satisfactorily for the phenomena of life. In *Possible Worlds and Other Essays* (1927), Haldane acknowledges the materialist tenet that "consciousness depends on the physical and chemical conditions of [the] brain" (204–05). However, he contradicts this comment almost immediately with the declaration that it is "immensely unlikely that mind is a mere by-product of matter" (209). In the absence of conclusive evidence, Haldane is reluctant to adopt either view exclusively. Finally in *Fact and Faith* (1934) Haldane announces a shift in his philosophical views, explaining that advancements in science have convinced him of the validity of materialism (v–vi).

We know that Clarke is familiar with Haldane's works and carried on a written correspondence with him.[6] Clarke refers to Haldane as a "great biologist" (*Greetings* 359) and praises Haldane's *Daedalus or Science and the Future* (1924) as one of the finest books ever written about the future (497–98). Clarke also often refers to Haldane's 1927 comment: "my ... suspicion is that the universe is not only queerer than we suppose but queerer than we *can* suppose" (Haldane, *Possible* 286). In particular, Clarke alludes to this statement in his 1982 novel *2010: Odyssey Two* (219).[7] Haldane's recognition of the infinite wonder of the universe, and his subsequently open-minded examination of a range of different theories, aligns with Clarke's own philosophical approach.

Like Haldane, Clarke becomes increasingly skeptical of mystical philosophies and his later novels, including *The Fountains of Paradise* (1979) and the sequels to *2001*, tend toward materialist explanations of the universe. However, throughout his corpus, Clarke hints at the possibility of transcendent evolution and the existence of highly evolved, godlike entities in the universe, who seek to intervene in human affairs.[8] The incorporation of mystical ideas in Clarke's SF is particularly evident in *Childhood's End*, *The City and the Stars* (1956) and *2001* but it is a tendency that can also be witnessed in Clarke's later novels. Furthermore, one of the most enduring images of twentieth-century SF is the externally controlled transcendent evolution of Dave Bowman in *2001*. Such representations of mystical, immaterial forces in the universe reinscribe, rather than resist, traditional, religious narratives that conceive of an all-powerful deity guiding humankind.

An examination of how life, evolution and religion are represented in Clarke's novels illustrates that, by engaging with contemporary theories in science and philosophy, SF necessarily deals with the dialectical coexistence of spiritual and materialist myths in twentieth-century society. It will also demonstrate the difficulty of escaping traditional beliefs that regard humankind as under the guardianship of spiritual beings when hypothesizing about the nature of the universe and developing new myths for modern humanity.[9]

What Is the Mind? Mechanism, Materialism and Vitalism in Clarke's Early Novels

In exploring the future of humankind and constructing new myths, Clarke's SF must consider what it means to be an intelligent life form. It thus engages with the various theories of life extant in early-twentieth-century biology. In Clarke's novels we see the mechanistic and materialist philosophies that inform his representation of machine intelligences counterbalanced by vitalist notions, which canvas the possibility of immaterial minds and paranormal forces in the universe. Indeed, in *2001* contradictory conceptualizations of life underpin the representation of the two most memorable figures in the novel: the astronaut Dave Bowman, who is ultimately transformed by aliens into an incorporeal mind, and Hal 9000, the intelligent machine responsible for controlling Bowman's spacecraft. While Hal's existence suggests that consciousness can be created by mechanical processes, Bowman's transformation into a disembodied consciousness invokes the vitalist notion that the mind can exist beyond matter. We also see vitalist forces at work in *Childhood's End, The City and the Stars* and the rest of the *Space Odyssey* series. By engaging with mechanistic, materialist and vitalist theories, Clarke's novels reflect the scientific discourses of the early twentieth century, illustrating the author's scientific standpoint. However, the incorporation of the paranormal also works to reinscribe spiritual myths.

The opposition between vitalism and mechanism can be traced to René Descartes (1596–1650). Descartes argues that organic creatures are elaborate automata whose actions are determined by involuntary, mechanical processes. He compares the human body, with its multitude of bones, muscles, nerves and arteries, with the many automata devised by the industry of humanity ("Discourse" 73). He sees the parts of the human body as permitting action in the same way that moving parts in clocks, mills and other man-made machines afford them power to move ("Treatise" 99). Descartes recognizes that the human body is a mechanism "incomparably better ordered" ("Discourse" 73) than any man-made machine but he maintains that it is largely the material resources of the body that determine behavior. His statement that "the soul can cause no movement in the body unless all the corporeal organs required for that movement are properly disposed" ("Description" 171) is crucial to mechanist theories. Although Descartes' mention of a soul belies a vitalist tendency in his writings, his observations illustrate that the study of concrete, corporeal mechanisms can provide a working theory of the human body.

In his 1940 work *Keeping it Cool and Other Essays* Haldane identifies mechanistic theory as a persistent force in twentieth-century biology and, although he argues that the theory does not adequately encompass the complexity of life, he recognizes that "there is a good deal of truth in it" (49). Haldane readily acknowledges that consciousness depends on the physical and chemical conditions in the body, so that it is lost when brain function is impaired (*Possible* 204–05). This recognition of the reliance of life and consciousness on corporeal processes also coincides with materialism, a theory that regards all phenomena as a result of material interactions. Haldane observes that, by 1940, "most biologists [had become] materialists" (*Keeping* 104). Haldane himself remained unconvinced of the theory's validity until the 1930s and, until that point, continued to speculate on the validity of more spiritual explanations for life (*Fact* v–vi).

Although materialist theory did not gain widespread dominance until the late 1930s, the seeds of the philosophy were sown in the first century B. C. by the Roman citizen Titus Lucretius Carus who was a student of Epicureanism. Lucretius is best known for his poem *On the Nature of Things*, which espouses a rationalist doctrine that declares that all knowledge is derived from the senses. R. E. Latham notes the continued influence of Lucretius' philosophy on contemporary society in the introduction of his 1951 translation of Lucretius' poem (9). He explains that, like twentieth-century materialism, Epicureanism looked to rationalist science to debunk the spiritual myths of the past (7). Lucretius describes Epicurus as undaunted by "Fables of the gods" (29) in his quest to uncover the nature of the universe and crush superstitious beliefs (29). Lucretius' materialist persuasion can be seen in his assertion that the "*minds of living things ... are neither birthless nor deathless*" (108) because they are a product of matter and subject to the health of the body (109).

We know that Clarke is familiar with Lucretius' poem and Haldane's writing, having referred to both in his *Space Odyssey* series (*3001:* 141; *2010* 219). Clarke's understanding of materialist theory is also clearly demonstrated in his non-fiction. In *Profiles of the Future: An Inquiry into the Limits of the Possible* (1962), a collection of essays written between 1959 and 1961, Clarke identifies Friedrich Wöhler's 1828 synthesis of urea as evidence that the chemical processes in the body can be replicated by science (233). He recognizes the shattering impact of such a discovery on those who had "believed that the mechanics of life must always be beyond human understanding or imitation" (233) and also argues that science can produce far more efficient systems than those found in the human body.

Clarke draws on the work of mathematician John von Neumann to assert that electronic cells can be ten billion times more efficient than protoplasmic ones, meaning that a computer equivalent to a human brain need be no bigger than a matchbox (236).

Clarke thus suggests in *Profiles of the Future* that, not only can the material processes of the body be replicated by science, they can be improved. He states: "precision scientific instruments simply cannot be manufactured from living materials" (237). This attitude is also reflected in his fiction. In *3001: The Final Odyssey* (1997) protagonist Frank Poole observes that "The kilogram of jelly inside a human skull ... [cannot] possibly be as efficient as a [computer] storage device" (45). This belief that science can replicate and outstrip nature leads Clarke to assume that consciousness can also be manufactured in the form of thinking machines (*Profiles* 233). This assumption is contingent on the materialist belief that the mind is a result of material mechanisms, rather than evidence of an immaterial soul.

We see this mechanistic and materialist doctrine illustrated in the representation of intelligent machines in Clarke's novels, especially in the case of Hal in the *Space Odyssey* series. The depiction of artificial intelligence in Clarke's fiction clearly draws on the theories of Alan Turing (1912–1954).[10] Turing founded the field now called "Artificial Intelligence." He argues, in his writings, that the human brain is analogous to a digital computer. Turing's term "machine intelligence" indicates his belief in the material basis for intelligence and, hence, the possibility of physically constructing a consciousness. Turing was experimenting with the concept of machine intelligence as early as 1941, when he circulated a paper on the subject among his colleagues at the Government Code and Cipher School (Copeland 353). In 1947, he delivered the earliest known public lecture to mention computer intelligence (Copeland 2). Turing had thus been researching machine intelligence for a decade before a Dartmouth College conference established Artificial Intelligence as a recognized field of study in 1956.

Turing espouses the same materialist rhetoric that is later adopted by Clarke. In a 1948 report Turing argues that "a ... reason for believing in the possibility of making thinking machines is the fact that it is possible to make machinery to imitate any small part of man" ("Intelligent" 420). He adds that he is unable to accept any part of the theological doctrines that regard thinking as a function of humanity's immortal soul ("Computing" 449). Rather, Turing sees intelligence in materialist terms, regarding it as the product of both the physical structures of the brain and the sociological conditioning to which every human mind is subjected ("Intelligent" 431–32).

Turing writes: "man is a machine ... that is subject to ... interference" ("Intelligent" 421). He goes on to explain that "the cortex of an infant is an unorganised machine, which can be organised by suitable interference training" (424). Thus, for Turing, the human brain begins as a set of structures that are necessary for intelligent behavior but initially lack the coordinating thought systems needed to carry out complex tasks and respond to instructions. Turing argues that it is by external interference, in the form of communication with other humans and the receipt of sensory stimuli, that the child brain becomes capable of intelligent action (422; 431). Turing therefore suggests that instead of trying to produce a program analogous to the adult mind, a program that simulates a child's brain should be developed based on the assumption that "If [it] were then subjected to an appropriate course of education one would obtain [an] adult brain" ("Computing" 460). In *2001*, Hal is created and educated in accordance with this method. He is taught to speak during his "electronic childhood" (99) so that he can communicate with humans and acquire an education. Hal is eventually capable of communication that is indistinguishable from that of an intelligent adult human (99).

Furthermore, just as the human mind is impaired when the brain is damaged, when Bowman carries out a "lobotomy" (170) on Hal by destroying his material systems, Hal regresses to childish unintelligence. Hal pleads with Bowman to spare him, saying: "You are destroying my mind.... I will become childish... I will become nothing" (170). Hal's physical destruction, accompanied by his mental regression to childishness, reflects Lucretius' materialist notion that "mind and body are born together, grow up together and together decay" (109) so that "when the body is palsied ... the understanding limps ... and the mind totters: everything weakens and gives way at the same time" (109–10). Hence, in Clarke's representations of artificial intelligence, consciousness is presumed to be a product of the material world. As Dr. Chandra puts it in *2010*, whether the mind is "based on carbon or silicone makes no fundamental difference" (239) because both organic and manufactured consciousnesses are simply the product of elaborate machinery.

Interestingly, Hal's education at the hands of an intelligent and, at least initially, superior race is reflected in Clarke's representation of the evolution of primitive man in part one of *2001*. As we have seen, Turing's theory suggests that, while the capacity for intelligence is innate, intelligent behavior is contingent on an appropriate education. This concept is applied

2. Materialism and Mystery

to primeval man in *2001*. The "man-apes" of Pleistocene Africa are represented as nearing extinction because the "meat roaming ... the savannah ... [is] not only beyond their reach; it [is] beyond their imagination" (7). Although the "first intimations of intelligence" (4) are emerging in these creatures, they lack the creativity to make weapons and hunt. It is not until the alien monolith mysteriously appears and "program[s]" (20) the man-apes to perform fine motor tasks and use tools that the creatures begin to behave in a way that suggests intelligence beyond animal instinct.

Just as Hal's intelligence is cultivated by his human creators, the alien monolith "educates" primitive humankind, teaching them to utilize their physical structures in an organized way. We are told that the man-apes "might by their own efforts have come to the awesome and brilliant concept of using natural weapons as artificial tools. But the odds were all against them" (21). Certainly, in the context of the novel, it is only through education that intelligence is achieved. While we can see the roots of this representation of taught intelligence in Turing's computer science, the depiction of externally inspired cognition becomes problematic when applied to the origins of the human race. By contemplating the catalyst for human intelligence and representing a higher species as responsible for the creation of humanity, *2001* veers away from materialist theory toward more spiritual constructions of the universe. The seeming contradiction in Clarke's illustration of intelligence harks back to a similar dilemma in Descartes' writing.

In his "Treatise on Man," Descartes presents a materialist description of the human body as a machine but goes on to state that the machine is formed by God (99). He makes a similar statement in his "Discourse on the Method of Properly Conducting One's Reason and of Seeking the Truth in the Sciences" when he argues that the human body is "made by the hands of God" (73). Descartes further asserts that the Creator fashions a "reasonable soul" (76), which is "not in any way ... derived from matter" (76) and lodges it, during life, in the body to give humans the consciousness that distinguishes them from animals. This representation of a coordinating deity who provides the soul, or vital spark, that produces conscious intelligence, continued to influence biology well into the twentieth century.

Philosophies such as vitalism adopt Descartes' notion of a guiding force to argue that the processes that we observe in organisms are administered by a force that is only present in living creatures. In his study of mechanistic theory in *Mechanism, Life and Personality* (1913) physiologist, J. S. Haldane explains that "Vitalism raises no objections to physical and chemical explanations applied ... outside the intimate vital processes of living organisms. It assumes, however, that these intimate processes are guided or controlled by an influence which is manifested only in living organisms" (22). He observes that, while mechanism is the prevailing theory in the early twentieth century, vitalism continues to be espoused by an outspoken minority (18). He further writes that cooperation among living beings "has been taken as strong evidence for the presence in living organisms of some co-ordinating influence apart from blind physical and chemical forces" (9). Thus vitalist discourses believe in a vital spark, or soul, coordinating activity.

J. S. Haldane further asserts that materialism and mechanism are insufficient to explain life. He writes, "the idea of the physical universe as a world of self-existent matter and energy is only a temporary working hypothesis ... [that] breaks down in connection with the phenomena of life" (104). In other words, J. S. Haldane argues that, although living organisms can be examined based on their material processes, there remains a gulf between mechanical action and life that neither mechanistic theory nor materialism can account for (110–11). This appraisal of materialist and mechanistic discourses as incapable of encompassing the nature of being allows for the continued inclusion of vitalist ideas and religious myths, which regard life as guided by divine principles, in twentieth-century thought.

Bergson, too, recognizes the incompleteness of early-twentieth-century biological theories. He writes that "our thought ... is incapable of presenting the true nature of life, the full meaning of the evolutionary movement" (*Creative* xxxv). He regards the mechanistic belief that "there is nothing in the universe which is not mathematically calculable" (*Mind-Energy* 203) as "too rigid" (*Creative* xxxv). Bergson also acknowledges the limitations of vitalism but observes that "the 'vital principle' may ... not explain much, but it is at least a sort of label affixed to our ignorance ... while mechanism invites us to ignore the ignorance" (27) by concluding that all phenomena are mappable in physical and chemical terms.

This argument that vitalist notions hold as much scientific validity as materialist and mechanistic principles is clearly reflected in Clarke's early novels.[11] In particular, *Childhood's End*, which represents the human race evolving into an immaterial group mind, presents paranormal explanations for evolution. The novel depicts a future human society in which citizens assume that "Science ... [can] explain everything" (196) by "uncover[ing] the secrets of the physical world" (196). However, it is soon revealed that materialist science fails to present a complete picture of the universe because spiritual phenomena are also "part of the truth" (197) and materialist frameworks fail to incorporate such aspects of reality. It is asserted in the novel that "strange phenomena—poltergeists, telepathy, precognition" (197), which tend to be ignored by science, need to be acknowledged in any comprehensive theory of the universe (197).

Haldane presents a very similar argument in *Possible Worlds*. He writes: "Religious experience is a reality. Hence it affords a certain insight into the nature of the universe" (237). As previously mentioned, when Clarke wrote *Childhood's End*, in the early 1950s, he was willing to countenance the reality of the paranormal so made telepathy and immaterial intelligence a major theme in the novel. Both Haldane and Clarke thus acknowledge, in their early writings, phenomena that defy the laws of the physical universe and cannot be explained in materialist terms. Their stance reflects the scientific engagement with the paranormal that was encouraged under the vitalist approach. As Bergson observes in a 1913 address to the London Society for Psychical Research, an increasing number of scientists in the early twentieth century were recognizing paranormal investigation as relevant to the study of life and the mind (*Mind-Energy* 60).

The nature of the mind, or consciousness, is a point of contention in Clarke's works. Although we see intelligence mechanically constructed in the case of Hal in *2001*, the *Space Odyssey* series also represents mind as immaterial and capable of existence outside the physical body. Indeed, incorporeal consciousnesses are persistently depicted throughout Clarke's corpus. Again we see the origins of this contradictory representation of the mind in Descartes' philosophy. Descartes acknowledges the connection of mind and body while simultaneously arguing that the mind is immaterial in the statement: "I have a body to which I am very closely united, nevertheless ... my mind ... is entirely and truly distinct from my body, and may exist without it" ("Meditations" 156). This blatantly contradicts mechanistic theory and illustrates that, as Henderson puts it: "Descartes was far from being a mechanist" (284). We see scientists like Haldane engaging with Descartes' more vitalist notions. Haldane argues in *Possible Worlds* that he believes that "mind is not wholly conditioned by matter" (209).[12]

Many of Clarke's novels make the assumption that mind can exist without matter. In *Childhood's End*, human children break through into a world of telepathic unity, becoming a group mind and, eventually, transcending physicality. The humans in *The City and the Stars* similarly master telepathy and manage to create a "disembodied intelligence" (239). Of course, the most iconic representation of a transcended mind in Clarke's corpus is that of the Star-Child in *2001*. Although protagonist Dave Bowman transforms into a baby, the form is no more than "his mind's ... image of itself" (249), a projection, rather than a corporeal structure that generates his consciousness. In at least the first two novels of the series, Bowman has the potential to "[pass] beyond the necessities of matter" (*2001* 249; *2010* 159).

Although the representation of Bowman's physicality changes over the course of the series, the representation of the immaterial beings that created the monoliths remains consistent throughout. In *2001*, *2010* and *3001*, the beings are described as "pure energy" (*2001* 209; *2010* 274; *3001* 3). Although originally flesh and blood, these extra-terrestrials evolved into "creatures of radiation, free ... from the tyranny of matter" (*2001* 209; *2010* 274). This marks a sharp departure from materialist philosophy. This depiction of transcended beings, alongside the mechanist representation of Hal's intelligence, reflects the conflicting discourses at work in early-twentieth-century biology.

Clarke's fantastic depictions of telepathic connections, group minds and incorporeal intelligences are not without precedent in scientific writing. In *Possible Worlds*, Haldane argues that the mind is more than just a material mechanism. He states: "Without the body [my mind] may perish altogether, but it seems ... quite as probable that it will lose its limitations and be merged into an infinite mind" (210). Haldane also tries his hand at SF in the closing portion of *Possible Worlds*. Like Clarke in *Childhood's End*, he imagines future humankind becoming telepathically linked to form a group consciousness (304; 310).

Thus, Clarke's seemingly unscientific representations of immaterial minds do in fact spring from scientific contexts. The twentieth-century debate over the plausibility of materialist, mechanistic and vitalist philosophies clearly informs his representations of intelligent life. The question remains, however, as to whether, by incorporating mystical notions, Clarke's novels inadvertently return to traditional, spiritual conceptions of the universe in spite of his scientific standpoint. An examination of Clarke's representation of other pivotal scientific notions, such as evolutionary theory, is needed to offer further clarification.

Evolutionary Transcendence

Clarke's novels consistently speculate about the path that human evolution will take in the future. Evolutionary transcendence, whereby human beings transcend physicality to become immaterial minds, is a recurring trope in Clarke's early SF and is frequently depicted as the most desirable course for humanity's evolution. The notion of evolutionary transcendence was already being explored in SF and biology before Clarke began producing SF. However, it is Clarke's fiction that facilitated the widespread dissemination of the concept in twentieth-century society. As we have already seen, representations of immaterial intelligences can be problematic because they tend to contradict materialist philosophy, which was gaining dominance in early-to-mid-twentieth-century science. It is important, therefore, to consider the rationale provided for transcendent evolution in Clarke's novels.

Like other scientists and writers of his time, including H. G. Wells, Clarke recognizes that natural, blind evolution cannot offer the rapid change that is needed to avoid downward evolution. However, while early-twentieth-century scientists, including Haldane and J. D. Bernal, imagine humankind harnessing applied science to control their future, Clarke's early SF depicts mysterious alien forces directing the evolution of humanity. This constitutes a step beyond the religious myths espoused in Wells' SF because, whereas Wells conceives of humanity actively working toward a divine plan, Clarke's early novels represent humankind's successful evolution as contingent on their total surrender to external forces.

Evolutionary theory dominated early-twentieth-century thought. As Haldane explains, by 1927 there was "universal agreement among biologists that evolution [had] occurred" (*Possible* 27). That evolution had occurred and, by extension, would continue to occur was a conclusion that sparked much speculation about the future course of human development. It was soon recognized that, although there is a tendency to regard progress as the rule in evolution, decline is actually the norm (Haldane, *Possible* 28). Haldane argues in *The Inequality of Man* (1932) that, not only is the course of evolution for most species downward toward extinction, but that humanity itself is set on a destructive path (145). He states that "If, as appears to be the case at present in Europe and North America, the less intelligent of our species continue to breed more rapidly than the able, we shall ... go the way of the dodo" (145). Haldane argues that humankind's fate will be sealed within a few centuries and fears that, unless humanity's evolutionary course can be altered, the species will lose its intelligence, return to barbarism and become extinct (145–46).

These fears of downward evolution are reflected in Clarke's fiction. In *Childhood's End* humankind, governed by alien Overlords, achieves world peace, rapid technological progress and seeming utopia. However, cultural stagnation accompanies this utopia and leads to racial decline. The planet is transformed into "one vast playground" (117) and entertainment becomes the greatest global industry. Social decay soon becomes apparent in every avenue of human endeavor. The lack of discontent and ambition "destroy[s] the soul of man" (156) so that the utopians are eventually unable to match the achievements of previous centuries in any field. As John Huntington notes, there is a correlation between the utopian stagnation represented in *Childhood's End* and that experienced by the Eloi in Wells' *The Time Machine* ("From" 211), illustrating SF's consistent recognition of the potential dangers of technological and social perfection.[13]

This representation of utopia as a trigger for downward evolution echoes Haldane's concerns in *The Inequality of Man* when he comments: "It is ... likely that, after a golden age of happiness and peace ... mankind will ... gradually deteriorate" (146). Like Clarke, Haldane regards being "out of harmony with [one's] surroundings" (*Possible* 302) as the motivation for positive evolution. Without it, humanity stagnates in a temporary utopia, which is necessarily followed by decline. This notion is also illustrated in Clarke's *The City and the Stars*, which describes the citizens of Diaspar, who have been genetically purged of ambition and made immortal, as "content in their eternal autumn" (10).

While recognizing the dangers of complacency, Clarke's novels also suggest that human ambition is equally damaging to the species' evolution. In *2001* the "dissatisfaction with ... life" (17) that makes the man-apes receptive to education also inspires aggression. We are told that, although "Man would never have conquered his world [without tools]" (31) the application of such tools as weapons means that the human race "live[s] on borrowed time" (31).[14] The tribal warfare in the Pleistocene is mirrored in *2001* by the modern protagonists' twenty-first-century context. We learn that, since primeval times, "the human race [has] lost few of its aggressive instincts" (38) and exists in a temporary state of peace while the "nuclear powers [watch] each other with belligerent anxiety" (38). Thus, in Clarke's fiction neither stagnant utopias, nor ambitious nation states can offer positive avenues for human evolution. For Clarke, the road to social and physiological progress lies in one direction: outer space.

In a 1938 brochure for the British Interplanetary Society Clarke writes: "Looking out across immensity to the great suns and circling planets ... can you believe that man is to spend all his days cooped and crawling on the surface of this tiny earth?" (McAleer 28). He believes humanity's destiny to be among the stars (28) and that space exploration will facilitate positive social change. In his 1969 coverage of the moon landing for CBS

News with Walter Cronkite, Clarke further states: "[space exploration] is making our stupidities here on Earth seem more and more intolerable." He asserts that "the greatest result of the space program" is its power to highlight the triviality of terrestrial rivalries. Clarke hopes that, as humankind moves into space, "they [will] forget their original nationalities" and develop a sense of peaceful collegiality.[15] We see Dave Bowman liberated from Earthly pettiness in *2001*. As he races across the Solar System in search of extra-terrestrial life, he is struck by the "ludicrously parochial" (186) nature of Earth's politics.

Clarke thus argues that, "By providing an outlet for man's exuberant and adolescent energies, astronautics may make a truly vital contribution to the problems of the present world" (*Greetings* 42). In other words, for Clarke, space travel provides a benign avenue for humankind's ambition and thus offers salvation from both racial aggression and social stagnation.[16] The vacuum of space poses an obstacle to humanity's advancement into the void and means that only a small fraction of the universe is directly accessible to humankind without mechanical aids (Clarke, *Profiles* 238–39). For this reason, Clarke believes that the evolution of humanity to exist in vacuum conditions is essential for the survival of the species.

Mechanization as a means to achieve this evolutionary step is considered by early-twentieth-century biologists. Bernal describes the mechanization of human physiology in his 1929 work *The World, the Flesh and the Devil: An Enquiry into the Future of the Three Enemies of the Rational Soul*. In *Profiles of the Future* Clarke praises Bernal's vision, declaring him the first writer to predict that the limitations of the human body might be overcome by the use of mechanical attachments and substitutes (242).[17] Bernal envisions humanity's future evolution as involving the use of an organic brain as the directive center of a mechanical system of manipulators and sense organs (36–37). He also predicts the connection of two or more minds to function as compound organisms so that common endeavors may be easily coordinated (42).

Bernal further imagines that, as a compound organism, humans will become immortal. He states that, while each mentally directed mechanism will eventually die as its brain cells deteriorate, the "multiple individual [will] be ... immortal" (43) because the memories of older members will be transferred to the common stock so that the collective consciousness will maintain a "continuity of ... self" (43). Bernal also speculates that humanity may become "completely etherealized" (47), losing the physical organism altogether and becoming masses of atoms in space, communicating by radiation, before "ultimately ... resolving ... entirely into light" (47).

A similar path from mechanization to transcendent evolution is described in *2001*, albeit for aliens not humans. We are told that, in their evolutionary past, the beings who installed the monoliths reached the limits of flesh and blood, so moved "First their brain, and then their thoughts alone ... into shining new homes of metal and of plastic" (208–09). They thus became spaceships, capable of navigating the void, first as machine entities and then as "pure energy" (209). Again, the representation of evolutionary transcendence is not unique to Clarke's SF. We know that Haldane suspected that, after death, individual minds would merge with an infinite, immaterial mind (*Possible* 210). Thus the representations of transcendent evolution in Clarke's novels are also drawn from scientific writing.

However, Clarke's novels and early-twentieth-century biology describe very different methods for achieving transcendent evolution. Haldane consistently emphasizes the need for the scientific control of human development. In *The Inequality of Man*, he states: "civilization as we know it is a poor thing. And if it is to be improved there is no hope save in science" (143). He goes on to explain that, "unless [man] can control his own evolution as he ... [controls] that of his domestic plants and animals, man and all his works will go down into oblivion and darkness" (147). This sentiment is also articulated by Bernal who asserts that meaningful progress depends on "man ... actively interefer[ing] in his own making ... in a highly unnatural manner" (29). Bernal goes on to describe how human physiology might be artificially modified and mechanized, arguing that the future of humanity "depends ... on the reaction of intelligence on a material universe" (49). Thus, according to Bernal, modern humanity's future need not be dependent on the slow movement of natural evolution. Rather, it will be determined by the extent to which scientific knowledge is utilized to transform human bodies.

As previously mentioned, we see science used to facilitate evolution in the case of the creators of the monoliths in the *Space Odyssey* series. It is through "ceaseless experimenting" (*2001* 208) that they transform first into mechanized brains and finally into pure radiation. There are also instances of humans using applied science to manipulate their evolution in Clarke's other novels. For example, in *The City and the Stars* we learn that, prior to the stagnation of society in Diaspar, the human race used "genetics and the study of the mind" (238) to push the species to its evolutionary limits. However, the novel also presents scientific manipulation of evolution as dangerous. We learn that, when experimenting with consciousness, the humans created an insane intelligence that laid waste to

2. Materialism and Mystery   69

the universe. This catastrophe led to downward evolution: science was used counterproductively to deliberately "[redesign] the human spirit, [by] robbing it of ambition" (246) so that such disasters could never happen again.[18]

Thus, in Clarke's early fiction, we see the success of scientific endeavors undermined by representations of the misapplication of science. The majority of successful cases of human evolution in Clarke's early novels are facilitated by mysterious forces, rather than by human science. Huntington also identifies the tendency for Clarke's novels to represent myths that conceive of human evolution as contingent on suprahuman intervention ("From" 213). He writes that "Clarke's myth of progress consists of two stages: that of rational, technological progress, and that of transcendent evolution" (211).[19] However, Huntington observes that "the transcendent state is not simply the highest stage of technological progress" (212), explaining that, in Clarke's novels, scientific achievements simply act to demonstrate humankind's worthiness to receive transcendence at the hands of a higher being (213). He notes the spiritual overtones of this representation of transcendence, writing that, in *Childhood's End*, "the leap from human to Overmind is achieved by grace, not by man's own works" (213).[20]

Indeed, not all representations of transcendence in Clarke's novels present biological mechanization or genetic engineering as a necessary intermediately step to evolutionary change. In fact, the aforementioned self-engineered evolution of the aliens in *2001* is an exceptional case. In the majority of illustrations of human transcendence in Clarke's works there is a direct and sudden transition from organic physicality to immateriality. Of course, the most famous example of such a transformation is that of Bowman in *2001*, which concludes with Bowman's consciousness merging with Hal's in *2010*. We also see blended minds in Clarke's earlier novel *Childhood's End*. The novel asserts that "In suitable circumstances minds can merge and share each other's contents" (189) and concludes with all human children achieving "Total Breakthrough" (188–89) into telepathic unity. This sudden transition leads to the transcendence of Earth's children as an immaterial group mind. They are thus able to travel into space and join with another such mind. This representation of telepathy and disembodied intelligences illustrates again the incorporation of vitalist notions in Clarke's early fictions, which regard mind as a force that can exist outside of the body.

In favoring vitalistic notions, Clarke's representations of evolutionary transcendence often fail to align with Darwinian science. As noted by

Rabkin, the mutation of the human children in *Childhood's End* into a collective, immaterial consciousness is not supported by modern genetics (*Arthur* 26). Rabkin explains that contemporary science indicates that no mutation can occur after the moment of conception (26–27). In Clarke's novel, however, the human children transcend physicality in a "cataclysmic" (*Childhood's* 199) and "instantaneous" (199) transformation that occurs during early childhood.[21] Rabkin comments: "It is just barely conceivable, despite his obvious scientific erudition, that Clarke does not understand mutations" (*Arthur* 27). However, Rabkin suspects, as I do, that Clarke is familiar with the established laws of evolution but chooses to discard them in favor of vitalist themes (27).

We know that, during the 1950s, Clarke was open to the possibility of paranormal events. His meditation on supernatural phenomena is illustrated in the representation of a pure consciousness that provides a telepathic trigger for humanity's evolution in *Childhood's End*. No scientific explanation for this catalyst is offered in the context of the novel but, unlike the scientifically engineered evolution represented in *The City and the Stars*, the supernatural transcendence of all human children in *Childhood's End* is a complete success. Similarly, Dave Bowman's successful evolution in *2001* is far from scientifically plausible, being instead facilitated by a mysterious alien species.[22]

Interestingly, the blending of scientific and paranormal illustrations of transcendence in Clarke's early novels reflects a similar trend in other SF of the period, including Olaf Stapledon's *Last and First Men* (1930) and *Star Maker* (1937). Clarke read *Last and First Men* as a teenager in 1931 and credits his depictions of non-material minds to Stapledon's influence. He declares in a 1986 interview that, of all SF writers, Stapledon left the greatest mark on his imagination and influenced "*all*" ("Playboy" 65) of his writing.[23] *Last and First Men* presents a future history in which humankind uses science to "research into practical means of remaking human nature" (130). The scientifically manufactured mutations that are described in Stapledon's novel adhere to evolutionary theory and are highly plausible.

If we only consider *Last and First Men* in relation to Clarke's corpus there appears to be a disparity between the philosophy that informs Stapledon's work and that which underpins illustrations of evolution in Clarke's early novels. However, it is important to note that Stapledon departs from materialist science in his later novel *Star Maker*. The novel describes the protagonist's ascension into space as a pure mentality that merges with other minds and embarks on a quest to find the Creator of the universe. Thus, Clarke is not alone in blending materialist and mystical representations of evolution in his works. The paradoxical mixing of discourses instead provides further evidence of Clarke's participation in the scientific and SF debates of his time, in which vitalistic notions vied with materialism for dominancy.

Thus the incorporation of materialist and paranormal ideas in Clarke's SF represents an attempt to speculate on the future of humanity in such a way as to incorporate all contemporary theories about life. In producing myths for modern society, Clarke's early novels engage with the SF and science of his time, and reproduce their juxtaposition of vitalist and materialist worldviews. Clarke draws on the science writing of Haldane and Bernal to illustrate the importance of humanity's positive evolution. However, mystical forces are represented as interfering in humankind's evolution in some of Clarke's most influential novels so that the evolutionary changes presented in these fictions are the result of paranormal events rather than material interactions. Furthermore, transcendent evolution becomes a spiritual movement toward a cosmic mind in Clarke's fiction. This presentation of mystical forces at work in the universe leads to the reproduction of spiritual tropes in spite of the clear denigration of traditional religion in Clarke's novels.

Religion, Gods and Men

Clarke's novels are consistent in their representation of organized religion as deleterious to progress. However, illustrations of transcendent evolution facilitated by godlike forces permeate his SF. Such representations rework mythical tropes traditionally associated with religion. So, in Clarke's early SF, organized religion is dismissed while spiritual notions are repurposed to create new myths. By presenting materialist and mystical ideologies alongside one another, Clarke's SF advocates the scientific standpoint, which impartially considers all theories until they are discredited by new information. However, these new myths also risk perpetuating the religious attitudes they seek to criticize. Clarke's novels tend to envision humankind being shepherded by a more advanced race, rather than autonomously determining their own evolutionary future. Such representations replace the interventionist God of traditional Christianity with intrusive alien species. Representations of humankind passively molded by benevolent external forces create myths that reaffirm religious ideas.

In an interview for *Playboy* in 1972 Clarke declares: "I have a long-standing bias against religion" ("At the" 257). Unlike Wells, who sees religion as an effective means of inculcating moral values, Clarke writes that "The greatest tragedy in mankind's entire history may be the hijacking of morality by religion. However valuable—even necessary—that may have been for enforcing good behaviour on primitive peoples, their association is now counterproductive" (*Greetings* 360). Clarke's opposition to religion is based on his belief that it espouses inflexible worldviews. He declares: "My objection to organized religion is the premature conclusion to ultimate truth that it represents" ("Playboy" 66). Of course, the scientific outlook to which Clarke adheres resists any suggestion that complete knowledge has been attained. We see Clarke's personal disapproval of established theologies reflected in *The City and the Stars* when organized religions are described as claiming "with unbelievable arrogance" (131) to be the "sole repository for the truth" (131). It is of note, however, that Clarke's objection to religion springs more from his disapproval of its claim to hold absolute truth than from its presentation of mystical forces.[24]

Haldane also articulates concerns about religion in *Possible Worlds*. Like Clarke, he states that his "main objection to religious myths is that, once made, they are so difficult to destroy" (231). He elaborates, saying that, "while serious attempts are constantly being made to verify scientific myths, religious myths ... have become matters of faith" (231) that are impervious to empirical evidence. Both Clarke and Haldane thus regard religion as presenting myths that are immutable and, therefore, limiting, whereas science is based on a methodology that insists on constant reappraisal through empirical analysis. Haldane further laments what he describes as a "god-making tendency" (*The Inequality* 187) in humankind. He regards humanity's persistent desire for divine guidance as "one of the most unfortunate vices to which the human intellect is subject" (187), because it leads humankind to passively relinquish their powers of action to a higher being. Haldane accuses his 1927 milieu of "suffering from too much ... faith" (*Possible* 211) and demands that it resist the ingrained habit of taking established belief systems for granted.

Clarke and Haldane also note the human cost of religious myth. Haldane observes that ideological change in religious societies is often only achieved "at the expense of a sufficient number of martyrs" (*Possible* 224). Similarly, Clarke states that "few physicists have been murdered by other physicists ... nor have they slaughtered scores of innocents" ("At the" 256) over a difference of opinion. In this regard, Clarke and Haldane are not simply advocating the substitution of religious philosophy with scientific theory. Rather, they argue that science offers a more sophisticated method for producing myth because it allows for the easy modification of ideas to suit humanity's ever-developing knowledge of the universe. As Haldane states in *The Inequality of Man*: "science can do something far bigger for the human mind than the substitution of one set of beliefs for another" (1): it can spread among humanity "the point of view that prevails among research workers" (1). Thus, for Haldane, science offers humankind a mythic system that is infinitely plastic and is capable of evolving to encourage and accommodate new discoveries.

Clarke's SF notes that the limitless questing of the scientific outlook has not always been welcomed by the mass populace, which tends to seek fixed absolutes as opposed to embracing the mysterious nature of the universe. In *The City and the Stars* we are told that religious cults "[thrive] with particular strength during ... periods of confusion and disorder" (132) because, "When the reality is depressing, men [try] to console themselves with myths" (132). Clarke further argues that "religion [is] a by-product of malnutrition" ("At the" 256). He elaborates, saying: "when you have a society in which millions of people live in hunger and poverty, it may be necessary to develop ... a belief in reincarnation, a belief in a better life" (256).[25] This appraisal of religion as fulfilling a psychological need is also presented in *3001* when Dr. Ted Khan argues: "Lucretius hit it on the nail when he said that religion [is] the by-product of fear—a reaction to a mysterious and often hostile universe" (141). Here Dr. Khan is referring to Lucretius' assertion that, when primitive humans could not explain the awesome power of natural phenomena, they were filled with "shuddering dread" (208) and "took refuge in handing over everything to the gods and making everything dependent on their whim" (207).

Thus, for Clarke, organized religion is a mythic system that is characteristic of those societies that lack the maturity and civilization necessary to actively engage with their environment through scientific endeavor. Indeed, we see Dr. Khan in *3001* go so far as to suggest that religion is a form of mental disorder (141). He argues that nothing but widespread psychopathology can explain the "irrational behaviour" (141) that leads to the violent conflicts over "trivial points of doctrine" (141) that litter human history. Religion here is represented as a particularly persistent form of insanity that has been inherited from ancient man. This notion is also articulated by Haldane who argues that "Religion ... endows ... the laws of primitive peoples with eternal significance" (*Fact* viii).

In *The Fountains of Paradise* religion is dismissed as a system that should have been outgrown by modern humanity. In the novel Sigmund

Freud is quoted as having stated that religion "seems not so much to be a lasting acquisition, as a parallel to the neurosis ... pass[ed] through on the way from childhood to maturity" (67). This comment, taken from Freud's *New Introductory Lectures on Psycho-Analysis*, constitutes part of Freud's argument that religion fulfills the same function as the parental influence that governs the child by offering knowledge, comfort and regulation (62; 161). Freud observes that science and religion are rival doctrines because they both present explanations for reality, but states that science cannot compete with the ability of religion to offer the comforting promise of future salvation (161–62). For Freud, religion appeals to the childish need for reassurance in humanity and is, therefore, "an enemy" (160) of science. This notion is underlined in *The Fountains of Paradise* when the alien probe Starglider reveals that religion is not only more prevalent in less evolved cultures but is also unique to cultures that rely on mammalian reproduction (163–64).

Importantly, Clarke is not necessarily opposed to faith in a divine being, he is simply hostile to the passively receptive attitude that he believes is cultivated by organized religion. Indeed, Clarke observes in 1972 that "people tend to confuse religion with a belief in God.... whereas one could easily believe in a supreme being and not have any religion" ("At the" 257). This distinction is crucial to understanding the Clarke paradox. Clarke's SF consistently depicts humankind's eventual progression away from religious myths. However, his novels do not preclude the possibility of the existence of the divine. This is also the case in Haldane's early writings, in which he contemplates the possibility of a supreme mind "exist[ing] behind nature" (*Possible* 210).

A belief in the infinite possibilities of the universe is something Haldane and Clarke share. As previously mentioned, Haldane's statement that the universe is stranger than we can imagine is even quoted in *2010* (Haldane, *Possible* 286; Clarke, *2010* 219). Clarke invokes this quote from Haldane again in 1986 when acknowledging the recurring engagement with mysticism and godlike forces in his novels. He observes: "we constantly find new things out; but what we know may be such a small part of reality. ... one must always allow for the totally unexpected. So ... by talking about things that could be called mystical ... I ... try to allow for the idea[s] ... [articulated by] Haldane" ("Playboy" 65). Like Shakespeare's Hamlet, Haldane believes that "there are more things in heaven and earth than are dreamed of, or can be dreamed of, in any philosophy" (*Possible* 286).[26] Therefore, for Haldane and Clarke, static religious systems are particularly limiting because they fail to acknowledge the infinite mystery of the universe and the importance of a continuing quest for knowledge.

However, in his early works Haldane argues that a belief in a supreme being may not be deleterious to social progress. In *Possible Words,* Haldane comments that it may lead to the selfish deification of humanity if all mystical beliefs are abandoned and that "It is possible to become convinced on philosophical grounds of the supreme reality ... of the spiritual" (235) without depending on traditional religious tenets.[27] Haldane further argues that the existence of the spiritual is "supported by mystical experience[s]" (*Possible* 235) that continue to be reported in modern society.

Haldane not only speculates that a godlike consciousness exists in the universe but also asserts that this mind can be sensed in terrestrial life (*Possible* 210). He comments: "when I think logically ... or act morally my thoughts and actions cease to be characteristic of myself, and are those of an intelligent or moral being" (210). Haldane thus argues that, when he acts in accordance with higher values, he is "identifying ... with an absolute ... mind" (210) that he will ultimately merge with (210). He acknowledges that he has no scientific explanation of how his transcendence will be achieved but remains optimistic that telepathic unity on a cosmic scale is possible. This reflects J. S. Haldane's earlier hypothesis that "In our relations to fellow-men, fellow-animals, and Nature as a whole, we find ... this ... all-embracing personality which we call God" (135). Importantly, both Haldane and his father imagine that humankind will achieve oneness with God through autonomous action. J. S. Haldane states that humanity will participate in the cosmic personality by constantly "seeking for and acting on duty and truth" (146) while Haldane sees humankind's participation in the wider "Plan" (*Possible* 311) of the universe as contingent on their creation of new ideas and their pursuit of positive evolution (311).

Other early-twentieth-century thinkers also acknowledge the possibility of a divine force at work in the universe. In particular, philosopher S. Alexander speculates on the existence of a universe encompassing God in *Space, Time and Deity* (1920). He argues that "the body of God is the whole universe and there is no body outside his" (357). In this philosophy, humankind has already achieved oneness with the collective being that is God. For Alexander, God is not perfect but is an immortal being that is forever moving toward the next empirical quality, which Alexander calls "deity" (347). Alexander explains, "God ... is the universe ... tending to[ward] deity" (398). Therefore, the human race, as part of God, is also striving toward the next evolutionary leap.

Alexander's representation of humanity as part of a cosmic process correlates with the ideas articulated in *Childhood's End*. Importantly, however, humankind is endowed with far less self-determination in Clarke's novel than in the philosophies presented by Haldane and Alexander. Although Alexander describes all beings as part of the divine, he criticizes the pantheistic attitude that imagines the individual subsumed by the power of God (392). The opposite is the case in *Childhood's End*, in which the children of the human race are transformed and absorbed by an immaterial godlike principle that completely dominates their evolution. Thus, although the human race is liberated from traditional religion in *Childhood's End*, they are manipulated by immortal, alien powers. The Overlords are described as "shepherding mankind" (21) on behalf of a supreme being that manifests as a pure mentality. Far from encouraging humans to strive toward their own positive evolution through scientific and artistic endeavors, the Overlords discourage space flight and turn the Earth into a complacent Utopia. They deliberately "[interrupt human] development on every cultural level" (197) because they do not trust humanity to autonomously evolve in a successful manner. It is revealed that the Overlords are, in turn, controlled by an Overmind, which tops the cosmic hierarchy.

We discover in *Childhood's End* that the Overmind is "trying to grow, to extend its powers and its awareness of the universe" (199) by imbibing intelligent species and becoming a composite mind, or "the sum of many races" (199). The Overlords are enlisted to ensure that each species develops in such a way as to facilitate its absorption into the Overmind. The climax of the novel sees the Overmind trigger the telepathic connection of all human children so that it can "[train] them [by] molding them into one unit before ... wholly absorb[ing] them into its being" (220). This event signals the individual death of each child and the extinction of the human race. However, the novel presents this evolutionary progression as a cause for rejoicing. At the conclusion of the novel, Jan, the last surviving human adult, witnesses the transcendent evolution of the children and marvels at the glory the human race has achieved while pitying any species that fails to attain transcendence (235). The SF myth presented here is that human evolution is contingent on the patronage of God and that the relinquishment of individual liberty is an acceptable cost for transcendence.

We also see human evolution depicted as reliant on the intervention of a higher species in the *Space Odyssey* series. In *2001*, we are told that primitive man was unlikely to achieve intelligence without the aid of the monoliths. Further, the godlike entities responsible for the monoliths are at liberty to "dispassionately ... weed" (208) their creations, destroying those species that fail to meet with their approval.[28] Although we see human science produce an immaterial mind in *The City and the Stars*, the progress humanity makes in this novel does not compare with the transcendent intelligences depicted in *Childhood's End* and the *Space Odyssey* series. The human race itself does not achieve transcendence in *The City and the Stars* but creates two immaterial minds. The first, termed the Mad Mind, is "implacably hostile to matter" (240) while the other, named Vanamonde, is "a creature of tremendous knowledge, but ... little intelligence" (220). Eventually humankind abandons their scientific creations and some members of the species choose downward evolution in Diaspar while others set off on a quest "around the curve of the Cosmos" (241) in search of a "very strange and very great" (241) being that has made contact with them. Thus, *The City and the Stars* also represents the search for the divine as of paramount importance to the human race.

The persistent representation of humankind being guided by a supreme being in Clarke's early SF again reflects early-twentieth-century biology. In *The World of Life: A Manifestation of Creative Power, Directive Mind and Ultimate Purpose* (1911) Alfred Russel Wallace, who independently conceived of the theory of evolution through natural selection, studies terrestrial organic structures and, on observing the elaborateness of these systems, surmises the existence of a "Creative Power ... a directive Mind ... and ... an ultimate Purpose" (vi–vii). Instead of being the result of coincidence, Wallace believes the correlations in nature are evidence of an "organising and directive Life-Principle" (vi). He also asserts that a "supreme ... overruling Mind" (vi) is controlling evolution on Earth. Similarly, Henderson argues that the complex coordination of elements needed to generate an environment fit for human life cannot be reasonably assumed to be an accident (37). Henderson admits that "no explanation is at hand" (276) for the miraculous creation of a life-sustaining environment on Earth but suggests the existence of a mysterious, coordinating force. As we have seen, Clarke's novels also develop myths that represent external godlike entities controlling life.

Rabkin notes the continual return to spiritual myths in Clarke's novels. He states, "Clarke has an obvious desire to construct a world in which some kind of higher benign order makes clear the centrality and importance of humanity" (McAleer 385). Rabkin also observes in Clarke's SF a "persistent spiritual ... optimism concerning the place of humanity in the universe" ("Clarke" 141). While Clarke's novels consistently depict humankind as low on the hierarchy of intelligent beings, they suggest that humanity will find a place within the greater life of the universe. As we have seen, while Clarke dismisses organized religion as propounding limiting worldviews, his early SF tends to envision humankind's positive evolution as contingent upon the intervention of a godlike principle. Such representations of immaterial minds controlling the destiny of humanity are problematic because they imply a relinquishment of self-determination that is antithetical to the autonomous questing advocated by the scientific point of view. By veering away from materialist science and toward vitalist and mystical conceptions of the universe, Clarke's early novels articulate spiritual myths, which represent humanity's destiny as determined by the will of God.

Thus, although Clarke presents religion as deleterious to human progress and advocates a scientific approach to mythmaking, his incorporation of the myriad of contemporary theories on the nature of existence paradoxically results in the presentation of spiritual myths in his early SF. The image of the non-consensual transcendence of Bowman in *2001* has had a major influence on the SF genre, as have Clarke's representations of immaterial minds overseeing humanity's development in *Childhood's End* and the *Space Odyssey* series. Such myths of divine providence perpetuate the tendency for SF to return to traditional, spiritual frameworks when speculating about the nature of the universe and humanity's place in it.

A Learning Process: Increasingly Materialist Myths and a Consideration of Language in Clarke's Later SF

It is worth noting that Clarke's views on paranormal phenomena change over the course of his career. He grows increasingly skeptical of spiritual myths and comes to regard his ever-changing philosophy as a "long, and sometimes embarrassing, learning process" (Afterword 240). We can see a distinct movement toward materialism in Clarke's later novels. This transition is most obvious in the sequels to *2001*, in which key plot elements are altered between novels to make Bowman's existence align with materialist science. A shift toward materialism is another trait Clarke shares with Haldane, who admits to a change in philosophy in *Fact and Faith*. In their later writings, both Clarke and Haldane resist the notion that a spiritual realm or godlike mind might influence the material world.

Indeed, in *The Fountains of Paradise* and the later novels of the *Space*

Odyssey series, humankind's future evolution becomes far more reliant on human autonomy and technological ingenuity than on externally facilitated transcendent evolution. This shift in emphasis over the course of Clarke's career illustrates the way SF functions as a platform for exploring the nature of the universe. Like scientific theory, the premises underpinning Clarke's fiction change over time to accommodate progressions in human understanding. In this way, SF can be seen as emblematic of the scientific attitude. The genre strives to develop myths that incorporate the breadth of modern knowledge, ranging from the mystical to the mechanical.

Haldane modified his stance on materialism in 1934. In the preface to *Fact and Faith* he writes: "My philosophical views have changed, and ... will go on changing for ... years to come" (v). This statement signals Haldane's willingness to modify his views in response to changes in knowledge. He explains that "the progress of physics ... has rendered Materialism a good deal more plausible than seemed likely even ten years ago" (v–vi). Accordingly, Haldane alters his philosophy and declares an entirely atheistic stance (vi). He further outlines his alignment with materialist theory in *Keeping it Cool*, explaining that he believes that matter existed before mind and that the mind is destroyed with the death of the body (225).

Just as Haldane articulates a willingness to reframe his philosophy in accordance with scientific progress, Clarke also adheres to the scientific method by modifying his beliefs in response to new knowledge. Clarke states in 1972 that, having lived through several revolutions in half a lifetime, he understands the "imperatives of change, and the urgent need to prepare for ... inevitable revolutions in almost every field of human activity" (*Profiles* 9). However, Clarke is more hesitant to dismiss vitalist notions than Haldane. He continues to incorporate mystical themes in his novels several decades after Haldane rejects vitalism in *Fact and Faith*. Furthermore, in 1989 Clarke states that although he is "an almost total sceptic" (Afterword 240) he is skeptical of only "99 percent of ... 'paranormal' [phenomena]" (241) because "[they] can't *all* be nonsense" (241). Indeed, it was only after participating in several documentary series investigating paranormal activity, including *Arthur C. Clarke's World of Strange Powers* (1985), that Clarke declares the specious nature of most reported mysteries (Afterword 240). That said, we do certainly see a move toward materialism in Clarke's fiction after *2001*.

Roberts argues that in Clarke's fiction "what seems at first glance to be miraculous becomes, when properly analysed, only technological" (*The History* xiv). He cites the *Space Odyssey* series as evidence of this, stating that "the apparently 'transcendent' ... ending of *2001* ... is later rationalised in materialist, technological terms (in the three sequels...)" (xiv). However, I posit that the eventual rationalization of Bowman's transcendence was not premeditated by the author and, therefore, cannot be seen as representative of a consistent materialist pattern in Clarke's fiction. Clarke explains that for more than a decade after publishing *2001* he "indignantly denied that any sequel was possible, or that [he] had the slightest intention of writing one" ("Back to 2001" xvi). Thus Clarke originally intended the transcendent evolution of Bowman at the end of *2001* to represent a miraculous event facilitated by a godlike force.

In 1989 Clarke reflects that a major motivation for writing a sequel to *2001* was "the brilliant success of the [1977] Voyager missions" (xvi), which provided a wealth of new information about the planets in our solar system. Clarke decided to utilize this knowledge to create a new SF story about the Jovian satellites ("Back to 2001" xvi). By changing the location of the space monolith from Saturn's moon Japetus, where it had been in *2001*, to near Jupiter in *2010,* Clarke simultaneously established narrative continuity with Kubrick's film version of *2001* and furnished himself with a setting that could utilize the new information provided by the Voyager missions ("Author's Note" 15; "Back to 2001" xvi). Thus, while plot changes in the *Space Odyssey* series are influenced by developments within the SF genre, Clarke's admission that scientific discoveries were also a catalyst for his narrative choices means that we can, at least in part, attribute other major alterations in the plot of the series to progressions in science and subsequent changes in Clarke's worldview.

Narrative continuity, particularly in the representation of Bowman, is sacrificed for an increasingly materialist stance in the three sequels to *2001*, published in 1982, 1988 and 1997. For instance, in *2001* Bowman travels through the Star Gate, or monolith, at a speed "a million times [greater than] the velocity of light" (222). We are told that Bowman's evolutionary transcendence will allow him to eventually "[pass] beyond ... matter" (249) and that he can travel across the universe without the aid of the monoliths (249). In *2010: Odyssey Two* the story of Bowman's transformation is retold and he is still represented as a "creature of pure energy" (161). However, while Bowman can travel faster than light in *2010* he can only do so via the star gates and is not able to travel as freely through the universe (157–60). Rather, his consciousness is tied to the physical structure of the monoliths, which the alien race responsible for his evolution installed through space (159–61). He is able to transmit himself between monoliths and can manifest in electronic devices, including his former girlfriend's television set (171). This change indicates the first move toward a materialist representation of Bowman as a mind connected to matter.

By *3001: The Final Odyssey* (1997), Bowman can no longer travel faster than light. Clarke explains that "One of the assumptions ... in [*3001*] is that Einstein is correct, and that no signal—or object—can exceed the speed of light" ("Sources" 259). Although Clarke represents faster than light travel in the earlier *Space Odyssey* novels, he declares in 1997 that, if such a thing were possible, aliens would already have visited our solar system ("Sources" 260). Clarke's increasingly rationalist philosophy leads Bowman, or Halman as he becomes after merging with Hal in *2010*, to be reduced from an "embryo god" (159) in *2010* to a piece of data in *3001*. In *3001*, Halman is no longer a pure mentality, liberated from matter. His consciousness is tied to the Europan monolith, which is presented in *2061* as a kind of complex computer (292). Although Halman travels away "Sometimes for years" (*3001* 235), his travels seem to consist of movements between monoliths, rather than free flight through open space. When the humans decide to destroy the monolith on Europa, Halman's life is threatened and he must survive by "download[ing]" (240) himself into a man-made computer hard drive. Halman's inability to survive without having his mind grounded in a material form is underlined by his request that he be remembered if he fails to download and perishes (240). We are thus left with a materialist view of consciousness in *3001*.

In *3001* the human mind is also described as data. In the future society of the novel humans are experimenting with "data compression ... [to] store not only ... memories—but ... actual [people]" (45) within computer storage devices. It is suggested that such a method is responsible for Halman's seeming transcendence. The concept of storing a human mind inside a computer is based on late-twentieth-century science. Clarke refers to a 1994 paper from the *Quarterly Journal of the Royal Astronomical Society* to explain that the total mental state of a one hundred year old human could be represented by one petabit ("Sources" 260).[29] Thus, in *3001*, we are presented with a universe where even the most mysterious entities and objects "obey ... universal laws of logic" (222). This transition toward materialism illustrates Clarke's scientific approach, that is, his willingness to adapt his views based on new data.

Like Clarke's ever-evolving philosophy, SF expands and adapts the myths it produces to reflect changes in twentieth-century knowledge. Clarke argues that "[the SF writer] encourages in his readers ... [a] readiness to accept and even welcome change—in one word, adaptability" (*Greetings* 249). Clarke sees adaptability as perhaps the most important attribute of any species, saying, "We shall disappear if we cannot adapt to an environment that now contains spaceships and thermonuclear weapons" (249). In a 1972 interview Clarke further declares: "I believe the future is not predetermined, that to some extent we can determine our own destiny" ("At the" 258). This philosophy, which values human autonomy, is not reflected in Clarke's early novels that depict humankind submitting to the will of supreme beings. However, myths of human self-determination become increasingly important in Clarke's later fictions. Again this shift in emphasis can be most clearly observed in the *Space Odyssey* series, in which the creators of the monoliths are initially represented as benevolent, albeit mysterious, entities but are later depicted as negligent dictators against whom humankind must rebel.

In *2001*, it is hypothesized that "any advanced culture must be benevolent" (177) and, as in the case of the transcendence of humanity in *Childhood's End*, Bowman's non-consensual evolution is represented as a positive development. He returns to Earth in *2001* as an autonomous being who is "master of the world" (252). However, in *2010*, the human "hope ... that benevolent creatures from the stars might help mankind" (174) is juxtaposed with representations of Bowman being used as an emotionless "probe" (177) by "a vast mentality" (184) that is monitoring humanity's development. Bowman is "compelled to obey the overriding wishes" (177) of this "implacable will" (184) and becomes little more than a "hunting dog on a leash" (177). This servitude becomes increasingly troubling, particularly when Bowman's reconnaissance missions result in the destruction of Jupiter and all its life forms, which are deemed expendable by his controllers.

The hierarchy of intelligences that are "controlling and manipulating" (*2010* 205) life in the Solar System are thus depicted quite differently in the later *Space Odyssey* novels from the Overmind in *Childhood's End*. Far from representing the zenith of evolutionary progress, the immaterial minds in the sequels to *2001* are shown to make misjudgments and miscalculations. The revelation that they are "not omnipotent" (*2010* 216) thus becomes a catalyst for the human protagonists to "hope and dream— and act" (216) in such a way as to liberate themselves from their manipulators.

An emphasis on human self-determination becomes crucial in differentiating Clarke's earlier works from these later novels. In *The Fountains of Paradise*, for instance, the alien visitor from distant Starholme addresses humankind as its equals, exchanging information without seeking to interfere in human affairs. Meanwhile, the human characters use science and technology to better themselves, rather than seeking after transcendence at the hands of mysterious forces. The sequels to *2001* also represent the need for human-driven evolution as the protagonists struggle to escape the control of their alien guardians.

Furthermore, in *3001*, the creators of the monoliths are credited with establishing religion on Earth by leaving the monolith in Africa to become "The very first of all [humankind's] multitudinous gods" (58). Given the novel's criticism of religion, the conflation of the aliens with religious myth immediately establishes a relationship of manipulation and dominance between the humans and their guardians. It is suggested that, by presenting the developing minds of the ape-men with religion, the monolith created something "fundamentally wrong [in] the wiring of [humankind's] brains ... mak[ing them] incapable of consistent logical thinking" (153). Resistance against religious fanaticism and limiting traditional myths thus becomes synonymous, in the *Space Odyssey* series, with resisting external manipulation and control. With the help of Halman, who is "resentful of the way he's been collected, like a specimen" (215), humankind rebels against the aliens by destroying the monolith that was to eventually judge their fitness to survive. By the conclusion of *3001*, the human race is left unmonitored to autonomously continue its upward evolution. The species is even freed from the potential influence of Halman, who is ultimately locked inside an inactive hard drive.

The emphasis on human autonomy and materialist science in Clarke's later novels counterbalances the positive representation of paranormal, godlike rulers in his earlier works. We see, particularly in *3001*, a consideration of the influence of traditional myths on the present and an attempt to resist rigid belief systems. While earlier novels imagine secular futures, in which "science [has] destroy[ed] religion" (*Childhood's* 17), Clarke's later works represent the persistent influence of religion within seemingly secular societies. In the late twentieth century, Clarke was surprised by the continued, widespread faith in religions he himself had dismissed, albeit far more slowly than some of his scientific contemporaries. He observes that the close of the twentieth century saw a fin de siècle manifestation of beneficial changes, particularly in international politics, coupled with "a rising tide of irrationality and belief in superstitious nonsense" (*Greetings* 473).

J. S. Haldane also considers the societal forces that perpetuate traditional myths. He observes that "past perceptions are ... still directly active in the present" (107) so that "The personality of any individual represents a spiritual inheritance" (127) that is "continuous from generation to generation" (129–30). Haldane echoes this view in *The Inequality of Man*, when, in discussing the social importance of SF, he observes that "myths have a very real influence on the present" (196). He further argues that the perpetuation of traditional myths is facilitated by the nature of language itself (*Keeping* 48).

Clarke also explores the influence of linguistic structures on myth in *3001*. In the novel, Frank Poole, who died on the *Discovery* mission of *2001*, is resurrected and discovers that, in the thirty-first century, "'God' ... [has become] a dirty word" (48). Frank learns that, after traditional religions were discredited by materialist science, the word became impractical because of its suggestion of an interventionist Redeemer. However, instead of *3001* depicting a culture purged of religious rhetoric, it instead presents a society that still acknowledges a divine creator. Frank is told that, after ancient religions had been dismantled, humankind "still needed a word for the Prime Cause, or the Creator of the Universe" (60). The human race in *3001* is divided into Deists, who believe there is at least one God, and Theists, who believe there might be one God (61). The word used in this thirty-first-century culture to denote this creative mind is "Deus" (60). While it is asserted in the novel that this term is disconnected from religion, the fact that it is a word extant in traditional theology suggests its potential to develop new connotations of a religious nature and illustrates the power of persistent linguistic systems over human thought.

Thus, despite veering toward materialism and humanism in his later novels, as late as 1997, with *3001*, Clarke represents a universe in which a godlike principle is thought to exist. This reflects Clarke's ongoing scientific, impartial contemplation of all possibilities. Dr. Ted Khan observes in *3001* that atheism and a belief in God hold equal plausibility. He declares: "Atheism is unprovable.... Equally ... we can never be certain that God once existed—and [is now] ... where no one can ever find him" (140–41). Dr. Khan thus determines to "take no position on [the] subject" (141) of God's existence. Clarke's novels adopt a similar stance. *3001* ends with the homocentric observation that "Whatever godlike powers and principalities [lurk] beyond the stars ... for ordinary humans only two things are important—Love and Death" (247–48). This conclusion epitomizes the dialectic consistent throughout Clarke's fiction: a tension between human autonomy and the potential existence of awesome, transcendent powers in the universe.

While there are certainly materialist notions represented in Clarke's novels, divinely inspired transcendent evolution remains one of the most iconic concepts to emerge from his SF. Even *3001*, which dismisses traditional religious models on a linguistic level, represents the possibility of a divine creator. Clarke's works are thus characterized by a paradoxical blending of discourses so that materialist notions and spiritual myths coexist in his SF. Clarke himself argues that "Though it often serves to impart information ... [SF's] chief value is *inspirational* rather than educational" (*Greetings* 247). He further explains that "Science fiction encourages the cosmic viewpoint" (248), that is, an attitude that acknowledges the boundless possibilities of our vast cosmos. For Clarke, "The purpose of the Universe ... is the perpetual astonishment of mankind" ("At the" 274). Of course, this sense of wonder tends to result in the perpetuation of spiritual myths in the face of modern materialism.

Clarke's representation of immaterial intelligences and sudden evolutionary transcendence still informs SF narratives today, which frequently blend the spiritual and material. It cannot be denied that Clarke's SF inspires a sense of optimism and enthusiasm unrivaled among the best SF of the century. However, other SF writers, including Frank Herbert, see the incorporation of mystical ideas in SF, which is characteristic of Clarke, as representative of a tendency for SF to perpetuate traditional myths. Alternatively, as we see in the case of Philip K. Dick, other SF writers embrace the potential for SF to construct religious myths and seek to utilize SF to critique existing ideological systems and suggest alternative, spiritual belief systems.

Chapter 3

Science Fiction as Truth: Sociology, Philosophy and Theology in Philip K. Dick

In a private journal entry from early 1981 Philip K. Dick (1928–1982) reflects: "The core of my writing is not art but *truth*" (*The Exegesis* 693). This statement, which is reminiscent of the ideas H. G. Wells espouses about the novel,[1] exemplifies Dick's belief that SF is a vehicle for examining and describing the nature of reality. Like Wells, Dick utilizes the genre to explore sociological issues and to engage with a range of theological and philosophical questions. In particular, Dick's SF reflects the social disillusionment characteristic of the 1960s counterculture. His novels consistently depict bleak societies and examine the man-made ideologies that structure human life. Dick's SF frequently highlights the insubstantiality of perceived reality by depicting characters caught in webs of illusion, unable to discern the true nature of their environment. Importantly, Dick's SF does not only critique contemporary ideologies and dismiss reality as illusory. It attempts to formulate a mythology that represents the "true" reality that underlies the mundane world and, subsequently, to offer a narrative of redemption for modern society.

In seeking for a new mythic system, Dick draws on ancient myth, modern philosophy and religion. His works thus present an ever-evolving, cumulative myth, which incorporates sources ranging from the Presocratics to Martin Heidegger. For Dick, SF becomes a vehicle for theological speculation and the formulation of new spiritual myths. As in the writings of Arthur C. Clarke and Wells, Dick's SF tends to represent cosmologies that feature a divine structure and an interactive relationship between the human world and the spiritual realm. It is also of note that Dick, like Wells, developed a personal religion during his lifetime, which is reflected in his late SF.

Despite his incorporation of a wealth of philosophical material into his SF, Dick is by no means a philosopher. He is an autodidact who attended just one year at the University of California, Berkeley. Dick's worldview constantly changes and adapts in response to his personal experiences and private study. What is more, his interpretation of established theories and myths is not always orthodox, resulting in a sometimes surprising patchwork of seemingly contradictory theories.[2] Critchley notes that "Dick use[s] resources that he ha[s] at hand" including the complete set of *Encyclopædia Britannica*, which "permitted an ... untutored rapidity of association" so that "Skimming through and across multiple encyclopedia entries, Dick found links and correspondences of ideas everywhere." This has resulted in a synthesis of ideas in Dick's works that makes the task of examining the philosophical and theological underpinnings of Dick's fiction particularly challenging.

Novelist Steve Erickson observes in an annotation in *The Exegesis of Philip K. Dick,* a collection of Dick's private journals, notes and correspondence, that "[Dick's] 'philosophy' is erratic, even crackpot" (Jackson and Lethem 693).[3] However, the combination of religious, philosophical and mystical theories in Dick's SF makes his work a compelling example of how SF can be used to explore the diverse systems that inform human thought, and to formulate new myths. Critchley writes that "whatever [Dick] lacks in scholarly rigor, he more than makes up for in powers of imagination and in rich lateral and cumulative associations." This chapter charts the way that Dick's SF amalgamates diverse systems of thought to critique his society and produce new myths.

There has already been much critical examination of Dick's corpus, which consists of over forty novels and more than one hundred short stories, in both SF and mainstream genres, written between 1951 and 1982. The sheer quantity of Dick's writing presents a challenge to scholars seeking to provide an overview of his works. There has, therefore, been a tendency for critics to divide Dick's corpus into distinct periods and to focus either on Dick's earlier works, and the socio-political critiques they offer, or to examine the theological ideas in his later SF. For instance, in *Archaeologies of the Future: The Desire Called Utopia and Other Science Fictions* (2006), critic Fredric Jameson seeks to categorize Dick's works based on content and chronology in a deliberate attempt to "disconnect the religious thematics from the earlier [sociological] works" (363).

Jameson argues that Dick's writing falls into three thematic groups: the "mainstream novels" of 1955–1960, the "Science Fiction period" of 1961–1968 and the "religious novels" of 1973–1981 (363). Crucial to

Jameson's argument is the assertion that there is a clear disparity between Dick's early works and his later, religious novels (363). Jameson justifies this stance by asserting that the religious notions presented in *Do Androids Dream of Electric Sheep?* (1968) and *Ubik* (1969) are entirely different from those in Dick's later fiction (364). I posit, however, that such differences are merely evidence of Dick's evolving philosophy.[4]

As will be evident through an examination of some of the key SF novels written by Dick between 1964 and 1981, there is a logical progression of sociological, philosophical and theological ideas in Dick's writing, which means that we cannot separate his corpus into distinct, unrelated categories. As noted by critic Umberto Rossi, Dick "never lost sight of the sociological aspects of sf" ("The Holy" 154) so that, even in his later novels, theological ideas and social critiques are intertwined together.[5] Darko Suvin also observes that the ontological questions about the nature of being that arise in Dick's fiction have a genesis in socio-political critiques ("P. K." 15). This chapter demonstrates that the countercultural notions in novels such as *The Three Stigmata of Palmer Eldritch* (1964) and *Do Androids Dream* lead naturally to an exploration of the nature of reality, which in turn results in philosophical and theological speculation and the construction of new mythic systems in Dick's later works.[6]

In the 1960s, the American counterculture movement railed against the inequality inherent in Western capitalism. It protested against a system that afforded comfort and security to the privileged middle class while minority groups, both domestically and abroad, suffered civil rights violations, gender discrimination and poverty (McWilliams 1; 30). We see countercultural attitudes that denigrate consumer capitalism expressed throughout Dick's SF. Prominent thinkers of the time, including the German-American scholar Herbert Marcuse (1898–1979), also articulate sharp criticisms of Western social systems.[7] In *Eros and Civilization: A Philosophical Inquiry into Freud* (1955), Marcuse argues that all citizens living under capitalism are dominated by a system that robs them of autonomy. He writes: "intensified progress seems to be bound up with intensified unfreedom. Throughout the world of industrial civilization, the domination of man by man is growing in scope and efficiency" (23). He further argues that the social ideologies that are responsible for the repression of human instincts and the enslavement of humankind to the capitalist machinery generate an illusory reality, which perpetuates established norms (*One* 123).

Marcuse's arguments echo Immanuel Kant's eighteenth-century assertion that "Everywhere there is restriction on freedom" ("What" 85), facilitated by ideologies that construct man-made realities (*Critique* 41–42). As in the works of Kant and Marcuse, socio-political critique in Dick's SF is linked to an examination of the nature of existence and the insubstantiality of human ideological constructions. By examining reality and presenting it as an illusion, Dick's fictions interrogate the validity of the systems of thought that construct our perception of the universe and search for alternative ways of thinking.

Questions about the nature of Being and how reality is perceived are also explored in the writings of the Presocratic philosophers of the fifth and sixth centuries BC. Dick admits in a 1980 interview that "The Pre-Socratics always fascinated [him]" ("Philip" 46) and we can trace an engagement with Presocratic notions in his SF.[8] Heraclitus' suggestions that most men do not draw knowledge from experience but, rather, from opinion (29; D. 17; IV) reflects Kant's later philosophy and offers an illustration of the impact of ideology on human perceptions.[9] We see characters consistently blinded by the rhetoric of dominant political systems in Dick's SF in which the true nature of the universe is often occluded under layers of state-generated dogma. For Dick, SF offers an opportunity to resist "accepted" reality by highlighting the insubstantial nature of human society.

In a 1980 interview Dick observes that "the function of SF psychologically is to cut the reader loose from the actual world that he inhabits; it deconstructs time, space, reality" ("Philip" 45). Thus, in SF, established systems can be extirpated and new ideas can be explored. This function coincides with the objectives of the counterculture. Sociologist J. Milton Yinger comments that "counterculturalists can be thought of as the shamans of urban society, dreaming new dreams, formulating new myths, forging alternative paradigms" (9). I contend that Dick is just such a "shaman." His SF seeks to critique existing systems while offering new myths to replace established patterns.

The myths that Dick produces in his SF between 1964 and 1981 are increasingly religious. In drawing on Presocratic ideas about the illusory nature of reality to critique consumer capitalism, Dick also engages with Presocratic notions about spiritual matters. Just as the Presocratics posit a divine being behind the illusory veil of reality, Dick's novels increasingly explore the possibility that something true, real and divine underlies the phenomenal realm and seeks to intervene in the human world. Such a being is particularly evident in *Ubik* (1969), *A Maze of Death* (1970) and *VALIS* (1981). This incorporation of theology into Dick's SF can also be attributed to the influence of Platonic and Gnostic doctrines on Dick's writing, as well as to Dick's own personal religious journey.

Dick had an ambivalent relationship with established religion. In 1963 he abandoned atheism and joined the Episcopal Church (Mckee, *Pink* 13). Dick notes in a 1970 letter to an Australian fanzine that he joined the "Anglo-Catholic Church" ("Letter" 32) after experiencing a disturbing vision, which would later inspire *The Three Stigmata*. He further states that, although he "even took the rite of unction … it didn't help, and [he] wandered away from the Church" (32). However, critic Gabriel Mckee argues that Dick ultimately favors Judeo-Christian doctrines in his SF (Mckee, *Pink* 31).[10] In contrast, numerous critics, including Howard Canaan ("Metafiction" 391), Critchley, Robert Galbreath ("Fantastic" 332) and Roger J. Stilling (91; 96), emphasize the Gnostic notions present in Dick's SF.[11] There is no doubt that Dick's work incorporates both Gnostic and Christian notions but I will argue that the theologies presented in Dick's SF cannot be classified neatly into any particular orthodoxy. Rather, he incorporates a range of religious orthodoxies, Presocratic notions, pagan myths and modern philosophies into new, composite myths.

The myths presented in Dick's SF eventually blend with Dick's personal philosophy. In February and March 1974 Dick had a series of visionary experiences that he would spend the rest of his life trying to understanding. He represents these experiences, which he refers to using the abbreviation "2-3-74," in *VALIS* and describes them in his private writings. Importantly, Dick's interpretations of his mystical experiences strongly correlate with the mythic ideas presented in his earlier SF. This suggests that the myths presented in Dick's SF constitute a deliberate attempt to explore, through a fictional medium, the nature of the universe. It further indicates that Dick's interest in religious myth is grounded in his socio-political fiction, rather than finding its genesis in his 2-3-74 visions. Dick's SF reflects the social disillusionment of his historical context and seeks to represent the true nature of reality. Like the SF of Wells and Clarke, Dick's novels tend to ultimately depict a system in which a benevolent deity guides humankind. Here, again, we see some of the most influential SF of the twentieth century exploring theological issues and generating spiritual myths for the modern world.

Countercultural Revolt in a World of Androids

Like Wells, Dick recognizes the potential of SF to explore sociological issues.[12] In his 1955 article "Pessimism in Science Fiction" Dick writes, "[SF] has always been a protest medium" (54), and goes on to explain that, for SF writers during the Cold War, the self-destruction of human civilization is an often unavoidable theme. In Dick's SF in particular we see a representation of capitalism, and the ideological systems it supports, threatening humankind and repressing individual freedom. In *The Three Stigmata* and *Do Androids Dream* protagonists are manipulated by elaborate, dehumanizing systems that utilize medical technology and consumer products to pacify the populace. Significantly, Dick's SF does not simply criticize existing ideologies, it identifies the insubstantial core of human social constructs and, subsequently, the illusory nature of consensus reality. In *Ubik* and *A Maze of Death* protagonists are represented as trapped within layers of unreality, unable to trust their perceptions. Dick draws on Presocratic philosophy and the works of Kant and Heidegger to depict space and time as constructs through which individuals lose any authentic sense of self within a reality formed from repressive ideologies.

In 1955, Dick observes "a worldwide loss of faith in science and scientific progress" ("Pessimism" 54). He comments that this "loss of faith in the idea of progress ... extends over the whole cultural milieu" (54). While this sentiment may have been truer for Europe and the United Kingdom than for the United States during the 1950s, Dick is correct in his observation that, after World War II, SF was frequently dealing with stories of nuclear disaster and dystopia.[13] Certainly by the 1960s, which saw the rise of the counterculture movement, the United States was experiencing the lack of faith described by Dick. In the 1960s, the American counterculture rebelled against the Establishment's perceived perpetuation of conventional morality, civil rights violations, authoritarianism in universities, gender discrimination and the war in Southeast Asia (McWilliams 1). Critics of Western capitalism called attention to the lack of popular control over political, economic and educational institutions (McWilliams 30).

For the counterculture, Western capitalism was regarded as a system that reproduces itself through the manipulation and repression of the individual. Marcuse wrote in 1955 that "As the affluence of society depends increasingly on the uninterrupted production and consumption of waste, gadgets, planned obsolescence, and means of destruction, the individuals have to be adapted to these requirements" (*Eros* 11). This notion is echoed by Horselover Fat in Dick's 1981 novel *VALIS*. In the novel, Fat, having experienced a divine vision, seeks to make sense of his reality.[14] Fat observes that 1960s America "was totally fucked.... The authorities became ... psychotic.... They wanted to put all persons who were not clones of the establishment away" (12).[15]

This fear that the state's aim is to render its citizens compliant participants in the capitalist process is explored through Dick's representation of androids in his SF and nonfiction. In a 1972 speech, Dick observes that living men can become "analogues of machines" ("The Android" 187) by relinquishing their own desires and becoming soulless instruments of the social apparatus. He argues that, while society has always required the compromise of individual desires, "the production of ... inauthentic human activity has become a science of government and suchlike agencies now" (187). He further states that, while the limitation of human behavior serves the purpose of sustaining social stability, it "limits [individuals] ... to the fulfilling of an aim outside of [their] own personal ... destiny" (187). This "reduction of humans to mere use" (187) is regarded by Dick as "the greatest evil imaginable" (187).

Rick Deckard experiences this evil in *Do Androids Dream*. He is tasked with hunting and exterminating androids that have escaped slavery on Mars and are seeking refuge on Earth. However, Deckard's hyper-empathic nature means that he includes androids within his range of empathic identification and hates having to destroy them. To "retire" the androids contradicts Deckard's sense of morality. However, he is eventually advised that "It is the basic condition of life, to be required to violate your own identity" (155). Thus to live within contemporary human society is to compromise one's selfhood in deference to an organized system and to become "an unnatural self" (201). In arguing that developed civilization depends on "intensified regimentation and control" (*Eros* 77), Marcuse also observes this point. He writes that the full satisfaction of individual needs is sacrificed when the external reality of an overarching ideological system is imposed on the individual (77).

Marcuse further explains that civilization is "antagonistic to [individual] happiness" (*Eros* 33) in that it "involves the repressive modification ... of happiness" (33). In other words, the apparatus of the civilized society manipulates the populace into adopting a set of desires that will serve to perpetuate the status quo. Marcuse argues that the "Scientific management of instinctual needs" (11) has become vital for the reproduction of capitalism. He observes that consumer goods and services are used as a means of providing an inauthentic form of cathexis to pacify the populace by satisfying their libidinal needs in such a way as to maintain the dominant culture (11). We can see this manipulative use of consumer products in *The Three Stigmata*.

In *The Three Stigmata*, Mars colonists achieve an escape from their miserable existence through the purchase of accessories for their "Perky

Pat" layouts. These faddish dollhouses are sold in conjunction with the drug Can-D[16] to achieve "the miracle of translation" (37) whereby "the miniature artefacts of the layout no longer merely [represent] Earth but [become] Earth" (37) and the drug users join together psychically in a "fusion of doll-inhabitation" (37). Any women taking part in the hallucination collectively become Perky Pat while male participants merge to become Pat's boyfriend, Walt. They are then able to enjoy a temporary illusion of the idyllic life on Earth that they each crave. As protagonist Barney Mayerson comments, one plug of Can-D "provides a reason for living" (24) by offering an escape from the dismal reality of social duty and providing libidinal satisfaction, albeit briefly. Of course, this happiness is illusory, the transient satisfaction just enough to prevent rebellion, suggesting that any joy offered under consumer capitalism is superficial and ultimately false.

The inability to achieve real world, lasting catharsis via the Perky Pat layout leads the characters in *The Three Stigmata* to experiment with a new drug, Chew-Z, peddled by Palmer Eldritch, a mysterious traveller who has returned to Earth after a prolonged absence in the Proxima Centurai system. Eldritch promises his customers the ability to visit, and alter, their pasts. However, the slogan "God ... promises eternal life.... *I can deliver it*" (86) betrays the capitalist bent of Eldritch's endeavors. Similarly, his antagonistic relationship with Leo Bulero, who runs the company responsible for Can-D and the Perky Pat layouts, undermines the supposed spiritualism of the Chew-Z experience. Despite the mystical overtones of Eldritch's Christian name, Suvin also regards him as a "mad capitalist" ("P. K." 14).

We eventually learn that Eldritch's primary desire is to have his product consumed and, subsequently, to consume humanity. He aims to become "everyone on.... Mars" (204) through the commercial, and thus psychological, domination of the colony. By forcing his product on humankind, Eldritch gains access, both literally and metaphorically, to the social consciousness and can thus "guide ... civilization" (204). The power of consumer products, and their associated cultural behaviors, to manipulate society is also noted by Marcuse. He argues in 1955 that the manipulation of consciousness in supposedly free "popular cultures" (*Eros* 85) involves the coordination of public and private existence through the promotion of thoughtless leisure activities and anti-intellectual ideologies.

The civilization of Earth in *Do Androids Dream* is also manipulated using consumer items, medical intervention and state-sanctioned activities. The "mood organ" is used to generate artificial emotions in lieu of genuine environmental stimuli and the "empathy box" is a state-regulated means of connecting with other human beings.[17] In 1972 Dick admits that he is particularly worried about "establishment drugs, prescribed by reputable doctors or given in ... psychiatric hospitals" ("The Android" 200). He terms these substances "pacification drugs" (200) and describes them as a way that the state transforms humans into androids. In *Do Androids Dream* the chemical modification of human emotions has become a part of everyday life, the citizen self-regulating their emotional responses to cope with reality. Similarly, the technovisual empathy box provides citizens with a government-sanctioned form of spiritual catharsis.[18]

The empathy box allows citizens to experience the core narrative of Mercerism, a worldwide religion that follows the perpetual rise and fall of Wilbur Mercer. The cyclic narrative of Mercer's torture at the hands of the authorities, descent into a tomb world and eventual renewal represents a retelling of Christ's death and resurrection that acts as a parable for the post-holocaust world of the novel.[19] The surviving citizens of the nuclear war use the empathy box to psychically fuse with Mercer, and one another, and experience a sense of upward striving. Protagonist John Isidore describes the empathy box as "the most personal possession [he has]. ... [because] it's the way [he] touch[es] other humans" (57). Thus, the empathy box works to fabricate a sense of community in a world of isolation. It satisfies the human need for empathy without actually altering the status quo.

It is ultimately revealed that Mercerism, as experienced via the empathy box, is a "swindle" (182).[20] To Isidore's distress, it is proven that Mercer's upward climb is a fictional film produced on a "cheap, Hollywood ... sound stage" (182) while Mercer himself is played by a failed actor. Mercerism is simply a politically expedient form of social control. Earlier in the novel, the UN Secretary General endorses the religion, declaring: "Mankind needs more empathy" (65). Far from being a "superior entity ... from another star" (182), Mercer has thus been imposed on humanity by those in authority. We learn that the empathy box "reduce[s] crime by making citizens more concerned about the plight of their neighbors" (65). Furthermore, as critic Jill Galvan observes, Mercerism allows each citizen to empathize with Mercer, "a noble criminal" (Galvan 417), and, in doing so, vent any feelings of rebellion within a private, controlled space. Mercerism thus works as a means of repression by dissipating transgressive sentiments and preventing the rise of countercultural voices.[21]

Furthermore, the ability of the empathy box to generate genuine interpersonal connections is called into question in the novel and can be interpreted in contradictory ways. Critic Christopher A. Sims argues that the empathy box "shows us that technology can be used as a guide to return [humankind] to the humanity that they have abandoned for solipsistic individualism" (68). He thus asserts that Mercerism is a socially beneficial religion (79) and that the novel "protests against the dehumanizing effects of technology" (86) articulated by Heidegger (1889–1976) in *The Question Concerning Technology* (Heidegger, *The Question* 4).

However, it can also be argued that the empathy box fails to generate authentic empathic connections. I posit that genuine empathy, involving a true emotional connection between independent minds, cannot be achieved through the empathy box, which is exploitative rather than communal. After purchasing a much desired goat, Deckard is told by his wife, Iran, that they must fuse with Mercer, and the rest of the populace, to transmit their mood of euphoria to everybody else. We could read this, in light of Sims' comments, as an instance of technology being used to forge interpersonal relationships. However, while Iran believes it is immoral to keep positive emotions private, Deckard laments that "[the rest of the populace will] have our joy ... but we'll lose.... Our joy will be lost" (150; 151). This suggests that no true emotional equality is achieved through the empathy box. Rather the meager joy of the few is dispersed among the desperate community.[22]

Indeed, Jameson comments that the interactive televisual spectacles offered by both Perky Pat and Mercerism constitute a meditation on mass culture (371), fusion resulting in a loss of individual autonomy and immersion in a vast, state-regulated social system.[23] Heidegger observes that Being is always constructed by social relationships. Heidegger uses the term "Dasein" to signify human existence, which he regards as characterized as *"being-in-the-world"* (*The Concept* 7E). For Heidegger, Being is always connected to the social environment and there is no subjectivity that is free from being-in-the-world. He theorizes that "As ... being-in-the-world, Dasein is ... [also] *being-with-one-another*" (7E). This concept is highlighted by Isidore in *Do Androids Dream*. He believes that "You have to be with other people.... In order to live at all" (178). However, while human citizens in *Do Androids Dream* desire to exist in community with others, the empathy box ultimately sheds them of their individual identity and emotions.

Heidegger points out this problematic aspect of Being, stating: "Being-with-one-another dissolves one's own Dasein completely into the ... Being of 'the Others'" (*Being and Time* 164). Dasein thus "stands in *subjection*" (164) to the communal group and popular opinion determines the Being of each individual. Furthermore, with regard to the public environment, Heidegger notes that "In utilizing public means of transport and in making use of information services ... every Other is like the next" (164). We see this in the fusion involved in both the Perky Pat experience in *The Three Stigmata* and Mercerism in *Do Androids Dream*. The inherent empathic connection between humans is used here as a means of enslaving the population and transforming them into uniform instruments of the system.

The androids that Deckard hunts, which have been created for slave labor, represent the potential end point of socially conditioned humankind. In a 1981 interview with Paul M. Sammon, author of *Future Noir: The Making of Blade Runner* (1996), Dick says that *Do Androids Dream* stems from his "interest in the problem of differentiating the authentic human being from the reflexive machine ... [or] android" (Sammon 16). Dick declares, "android is a metaphor for people who are physiologically human but [behave] in a nonhuman way" (16). This inhumanity is, for Dick, the product of inauthentic Dasein: Dasein that has been deprived of true empathy and has been transformed into a cog in the social machine. Dick observes that the soldiers of the Nazi regime characterized this state. He comments that the Nazis operated under a "defective group mind, a mind so emotionally defective that the word 'human' could not be applied to them" (16).

The lethal potential of an unsympathetic being is represented in *Do Androids Dream* through the behavior of the androids. As Eric S. Rabkin observes, Dick's representation of the androids is absolutely unsympathetic ("Irrational" 164). The androids have "great intellect" (*Do Androids* 87) but are deplorably "cold" (86). Even Luba Luft, an android herself, regards the androids' lack of empathy as an irredeemable failing. She admits that her life "consist[s] of imitating the human.... Imitating ... a superior life form" (116). Although Deckard and Isidore exhibit empathy, in varying degrees, for androids and electric animals, their hyper-empathic responses serve not to elevate the androids to human status but to contrast the coldness of the androids with human warmth. The fundamental inhumanity of the androids is eventually emphasized through Pris' ruthless cruelty toward perhaps the last spider on Earth (179–80; 183).[24] Dick points out, in 1968, that "in the novel, Isidore has a naive love directed toward the androids; Rick Deckard's view is that the androids ... must be destroyed. ... when Isidore is confronted by the cruelty of the androids as they cut the legs off the spider ... Deckard's view [wins] out" ("Notes" 155).

Although Galvan cites Rachel Rosen's professed friendship with her fellow androids as evidence of android empathy (414–15), Rachel's words and actions are rendered suspect when it is revealed that she is using them to manipulate Deckard into allowing the androids to live. Furthermore, in describing her connection with Pris, Rachel says she feels "Identification; there goes I" (164). She elaborates, saying, "We *are* machines, stamped out like bottle caps…. I'm just representative of a type" (164). In recognizing Pris as simply a version of herself, Rachel is demonstrating a lack of authentic Dasein. Her own sense of self is subsumed by the Other and she is unable to regard the Other as anything but herself. Under such circumstances genuine empathy, the emotional connection of distinct beings, is impossible. Thus, the android represents the final transition of the individual, under consumer capitalism, from human to mechanism.[25]

In conflating Nazi soldiers with the androids created by American capitalism in *Do Androids Dream*, Dick's SF draws a link between American culture and Hitler's Germany. This correlation grows more marked in Dick's later writing. Indeed, in a 1973 letter to an Australian fanzine, Dick describes Richard Nixon's government as a "despotic gang of professional, organized criminals who came to power legally (as did Hitler in Germany)" (*The Exegesis* 48). Dick further adds that "We Americans are now faced with precisely the situation the German people of the 1930s faced: we elected a criminal government … and are stuck" (48). While these views could be regarded as paranoiac, Dick is not alone in likening Cold War capitalism to fascism. Marcuse writes in 1972 that Western capitalism has reached a new stage of development and that the defense of the capitalist system necessitates the domestic and international organization of counter-revolutionary action (*Counterrevolution* 1). He writes that "in its [current] extreme manifestations, [the capitalist system] practices the horrors of the Nazi regime" (1).

In justifying this claim, Marcuse elaborates thus: "Wholesale massacres in Indochina, Indonesia, the Congo, Nigeria, Pakistan, and the Sudan are unleashed against everything which is called 'communist' or which is in revolt against governments subservient to imperialist countries" (*Counterrevolution* 1). He further cites military and fascist dictatorships in Latin America; the military shootings of student protesters at Jackson State and Kent State universities in 1970; and the assassination of liberals, including Martin Luther King and John F. Kennedy, as further evidence of the horrors perpetrated by Western capitalism (1). Like Dick, Marcuse regards Nixon's government as endangering freedom. He writes,

"The Nixon Administration has strengthened the counterrevolutionary organization of society in all directions.... The normal equipment of the police ... resembles that of the S. S." (24). On the subject of police, Dick similarly writes: "something much like the police state I depicted in *Flow My Tears, the Policeman Said* [(1974)] has come to light" ("The Short" 33). He observes that, as early as the 1950s, the police apparatus was expanding in the United States. Dick asserts: "in ... about 1953, two FBI agents came to visit me and asked me to spy on my wife, who at that time attended the University of California at Berkeley and knew ... students ... who were politically active. From then on the secret political police apparatus grew" (33).

Marcuse fears that such counter-revolutionary measures, coupled with "the monopoly capitalist management of the population" (*Counterrevolution* 28), will lead to a worse form of fascism than that seen in Hitler's Germany (25). For Marcuse, "The capability to overkill and to overburn, and the mental behaviour that goes with it" (*Eros* 15) in the Cold War world is evidence of the technical and scientific overdevelopment of a capitalist society characterized by "exploitation and repression" (15). In light of these concerns, the pacification of the affluent population through consumerism becomes a sinister attempt to disguise the true nature of capitalist society, which Marcuse represents as a "society at war" (15).[26] The concern for Dick and Marcuse is that the expanding middle class is blind to the dystopian nature of their society. In *VALIS*, Fat conceives of the Western world as part of a "trans-temporal constant" (54), an empire, which he terms the "Black Iron Prison" (54). According to Fat, "Everyone who [has] ever lived [is] literally surrounded by the iron walls of the prison; they [are] all inside it and none of them [know] it" (54–55).

Pivotal to Dick's conception of the Black Iron Prison is that it is maintained by ideological apparatuses that keep the populace occluded, so that they are unaware of the truth of their oppression. In several 1974 letters, Dick refers to these apparatuses as "the Lie" (*The Exegesis* 18), stating, "The Lie deals with talk, written or spoken" (20), and explaining that "passivity, [and] resignation ... are intended by-products of the Lie" (18). In other words, the Black Iron Prison is maintained by ideologies, constructed through language.[27] Thus, the consensus reality through which Western capitalism maintains itself is regarded by Dick as insubstantial. For Dick, perceptual reality is an illusion, constructed via rhetoric. This notion becomes a fundamental thematic in Dick's SF, which consistently seeks to determine the nature of the "true" reality that lies beneath the obvious, man-made, structure.

Interrogating Reality: The Ideas of the Presocratics, Kant and Heidegger in Dick's Writing

In his 1975 work, *Early Greek Thinking*, Heidegger observes that "Since the beginning of Western thought the Being of beings emerges as what is alone worthy of thought" (76). This sentiment is central to Heidegger's work. In a lecture course presented from 1933 to 1934 he defines philosophy as "the unceasing, questioning struggle over the essence and Being of beings" (*Being and Truth* 9). Heidegger further states: "that in Greek antiquity the Being of beings became worthy of thought *is* the beginning of the West and *is* the hidden source of its destiny" (*Early* 76).[28] Interestingly, Heidegger regards the Presocratics as far more in tune with authentic Being than contemporary humanity is. He writes that it is difficult for twentieth-century thinkers to engage with the ancient Greek beginnings of Western philosophy "not because our sources are scant, but because our Dasein is impoverished" (*The Essence* 11). In exploring the nature of reality and Being, it is, therefore, unsurprising that Dick turns to the ancient Greeks and draws on Presocratic philosophy.

Dick was introduced to ancient Greek thought at the University of California, Berkeley, where he took a course in philosophy and read Plato (Dick, "Philip" 56). He was also fascinated by the Presocratics from a young age (46). In *VALIS* Fat states that "In all [his] reading [he has] ... never found anything more significant [than Edward Hussey's *The Presocratics*] as an insight into the nature of reality" (43). The Presocratics, and Heraclitus in particular, explore the notion that the perceived world is illusory and that the true structure of the universe is occluded, a concept that we see included in much of Dick's SF.

Fat incorporates Heraclitus' philosophy into his own worldview. He quotes Hussey's translation and commentary, declaring: "In *Fragment 123*, Heraclitus says, 'The nature of things is in the habit of concealing itself.' ... to which Edward Hussey adds, 'Consequently, [Heraclitus] ... agree[s] ... that reality [is] to some extend *hidden*'" (43).[29] Heraclitus argues that knowledge should come from experience (35; D.55; XIV). However, he notes that "Most men do not think things in the way they encounter them, do not recognize what they experience, but believe their own opinions" (29; D.17; IV). Significantly, these opinions are not private or unique to each individual, rather "The world of the waking is ... shared" (Heraclitus, 31; D.89; VI) and the individual "take[s] the mob as their teacher" (57; D. 104; LIX). In other words, our understanding of the world is not drawn from experience, but is based on dominant cultural beliefs. The appeal of such a philosophy for Dick is obvious: it correlates with his belief that humanity is deceived by the ideological systems that surround it.

The notion that "true" reality is concealed by appearances is also articulated by other Presocratic thinkers. Parmenides observes that "persuasion attends on reality" (56; fr. 3), indicating the malleability of consensus reality. This correlates with Kant's eighteenth-century statement that, although "knowledge begins with experience" (*Critique* 41), our mind tends to supply additional data that has not been derived from experience (42). He writes that this supplementary knowledge, which he terms *a priori*, is "absolutely independent of all experience" (43) yet becomes, in our awareness, indistinguishable from the raw material of experience (43). Kant asserts that all human beings are "in possession of certain modes of *a priori* knowledge, and even the common understanding is never without them" (43). The influence of Kant's philosophy on contemporary thought is unmistakable. Dick acknowledges Kant's influence in a 1964 article, saying: "It now is universally accepted that reality 'in itself,' as Kant puts it, is really unknown to any sentient organism" ("Drugs" 171). Marcuse also invokes Kant, writing: "Reason is the ... power ... that establishes ... the truth for men" (*One* 123). According to Kantian philosophy, the reason that creates truth is not based simply on experience but also on *a priori* knowledge, drawn from ideology. Thus, the true nature of reality remains veiled.

This notion becomes central to novels such as *Ubik* and *A Maze of Death* in which slippages of time and reality reveal the illusory nature of the world inhabited by the characters. In *Ubik* the protagonists are isolated in a version of America that is regressing back through historical time while the characters themselves fall victim to an entropic force that accelerates physical decay. As the characters witness elements of their environment revert to older, historical forms they realize that the changing reality they perceive is "*not a private vision*" (156) but is shared. They soon realize that their collective minds "exert some control" (125) over perceptual reality. However, it is ultimately revealed that their reality is "a pseudo-environment ... highly unstable and unsupported by any ergic substructure" (134). This novel suggests that the stability of reality relies on a highly structured collective consciousness. Thus, because the protagonists are trapped, alone, in an alternate world, there are insufficient minds to formulate a concrete reality. This highlights the constructed nature of perceived reality.[30]

Furthermore, Dick reflects in 1975 that "the world, was arrived at a priori" (*The Exegesis* 66). The *a priori* reality of *Ubik* breaks down as the protagonist's "perceptions ... [begin] to differ" (125) and they realize that systems of thought inform external reality. Prior to his death, one character, Al Hammond, sees before him a desert of ice before realizing that it is only a "projection on [his] part" (126). He reflects: "It isn't the universe which is being entombed by layers of wind, cold, darkness and ice; all this is going on within me, and yet I seem to see it outside.... When I blink out ... the whole universe will disappear" (126). Thus, *Ubik* suggests that the world, as we understand it, is nothing more than a projection, sustained by our minds.

Similarly, in *A Maze of Death* the protagonists' understanding is limited by a "veil of illusion" (107). In the novel, fourteen individuals are sent to the mysterious colony world, Delmak-O. They all subscribe to a religious theology that represents humankind as "mired in [a] quasi-reality" (102) in which they are "prisoners of [their] own preconceptions and expectations" (102). This point is adroitly emphasized by the final revelation that the Delmak-O universe is actually a virtual reality, which the characters enter and experience through "polyencephalic fusion" (178). We learn that the Delmak-O reality, and its culture, is a composite of all human knowledge, suggesting again that human reason constructs the insubstantial reality that we perceive.

During a theological discussion with other characters in the novel, Wade Frazer, a Delmak-O colonist, announces, "Nobody sees reality as it actually is.... As Kant proved" (*A Maze* 102). He goes on to argue that "Space and time are models of perception" (102). This assertion is a reference to Kant's description of space and time as belonging "only to the form of intuition" (*Critique* 68). He writes, "Space is not an empirical concept which has been derived from outer experiences.... Space is [an] ... *a priori* representation, which underlies all our intuitions" (68), and that "Time is not something that exists of itself" (76). In other words, in addition to the political ideologies and social norms that inform reality, clock-time and space act as structuring devices that humans have overlaid onto the universe. Dick reflects in 1964 that "the categories of organization, time, and space are mechanisms by which ... living [beings] ... [create] an environment that is relatively constant" ("Drugs" 171).

This point is demonstrated in both *Ubik* and *A Maze of Death* when reality unwinds as historical time breaks down. Seth Morley in *A Maze of Death* reflects that "Time ... is shutting down around us" (58) while Joe Chip in *Ubik* believes himself to be "outside of time entirely" (167). As the ordering principle of time ebbs away, the illusory nature of human reality becomes clear in *Ubik* and "past phases of reality" (123) resurface. It is thus revealed in Dick's SF that "Thoughts of the Brain are experienced by us as arrangements and rearrangements—change—in the physical universe" (*VALIS* 24). According to Dick, this process has led to the creation of the Black Iron Prison world.

Heidegger too regards clock-time as responsible for the construction of what we call reality. In a 1924 lecture, Heidegger appropriates Albert Einstein's relativity theory to assert that "There is no absolute time" (*The Concept* 3E). Heidegger states that "Once time has been defined as clock time ... there is no hope for ever arriving at its original meaning again" (18E–19E). In other words, clock-time, organized around human events, generates a reality that has been constructed by human perceptions. This adds greater significance to the disintegration of clock-time in Dick's SF, suggesting that liberation from time may offer an opportunity to escape inauthentic Dasein and achieve a greater understanding of Being. In 1977, Dick observes that "The basic theme in [*The Three*] *Stigmata*, *Ubik* and [*A*] *Maze* [*of Death* is] the ... illusory skin stretched over ... reality" (*The Exegesis* 218). The nature of the reality that underlies this illusory human world and the way humankind can obtain an understanding of this latent structure is another key theme in Dick's SF.

While the phenomenal world is represented as illusory in much of Dick's SF, there is a strong suggestion in his novels that a latent realm underlies perceived reality. Heraclitus states that "latent structure is master of obvious structure" (Hussey 35; D.54).[31] This belief underpins Dick's SF. Fat directly quotes this fragment in *VALIS* (43) while in *Do Androids Dream*, *The Three Stigmata*, *Ubik* and *A Maze of Death* a spiritual realm exists and intrudes on the mundane world. Although these novels depict worlds of illusion and artificiality, there is a consistent suggestion that, beneath the thin veil of seeming reality, there is something real and true.[32]

In *Do Androids Dream*, a clear distinction is made between the real and the artificial. As we have already seen, human beings are privileged in the novel over the androids. A differentiation between state-imposed ideology and the true nature of the universe is also made apparent, through the representation of Mercer. As previously pointed out, Mercerism, as mediated through the empathy box, is debunked. However, Deckard's and Isidore's personal encounters with Mercer suggest that a divine realm exists. When the state religion is exposed as a sham, Isidore's reality begins to break down. He "[sees] the dust and ruin of [his] apartment ... spreading out everywhere. ... [and] he [feels] the floor beneath his feet give [way]"

(185). This destabilization of consensus reality allows Isidore to glimpse the latent structure beneath. Isidore falls into a tomb world, "a pit of corpses and dead bones" (20), where he encounters Mercer and is raised back into life.

Mercer explains to Isidore that, although the government-endorsed version of Mercerism is false, "nothing has changed" (187). In other words, the divine exists regardless of human ideology. Mercer declares, "I'm still here…. I lifted you from the tomb world … and I will continue to lift you…. I will never stop searching for you" (187). This relatively early representation of a deity who pursues humankind and seeks to penetrate the illusory reality of Earth establishes a trope that is explored in more detail in Dick's later works, especially *Ubik* and *VALIS*. Dick reflects on Mercer's realness in his private writing. In 1978 he writes that the "Bottom Line" (*The Exegesis* 367) is that Mercer is real. He calls the fact that Mercer actually exists, beneath the fakery of the state religion, a "secret within a secret" (367).[33]

A layering of illusion and truth is also presented in *A Maze of Death*. During the Delmak-O experience, the characters espouse a theology based on a "composite religion" (181) that synthesizes all aspects of advanced Earth religions.[34] The religion describes a triune deity consisting of the creative "Mentufacturer," the supportive "Walker-on-Earth" and the "Intercessor," who takes the place of supplicants in pain. The "Form Destroyer" offers a malign counterpoint to this benevolent trinity. As previously mentioned, the Delmak-O experience, and its theology, are ultimately revealed to be a shared hallucination. However, at the end of the novel protagonist, Seth Morley encounters the Intercessor outside of the virtual world. Like Mercer in *Do Androids Dream*, the Intercessor promises to help humankind, saying, "you will die and be reborn. I will guide you to what you want, and to what is fitting and proper for you" (187). Thus, here again, we have the suggestion in Dick's SF that a spiritual realm exists beyond the phenomenal world and influences the human realm.

Although *The Three Stigmata* does not incorporate any suggestion of a benign deity, it does present the reality of a latent, spiritual structure in the universe. As in *Do Android Dream*, characters in *The Three Stigmata* are aware of a tomb world that threatens to overwhelm humankind. They acknowledge that "Below [is] the tomb-world, the … world of the demonic. At median extend[s] the layer of the human, but at any instant man [may] plunge … into the hell-layer beneath. Or … ascend to the ethereal world above" (71). Importantly, it is not simply after death that individuals experience these other realms (71). Rather, these different planes exist simultaneously, with the "possibility of ascent" (71) always available. The pivotal question in this novel becomes how to avoid the tomb world and achieve ascendance.

Thus, although the "near-sacred" (*The Three* 37) ritual of doll inhabitation is revealed as a consumer scam, the characters' search for a "purifying experience" (41) and an escape from corporeality in *The Three Stigmata* is valid, and the supernatural forces they encounter when translated are real. Anne, a Mars colonist, remarks upon her first use of Can-D that the experience is "*the only hint we can have*" (149) of what it is like to be "born again, with new bodies ... incorruptible" (148) in the ethereal world. The capitalist endeavors of Eldritch and Bulero are ultimately eclipsed by the wider spiritual implications of translation. As Leo Bulero admits, in spite of the exploitative motives of the drug peddlers, translation does offer a glimpse of "The light ... that underlies the play of phenomena which we call 'reality'" (106).

Dick's SF suggests, then, that, although religion can be exploited for capitalist and ideological purposes, the universe is indeed shaped by a latent, divine structure. In his novels, there is a consistent representation of a higher realm, containing godlike entities, that underlies the illusory reality constructed by human society.[35] The exploitation of theology by government and consumer bodies does not eliminate the reality of the divine in *The Three Stigmata* and *Do Androids Dream*. It does, however, mask the truth from view. Dick's characters frequently exist in a state of occlusion, unable to discern truth from illusion. The search for the means to transcend the illusory world of ideological repression is a core question throughout Dick's corpus, from his 1960s novels to his later, overtly theological SF.

The Presocratics were pessimistic about the possibility of achieving enlightenment. Xenophanes wrote: "clear and certain truth no man has seen nor will there be anyone who knows about the gods" (39; fr. 34) because "all things are wrapped in *appearances*" (Hussey 35; fr. 34).[36] In Dick's SF, however, there is a constant search for ways to lift the veil of seeming reality that clouds the truth from view. In the 1955 article "Pessimism in Science Fiction," which examines the prevalence of doom stories in SF, Dick writes that "Rather than writing stories about doom, perhaps we should take the doom for granted and go from there" (55). We can see this logic in action in the way Dick's novels incorporate a search for divine truth. The debased and illusory nature of consensus reality is taken for granted. The characters live in worlds where the truth is hidden. However, Dick's SF also explores ways that occlusion may be overcome and seeks to present new myths to explain the underlying nature of the universe.

Dick's SF incorporates elements from pagan myths and modern religions in its examination of ways to achieve enlightenment. In particular, Dick's novels draw on the works of the scholar of comparative religion Mircea Eliade to generate new myths of spiritual transcendence.[37] In *Myth and Reality* Eliade examines "societies in which myth is—or was until very recently—'living,' in ... that it supplies models for human behaviour and ... gives meaning and value to life" (2). Eliade, then, does not view myth in the conventional sense, as an archaic fiction, but rather, sees myth as it was regarded by ancient societies, as a "true story" (1) that provides revelations and behavioral models. It is this kind of myth that Dick's SF can be regarded as producing for modern society.

Given that *Do Androids Dream* is set in a post-nuclear-war society, it is fitting that it draws on "end of the world" myths to explore the possibility of rebirth after collapse. Eliade writes that "Myths of cosmic cataclysms are extremely widespread" (*Myth* 54) and observes that most ancient "American myths of the End imply either a cyclic theory (as among the Aztecs), or the belief that the catastrophe will be followed by a new Creation, or ... universal regeneration" (58). Such myths inform Mercerism, which involves the "eternal" (*Do Androids* 66) cycle of Mercer's uphill journey. As Isidore explains, "At the top of the hill he's struck down; he sinks into the tomb world but then he rises inevitably. And us with him" (66). There is thus a cyclic sense of impending disaster inherent in the Mercer myth that describes entropy as constantly at work.

The association of the cataclysm myth with human failure (Eliade, *Myth* 54–55) makes its inclusion in the post-nuclear, capitalist setting of *Do Androids Dream* a pointed statement against Cold War politics. However, the cyclic end of the world myth offers the hope that a divine force will ultimately reverse entropy. Eliade notes that although "The belief that [a] catastrophe is the inevitable consequence of the ... decrepitude of the World appears to be ... common" (59), such myths also "announc[e] the imminent re-creation of the World" (60). The reversal of death achieved by Mercer suggests that social rejuvenation is possible, generating a myth of rebirth and escape from a doomed world.

Mercer's ability to reverse decay also draws on the Buddhist and Taoist belief in the individual's potential to conquer time. As we have previously seen, Dick's novels present time as a construct that allows humankind to organize reality within fixed parameters. The importance of overcoming time is explored in ancient myth, modern spiritual discourse and philosophy. Heidegger argues that "The clock shows us the now, but no clock ever shows the future or ... the past" (*The Concept* 17E). In other words, clock-time limits Being to the present and prevents a recognition of the relation of Being to all of time. Heidegger argues that, by grasping that "Dasein is the whole of time" (16E), the individual can come to a truer comprehension of the forces that have created their Being (*Being and Time* 437). This active apprehension of Being allows the individual to be "authentically ... what it can be" (*The Concept* 10E).

Similarly, according to Eliade, many mystical religions advocate a transcendence of time. Eliade observes a "continuity of human behaviour in respect to time, both down the ages and in various cultures" (*Myth* 87). He states that Indochinese mystical techniques and primitive therapies act on the principle that "*To cure the work of Time it is necessary to 'go back' and find the 'beginning of the World'*" (88). In Buddhism in particular, to attain the beginning of Time is to enter "the Timeless—the eternal present which preceded the temporal experience inaugurated by the 'fall' into human existence" (86). This technique of going back also allows for the discovery of one's past lives (86). Eliade explains that, for Buddhists, "To re-live one's past lives [is] to understand them and ... 'burn up' one's 'sins' ... the deeds done in the state of ignorance" (86). It is this escape from karmic law that Palmer Eldritch offers through the use of Chew-Z in *The Three Stigmata*.

As we have seen, Eldritch promises that Chew-Z will allow the user to relive their personal history and change the events of their past (176). However, his claim is false. No time-conquering catharsis is achieved by the characters in *The Three Stigmata*. Rather the drug-takers relive their history without any true ability to change it. Instead of freeing them from karmic law, the experience traps the user in Eldritch's fantasy world, which is "like being in hell. ... recurrent and unyielding" (176). The reality produced by Chew-Z is merely an "illusory world in which Eldritch holds the key positions as god" (176). The all-consuming nature of Eldritch's reality means that "once you get into ... [it] you can't quite scramble back out" (185). This representation of consumers who are absorbed into an illusory world constructed by an exploitative ruler can be read as a critique of capitalism, a comment on the drug culture of the 1960s, and a chilling representation of the unseen spiritual structure of the universe.[38]

In *The Three Stigmata*, we have a clear indication that neither knowledge nor spiritual renewal can be achieved through drugs. Although Dick was prone to exaggerate his LSD usage during the 1960s, he actually found the drug frightening and only tried it on a few occasions (Sutin 51). In

1972 Dick admits, "I was interested in experimenting with psychedelic drugs. That is over for me. Too many suicides, psychoses ... [and] irreversible damage to both heart and brain" ("The Android" 200). Dick reiterates this point in the author's note of *A Scanner Darkly* (1977), a novel about the effects of a drug called Substance D. Dick writes, "Drug misuse ... is a decision.... When a bunch of people begin to do it, it is a social error, a life-style. In this particular life-style the motto is 'Be happy now because tomorrow you are dying,' but the dying begins almost at once" (218). Dick regards the drug culture as exacting a "punishment [that is] beyond belief" (218). This is certainly the case for the characters in *The Three Stigmata*. Any fleeting satisfaction gained through Can-D or Chew-Z is outweighed by the resultant enslavement of both body and mind. This reflects Fat's statement in *VALIS*: "There is no door to God through dope; that is a lie peddled by the unscrupulous" (20).

Of course, Eldritch is far more than just an unscrupulous capitalist. His presence in *The Three Stigmata* raises unsettling spiritual questions. It is ultimately revealed that Eldritch is a malevolent deity. We learn that Eldritch "[went] to Prox a man and returned a god" (192). Eldritch encountered an incorporeal deity in intersystem space and became its host (186). As a god, Eldritch rules over a domain that is "absolutely evil" (149). Like the original curse following the Fall, Eldritch is described as the "price" (219) for accepting the impure sacrament of Chew-Z. The appearance of Eldritch's artificial hand, synthetic eyes and metallic jaw as stigmata in the human world is evidence of the deity's penetration and control of perceptual reality. The correlation of Eldritch with both capitalism and the divine suggests that, while the mundane world is, in part, constructed by human ideologies, a spiritual realm also underlies reality and influences the lives of men. The figure of Eldritch is thus illustrative of how sociological critique, in Dick's SF, leads naturally into a consideration of how other, spiritual factors influence reality.

The overwhelming figure of Eldritch represents the power of the spiritual structure of the universe, upon which humanity has no influence. Eldritch's "negative trinity of alienation, blurred reality, and despair" (229) finds no opposition in *The Three Stigmata*. Leo Bulero, who has undergone artificial evolution and has thus "lived a hundred thousand years" (229) of human development, initially considers himself a match for Eldritch. However, at the close of the novel, Bulero starts to exhibit the stigmata of Eldritch. Thus, while humanity has some influence over the ideological frameworks of the phenomenal world, it is unable to effectively manipulate the latent structure of the universe.

Interestingly, though, there is a suggestion in the novel that religious ritual can be used to mediate between human and spiritual structures. We learn that, because Eldritch is a previously unknown deity, humankind has had no opportunity to develop "mediating sacraments through which to protect [themselves]" (219) from him. Much of Eldritch's pervasive influence stems from this fact. The human characters are unable to "compel" (219) Eldritch through "careful, time-honored ... painstaking rituals" (219). Religion and mystical rituals thus become more than means of political, economic and social control. Religion is represented in *The Three Stigmata* as a legitimate means of understanding and interacting with the spiritual realm.

Eliade notes that, in ancient cultures, an elite few became experts in interacting with the latent structure of the universe. He writes: "Shamans are the 'elect,' and as such they have access to a region of the sacred inaccessible to other members of the community" (*Shamanism* 7). Shamans thus constitute a small group that "not only directs the community's religious life but ... guards its 'soul'" (8). The difficulty in *The Three Stigmata* is that none of the human characters are equipped with a shamanistic knowledge of the divine. We do, however, see the shaman figure appear in *Do Androids Dream* when Mercer acts as a spiritual guide for Deckard and Isidore. Mercer exhibits many of the shamanistic traits outlined by Eliade. Like the shamans of Native America and Indigenous Australia, Mercer has a "mystical solidarity" (Eliade, *Shamanism* 94) with animals. He also undergoes a ritual death and resurrection in the tomb world in which he "reverse[s] time and bring[s] things back to life again" (*Do Androids* 212). Eliade writes that in Siberian and Eskimo tradition "reduction to the skeleton indicates a passing beyond the profane human condition and, hence, a deliverance from it" (*Shamanism* 63). It is deliverance from the illusory, human realm that Mercer offers his followers.

In reversing the decay of the bones in the tomb world Mercer illustrates his power over the material world. He also lifts Isidore and Deckard out of inauthentic Dasein by overcoming time and showing them his true nature. For Eliade, shamans are "great specialist[s] in the human soul" (*Shamanism* 8), able to see its form and destiny. Mercer heals Deckard's soul by revealing to him the latent structure of the universe, beyond the state-mediated world of the empathy box. Importantly, however, the encounters that Deckard and Isidore have with Mercer are deeply personal and the wider society remains untouched by their interactions. Thus, although *The Three Stigmata* and *Do Androids Dream* both depict spiritual structures underlying and influencing the phenomenal world, neither novel presents a complete image of how the spiritual realm is organized or how enlightenment can be achieved by humankind. These issues are, however, explored in detail in Dick's later SF.

Constructing Theology: New Religious Myths in Dick's SF

In *Ubik* and *A Maze of Death*, we see a shift in Dick's SF toward narratives that incorporate increasingly complex theological systems. While earlier novels, including *The Three Stigmata* and *Do Androids Dream*, suggest that a spiritual realm exists, Dick's later SF incorporates more detailed and cohesive representations of the divine structure of the universe. These novels amalgamate a network of spiritual systems, including Presocratic, Platonic and Gnostic models. The primary concern in *Ubik* and *A Maze of Death* is how to reconcile a belief in a powerful, benevolent deity with the contradictory universe, in which light and dark seem to coexist.

Presocratic philosopher Xenophanes wrote that "One god is greatest among gods and men" (31; fr. 23).[39] He further describes god as all-knowing and all-seeing, saying: "whole he sees, whole he thinks, and whole he hears" (31; fr. 24). In a 1980 interview Dick declares himself a subscriber to Xenophanes' philosophy, stating: "I still view God as Xenophanes viewed him" ("Philip" 46). He further says that "the truth was first uttered ... [by] Xenophanes [in fragment 23]" (46).[40] However, as Hussey points out, Xenophanes' belief in one, all-encompassing deity poses the "problem of explaining the diversity, transience and apparent imperfection and self-contradiction of ... the observable world" (46). Heraclitus seeks to unify these contradictions by regarding them all as facets of one god. He describes "the god" (85; D. 67; CXXIII) as "day and night, winter and summer, war and peace, satiety and hunger" (85; D. 67; CXXIII), saying that "[god] alters ... [and] gets named according to the pleasures of each one" (85; D. 67; CXXIII). For Heraclitus, then, god is "convergent divergent, consonant dissonant, from all things one and from all things all" (85; D. 10; CXXIV).[41]

Heraclitus' conceptualization of god is explored in *Ubik* and *A Maze of Death*. In *Ubik*, Joe Chip obverses that "An unnatural and gigantic force, haunt[s] [his life]. ... controlling what [he] experience[s]" (137). While he posits that this force may not be responsible for the entropic decay he and his friends are threatened by, he also admits that an all-powerful deity would likely be simultaneously responsible for both entropy and renewal (137). Joe thus recognizes, as the Presocratics do, that an all-encompassing, ubiquitous entity would have control over all matter and all experience, both positive and negative.

This belief that the universe may be controlled by one god is also represented in *A Maze of Death*. During the Delmak-O experience, the characters inhabit a universe in which humankind has "proof of the Deity's existence" (88). However, there are competing explanations of the nature of the triune deity and its relation to the Form Destroyer. The characters acknowledge that "it is ... not possible to declare whether ... [the Form Destroyer is] a separate entity from God, uncreated ... but also self-creating, as God is, or ... is an aspect of God" (9). The characters debate this issue but fail to come to a consensus. However, one character, Tony Dunkelwelt, experiences a divine vision that reflects Heraclitus' philosophy. Tony explains that his vision reveals that there is a "deity above the Deity. One who embraces all.... Manifestations. ... [of God, including] the Form Destroyer" (90). Tony states that "the Form Destroyer ... is absolutely-not-God" (91) but nevertheless "God contains all categories of being. Therefore God can be absolutely-not-God" (91).

Similarly, in *Ubik*, the supernatural being, variously termed Ubik, Runciter and Ella, declares: *"Before the universe was, I am. I made the suns. ... the worlds. ... the lives and the places they inhabit. ... they do as I tell them"* (223). There is an obvious correlation here between the representation of Ubik and the Biblical account of the Christian God as "I AM THAT I AM" (*Authorized King James Version*, Exod. 3:14). Ubik is also referred to as *"the word"* (223), a reference to John's gospel, which states, "In the beginning was the Word, and the Word was with God, and the Word was God.... All things were made by him" (1:1–3). However, the description of Ubik as *"the word"* (223) also correlates with Heraclitus' use of the term *logos* to denote a rational, divine causal principle in the universe. Heraclitus writes, "This account [*logos*] holds forever. ... all things come to pass in accordance with this account" (97–98; D. 1; I).[42] Dick's SF thus utilizes both Christian doctrines and Presocratic philosophy to explore the nature of the divine.

The amalgamation of different philosophies into an, often contradictory, unity is characteristic of Dick's SF. While both *Ubik* and *A Maze of Death* incorporate Heraclitus' vision of an all-encompassing deity, they also include references to an entirely different, binary system. In *Ubik* it quickly becomes apparent that two contradictory forces are vying for power over matter. We are told that two "processes are going in opposite directions. One is. ... [a] going-out-of-existence. ... the second ... is ... a coming-into-existence" (113). These processes manifest themselves in the physical world inhabited by the protagonists. The accelerated decay and disintegration of matter represents the first process at work while the appearance of a new currency and spray cans of the restorative substance "Ubik" represent the creative process.

Despite his early supposition that an all-encompassing deity is responsible for both entropy and renewal, Joe ultimately concludes that "two agencies [are] at work" (208). Entropy is attributed to Jory, a malevolent being responsible for creating the illusory reality in which the characters are trapped. Rejuvenation is facilitated by an entity, Ubik, who manifests as Glen Runciter and his wife, Ella. This representation of a dualistic system in which good and evil deities compete for cosmic dominance correlates with Gnosticism, a set of beliefs with which Dick sympathised.[43]

In 1978 Dick states: "I have been accused of holding Gnostic ideas. I guess I do" ("How" 264). This fairly dismissive comment belies the wealth of Gnostic notions canvassed in Dick's SF, particularly *A Maze of Death*, *Ubik* and *VALIS*. There was a growing interest in Gnosticism during the mid–twentieth century, prompted by the discovery of Manichean and Gnostic manuscripts in Turfan, (1902–1914), Medinet Madi (1930) and Nag Hammadi (1945–1948). In 1966, an international congress was held in Messina by scholars seeking to define Gnosticism. There was no Gnostic church or normative theology in antiquity (Rudolf 53). However, the Messina congress concluded that the term "Gnostic" could be applied to a group of second-century AD sects that subscribed to the "idea of a divine spark in man, deriving from the spiritual realm, fallen into this world of fate, birth and death, and needing to be awakened by the divine" (King 14; 169). Gnosticism thus encompasses a range of dualistic belief systems that oppose the material world and seek the deliverance of humanity from the constraints of earthly existence through knowledge of the supermundane realm of freedom (Rudolf 1).[44]

We can observe a correlation between Presocratic and Gnostic beliefs in that both philosophies regard humankind as living in a state of occlusion, unaware of their estrangement from the latent, spiritual realm. However, in Gnosticism, and its Manichean derivative, as in *Ubik* and *A Maze of Death*, a malevolent divinity is responsible for the debasement and occlusion of humankind while an opposing deity seeks to penetrate the material world of illusion and redeem humanity. The Manichean branch of Gnosticism declares that "there are two basic principles existing from the very beginning ... the kingdom of light and the kingdom of darkness" (Rudolf 65). We see this kind of dualism represented in *Ubik*. Both Jory, who represents darkness, and Ubik/Ella/Runciter, representative of light, are eternal. Upon meeting Ella and Jory, Joe realizes that he has "reached the last entities involved" (214). He observes that "Behind [Ella] there's no one, just as there's no one behind Jory" (214). These warring entities are both immortal divinities that predate creation. Jory creates the material world of illusion while Runciter "break[s] through from the outside" (206) and seeks to rejuvenate the characters by saving them from the tyranny of matter and providing them with gnosis.

In contrast, *A Maze of Death* presents an Iranian-Zoroastrian dualism of the kind represented in the Nag Hammadi codices.[45] In this system, evil is not a pre-existing principle but instead comes into being as the result of an error made by the creator, which results in the creation of the earthly world and the powers that hold it in subjection (Rudolf 65). Although Tony believes in an all-encompassing deity, in the style of Heraclitus, the other characters on Delmak-O subscribe to Iranian-Zoroastrian Gnosticism. Their prophet, Specktowsky, outlines a Gnostic creation narrative. He states that, as the Mentufacturer sought to reproduce himself,

> with each greater circle of power, good and knowledge on the part of God weakened, so that at the periphery of the greatest circle his good was weak, his knowledge was weak—too weak for him to observe the Form Destroyer, which was called into being by God's acts of form creation [9].

The Form Destroyer subsequently controls the fate of matter, subjecting it to decay. We learn that "entropy, the method of the Destroyer of Forms, retract[s] the stars into dull reddish coals and then into dust-like silence" (57). Therefore, to consist of matter is to exist in the dark realm of the Form Destroyer.

In *A Maze of Death*, time is not only an ordering process devised by humanity; it is also the method of the Form Destroyer, imposed to hasten the decay of matter. Consequently, the Mentufacturer, in *A Maze of Death*, seeks to "[roll] back time" (23) as a restorative act that "abort[s] the decay process" (10). This notion that time is the result of a divine error is also canvassed in *Ubik*. In the novel, the environment mysteriously regresses through a variety of historical periods. The characters initially equate these temporal regressions with the entropic decay of their bodies. However, they ultimately observe the positive effects of the reversal of time, which they come to suspect is leading toward a rebirth, free from the tyranny of matter. In moving backwards through time, Joe witnesses the forces that enacted his own society. Unlike Walter Benjamin's "angel of history," who is "propel[led] ... into [a] future to which his back is turned" (259), Joe moves backwards into history and gains a more authentic understanding of the way his own Being has been informed by the past.[46]

Furthermore, in distancing himself from the technological, consumer culture of his present, Joe recognizes the desirability of a society based on "human values and compassion" (87) as opposed to artifice and bureaucratic control. However, Joe also observes that the psychology of Earth's historical past is entirely undesirable and is shocked by the flagrant racism displayed in the 1939 regression (157–58). The human world is thus depicted as consistently flawed and constantly building, through time, toward a world of degradation and despair. In *Ubik*, the benign deity is the only being with the power to stop this process by overcoming time. This notion is also represented in *Do Androids Dream* in which "the final disorder of all forms" (185), known as "kipple," is a "universal principle" (57) that no one can resist except with the aid of the divine Mercer, who has the power to resurrect the dead by reversing time (186; 212). It is interesting that, in these new myths of renewal in Dick's SF, a divine figure is required to intercede for doomed humanity. As in much of Clarke's SF, we see in Dick's corpus a consistent representation of supernatural figures intervening in the fate of humankind.

It is important to note that the novels that have primarily been examined thus far, *The Three Stigmata*, *Do Androids Dream*, *Ubik* and *A Maze of Death*, were all written prior to Dick's visionary experience of 2-3-74. Therefore, the myths presented in these texts cannot be attributed to Dick's famous prophetic experience. Similarly, although the novels written after 1974, particularly *VALIS*, do tend to incorporate Dick's visions, these later novels also draw on the mythologies already generated in Dick's earlier SF. Interestingly, Dick's 2-3-74 experience correlates in many ways with the ideas previously set forth in his SF.

Dick's life-changing visions commenced in February 1974 when, after receiving a dose of sodium pentothal during the removal of an impacted wisdom tooth, Dick returned home and later encountered a pharmacy delivery girl bearing pain killers. He was transfixed by the gold necklace the girl was wearing. It bore the fish symbol that, as the girl explained, was a sign used by the early Christians (Jackson and Lethem xiv; *VALIS* 121–22). Instantly, Dick experienced "a single moment of total knowledge" (*The Exegesis* 277) in which he became aware of "the *true* state of things" (277). Dick explains that "what [he] customarily saw ... vanished" (277) and was replaced by an awareness of a supermundane reality. This was the first vision of many. After this initial experience, Dick continued to hear voices and have prophetic dreams and visions, which he then sought to interpret.

In his private writing, Dick often reflects on the similarity between his visions and his SF novels. In a letter to Peter Fitting in June 1974, Dick admits, "the world has come to resemble a PKD novel; ... I sense *my* actual world as resembling the kind of typical universe which I used to merely create as fiction" (*The Exegesis* 12). Indeed, there is a striking similarity between the Presocratic, Gnostic and Platonic notions utilized by Dick to explain his 2-3-74 experience and the ideas that we have already seen presented in his SF. Dick uses the mythologies created in his SF to interpret his own experiences in a remarkable example of the power of SF to develop myths that are applicable to modern life. Dick himself came to regard his pre–1974 SF as an unconscious, symbolic representation of the latent structure of the universe (Jackson and Lethem xiii). His 1981 work *VALIS* is a deliberate theological endeavor in which we see a culmination of all of Dick's sociological, philosophical and theological explorations, and a search for a redemptive myth.[47] Dick's SF corpus can thus be seen as consisting of a constant search for myths that can be applied to modern society.

As in Dick's earlier SF, which highlights the illusory nature of perceived reality, Dick's post–2-3-74 writing often posits that what we see is a lie. This is the basic assumption of Fat's tractate in *VALIS*, which echoes many of the sentiments expressed in Dick's own private writings. As we have already seen, Fat describes the human world as the Black Iron Prison or "the Empire." His tractate reads, "The Empire is the institution, the codification, of derangement; it is insane and imposes its insanity on us by violence" (264). The Empire is conceived in both supernatural and mundane terms. It is the result of both an abortive creative process and the ideological degradation and sin of humanity.

Taking further the ideas already explored in *Ubik* and *A Maze of Death*, *VALIS* explicitly incorporates Gnosticism, as presented in the Nag Hammadi codices, to account for the degradation of the material world. According to the Nag Hammadi manuscripts the divine emanation, Sophia, spawned the darkness that originated matter and created the evil Demiurge, variously named Ariel, Jaldabaoth and Samael, that rules over matter (Rudolf 72–74). In the Nag Hammadi codices, the Demiurge declares, "I am God and there is no other apart from me" (75). In saying this, the Demiurge sins against the other immortals and becomes known as Samael, "the blind god" (75). Thus, in this cosmology, the creator is evil and all matter is tainted by his darkness.

Fat recounts this Gnostic narrative to his disapproving Christian therapist, Maurice, in *VALIS*. He says: "Yaldaboath. Sometimes called Samael, the blind god. He's deranged.... [He] is a monster spawned by Sophia.... He imagines he's the only god but he's wrong. There's something the matter with him.... He creates our world but because he's blind he botches the job" (97). For Fat, this failed creative act is the "origin of entropy, undeserved suffering, chaos and death, as well as the Empire, the Black Iron Prison" (104). Both Fat and the Gnostics regard the insanity of the Demiurge as the cause of the irrationality of the physical world. According to Gnosticism, all matter is contaminated by darkness and disorder, which originates in the supermundane realm and extends to creation, enslaving the world and its rulers (Rudolf 58). The world thus becomes a Black Iron Prison.

Importantly, however, Fat does not place the blame for the derangement of the world solely on the Demiurge. He writes that the Black Iron Prison is perpetuated by humankind on a socio-political level as the "Empire never ended" (53). Dick also perceives dictatorial regimes as evidence of humankind's active participation in the debasement of the world. He lists ancient Rome, the USSR and the "Fascist USA" (*The Exegesis* 256) as manifestations of the Empire. In a November 1974 letter to literature student Claudia Bush, Dick quotes John Calvin to describe modern humanity. He writes, "The natural talents in man have been corrupted by sin" (58), and humankind is hence "exiled from the Kingdom of God, in such a manner that all the affections relating to the happy life of the soul are also extinguished in him, till he recovers them by the grace of regeneration" (58).[48]

This suggestion that occlusion and imprisonment are the punishment, or Curse, brought on by humanity's sin is consistently implied in Dick's earlier SF. As we have seen in *The Three Stigmata*, Eldritch's dominion is the result of the humans, described as *"chooser[s]"* (103) deciding to subject themselves to Eldritch's capitalism. The curse becomes "a price" (219) they must pay, as Adam and Eve did with "the apple originally" (219). Likewise, in *Do Androids Dream*, humans fall victim to "the curse that feeds on all life" (155), and in *A Maze of Death*, the characters seek to "[rise] from the confines of the Curse" (45). The suggestion that humanity has fallen as a result of its own misdemeanors is a departure from Gnostic doctrine, which attributes the fall of nature solely to the creator (Campbell, *The Masks* 45). By attributing the Empire to human error, Dick's SF calls humanity to account for the atrocities of the twentieth century.[49]

Although the Black Iron Prison of falsehood and despair is represented as a result of both human and divine machinations, the chaos of the world is increasingly depicted, in Dick's SF, as something that cannot be altered by human endeavor. Fat declares, "To fight the Empire is to be infected by its derangement. ... whoever defeats a segment of the Empire becomes the Empire; it proliferates like a virus" (264–65). Therefore, the only hope for escape from the prison world of occlusion is through the intervention of another deity. We have already seen this situation depicted in *Ubik* and *A Maze of Death*. In both novels our protagonists fall victim to a malevolent deity and are protected by a restorative entity. In *VALIS* the idea of a redemptive suprahuman at work in the universe is further developed.

Variously named the Logos, Zebra, Ubik and VALIS, the savior deity in *VALIS* exists outside of the irrational creation of Samael and seeks to invade the deranged universe and transform it into a rational form (79). Fat believes that this change will occur via "transubstantiation" (79), a process whereby matter will be transformed into the likeness of the sane Logos. Here there is, again, a divergence from Gnostic teaching. According to Gnosticism, matter and its deranged creator are entirely evil (Rudolf 60). Redemption thus involves a deliverance from corporeal existence and the ascent of the soul. In the Manichean system, in particular, "The body is the dark, evil, component of man, which in death returns to its origins, the darkness" (Rudolf 338) so that the soul can escape the realm of matter and ascend to the spiritual universe. Death is thus the ultimate liberation for Gnostics (Rudolf 171). However, in *VALIS*, there is a sense that the phenomenal world can be changed into the image of the rational god.

Fat draws on Presocratic philosophy to present the possibility of transformation in the material realm. In contrast with Heraclitus' representation of one god that encompasses all contradictory processes in the universe, Parmenides argues that change and multiplicity are impossible. According to Hussey, it appears that Parmenides is seeking to directly refute Heraclitus' work by stating that the contradiction inherent in the assertion that "it is" and "is not" can be simultaneously true is impossible to sustain (87). Parmenides insists that reality is actually static and the material world of variety and change is, therefore, a falsehood (Warren 78). Parmenides' assertions are presented alongside Heraclitean and Gnostic conceptions of the universe in *A Maze of Death* when, during a chaotic theological debate, one character expostulates that "Nothing changes" (28).

Dick himself recognizes the influence of Parmenides on his SF. In a 1976 speech he reflects:

> There is internal evidence in at least one of my novels that another reality, an unchanging one, exactly as Parmenides and Plato suspected, underlies the visible

phenomenal world of change, and somehow ... we can cut through to it. Or, rather, a mysterious Spirit can put us in touch with it ["How" 270].

In referencing Plato, Dick is alluding to Plato's *Timaeus*, in which a cosmology is outlined that involves the interaction of a rational Demiurge with the chaos that is matter. Plato writes that all forms of matter "were in disorder and the god introduced ... every kind of measure ... in which it was possible for each one to be in harmonious proportion.... For at first they were without any such proportion" (*Plato's* 280). Plato declares that this deity is "good" (33) and, faced with the inherent disorder of the world, which he is not responsible for, "desire[s] that all things should come as near as possible to being like himself" (33).

Fat also engages with Plato's *Timaeus* via Francis Macdonald Cornford's 1937 translation and commentary, *Plato's Cosmology*. Fat observes that "it is Cornford who says that Plato believe[s] that there was an element of the irrational in the World Soul" (44). Cornford indeed expresses this point, saying:

> Plato's Demiurge ... operates upon materials which he does not create. ... [he is] confronted with "all that is visible" in a chaos of disorderly motion. For this disorder he is not responsible, but only for those features of order and intelligible design which he proceeds to introduce [37].

This is how Zebra/Ubik/the Logos operates in *VALIS*. Fat asserts that, "The true God, who is totally transcendent, did not create the world" (97), yet "sees [what Yaldaboath has done] ... and in his pity sets to work to save us" (97).

This redemption comes in the form of information that reveals the irrationality and falseness of phenomenal reality. This gnosis can only be achieved via the direct intervention of Zebra. Fat writes: "information will save us. This is the saving *gnosis* which the Gnostics sought. There is no other road to salvation. However, this information—or more precisely the ability to read and understand this information—... can only be made available to us by the Holy Spirit" (265). The impossibility of humanity discovering truth for itself is also canvassed by Heraclitus. In fragment 79, he writes, "man is found foolish by god, as a child by a man" (55; LVII). As noted by Hussey, however, this fragment implies that humanity can be educated by god in the same way that a child can be taught by an adult (36). While Heraclitus observes that most men remain blind to the truth, "Not comprehending" (29; D. 34; II) reality, he hopes that understanding may be gained by some. The Gnostics too hold that divine secrets will be revealed to a small elite (Rudolf 56).

The education of the elect is represented in *VALIS*. In the novel,

Zebra breaks into the prison world and "camouflages itself" (79). The immortal Zebra is described as "pure energy, pure living information" (135). Fat explains that this immortal information, also called "*plasmate*" (260) "replicates itself" (260) by "crossbond[ing] with humans" (260). In other words, Zebra educates humankind by instilling itself in human beings as living information. The elite individuals who achieve gnosis through this crossbonding are referred to by Fat as "*homoplasmate[s]*" (260). Dick echoes this theology in his private writing, commenting that "[Zebra] de-occludes us on an individual basis" (*The Exegesis* 432) so that "One by one he ... draw[s] us out of this world" (432) and away from the Black Iron Prison. This gnosis does not only come in the form of prophetic visions, like those experienced by Dick and Fat. Zebra also hides within the irrational structures of the human world and transmits information subliminally. For instance, while watching a television commercial for a supermarket chain, Phil Dick, in *VALIS*, becomes aware of "quick messages fired off by VALIS in rapid succession" (254).

As strange as this account of a camouflaged deity may seem, Dick is again drawing inspiration from ancient myth. In his private notes and letters, Dick reinterprets myths from a variety of cultures and sects and uses them to construct his messianic–Zebra model. In particular, Dick utilizes the Orphic Zagreus myth and combines it with Biblical narratives.[50] In a 1975 letter to Claudia Bush, Dick writes: "Zeus sent Zagreus ... to Earth *in order to hide him*. ... [Zeus] wanted his son to blend, to mingle ... to disappear" (*The Exegesis* 91). Dick then equates this Zagreus narrative with the Biblical concealment of the infant Christ from King Herod. He describes "Christ, disguised as a carpenter" (91) as the rational god's first attempt to penetrate the chaos of our universe. He writes, "If [Christ] lived long enough... He ... would [have begun] subtly to alter the Plan of this world" (92).

This cannibalization of ancient myth and traditional religion to fit a new pattern can also be seen in Dick's SF. In *VALIS*, Fat's tractate reads: "The Immortal One was known to the Greeks as Dionysus; to the Jews as Elijah; to the Christians as Jesus. He moves on when each human host dies, and thus is never killed or caught" (110). According to Fat, this new mythology explains Jesus' final words on the cross. Fat states that, as suggested by eye-witnesses, Jesus was indeed calling out to the immortal spirit of Elijah, to Zebra, which left him at the moment of his death to seek a new host (110). Fat thus assumes that "the Savior [will] soon be reborn" (138) and goes in search of the new messiah, the "plasmate" that has "returned and is creating new homoplasmates" (261).[51]

3. Science Fiction as Truth   119

Fat believes that, through the de-occlusion of the elect homoplasmates, including himself, Zebra will dismantle the world of the Black Iron Prison and reveal the true world beneath. Dick hypothesizes that those to whom Zebra reveals himself "*are going to link up*" (*The Exegesis* 46) and form a community "rooted in ... justice, truth and freedom" (48). He writes that Zebra seeks to "de-program" (230) humankind to save it from the stifling ideologies of the Black Iron Prison. Dick further believes that he personally channeled Zebra's transformative power in 1974 when Richard Nixon was removed from office. He writes: "The spirit which filled me ... in March [1974] ... looked around, saw Richard Nixon ... and was so wrath-filled that he never stopped writing letters to Washington until Nixon was out" (48). Similarly, Fat explains that the plasmate "thirsted for vengeance. ... against the modern day manifestation of the Empire, the imperial United States Presidency" (*VALIS* 181).

To make sense of his own visionary experiences and the historical moment in which he lives, Dick thus generates new myths that modify and amalgamate existing systems of thought. Hussey names Heraclitus as the first to suggest that language must be used in a highly unusual way in order to reflect the nature of things, which is, in reality, vastly different to anything previously supposed (34). Dick applies this logic to rationalize his use of SF as a vehicle for myth. He declares in 1975 that "What is needed is a harmonization of theology and S-F without a reduction of the former to the latter" (*The Exegesis* 177).[52] Dick's novels clearly achieve this correlation of theology and SF. His works consistently explore religious questions without attempting to answer them with materialistic solutions. Indeed, Dick's SF, culminating with Fat's theological tractate in *VALIS*, becomes increasingly spiritual, moving from concrete, sociological critiques to detailed cosmologies.

Dick declares: "the two modes of interpretation which I hover most between are S-F and theology, which surely tells us something about S-F.... The two must be related in some important way" (*The Exegesis* 177). As a mode that is fundamentally concerned with exploring human thought and action, and humanity's place in the cosmos, I agree that SF is inevitably linked with religion, a branch of thinking that is also intrinsically concerned with the structure of reality. Even before 2-3-74, Dick's SF was engaging with philosophy and religion to create new myths. Dick recognizes this, saying, "Starting in 1951 ... I began in my stories ... to make certain very serious *guesses* about the nature of reality" (250). Dick ultimately comes to view his novels as "progressive parts of *one* unfolding true narrative, in which ... the spurious world [is] discerned for what it is, and ... the true state of things [is] put forth" (402). Interestingly, the power of SF to articulate living myths is represented explicitly in *VALIS*, in which a SF film depicts Fat's theology and, in doing so, validates it in the eyes of his peers. Dick's writings illustrate that SF is an ideal vehicle for the exploration of existing myths and the articulation of new ones. Twentieth-century SF can thus be seen as a method of seeking and articulating "truth" in a world saturated by restrictive ideologies and competing philosophies.

Chapter 4

Resisting Tradition: The Messiah Myth and Authentic Dasein in Frank Herbert's Dune Series

"We live in a universe dominated by relativity and change, but our intellects keep demanding fixed absolutes that contain comforting reassurance" ("Listening" 9): such were the words of Frank Herbert (1920–1986) in a 1973 article for *Harper's Magazine*. Absolutes in all forms are dismissed in Herbert's *Dune* series. In particular, messiah myths, which represent humanity under the care of a divine being, are regarded as imperiling humanity's positive evolution. For Herbert, myths of messiahs, gods, heroes and kings project comforting, stable narratives onto the ultimate chaos of the universe and thus discourage humanity from collectively striving to meet the challenges of existence in a dynamic environment (Herbert, "Science Fiction and a World" 32).

The *Dune* novels suggest that blind acceptance of social structures, and the mythic patterns that inform them, leads to the intellectual stagnation of humankind. According to Herbert's philosophy, individuals experience inauthentic existence when they fail to recognize that their opinions, beliefs and lives are shaped by human constructs, which conceal the true nature of the universe. For Herbert, SF is a mode that "helps us understand what it means to be human" ("Men" 77) by examining established myths.[1] The *Dune* series is particularly concerned with the impact of religion and the hero figure on human psychology. It draws on the philosophical works of Martin Heidegger (1889–1976) and Karl Jaspers (1883–1969) to explore the nature of being and consider how an authentic awareness of the potentialities of existence can be achieved. Furthermore, Herbert's series considers the power of language in constructing selfhood and perpetuating traditional myths, drawing especially on the works of Alfred Korzybski (1879–1950), the founder of general semantics.[2]

The correlation between Herbert's SF and the philosophical writings of Heidegger and Jaspers has been noted by critics, including Timothy O'Reilly, who observes that Herbert's *The Santaroga Barrier* (1968) appropriates notions from both philosophers (*Frank Herbert* 140–46).[3] Surprisingly, neither O'Reilly nor other critics have addressed, in any detail, the incorporation of Heidegger's and Jaspers' ideas in the *Dune* series.[4] The lack of critical consideration of the Heideggerian concepts in the *Dune* novels could relate to the fact that the philosophical elements of *The Santaroga Barrier* are so overt,[5] whereas the *Dune* series offers a more subtle treatment of Heidegger and Jaspers. As O'Reilly observes, in *Dune* "the story itself is the message; the concepts are so completely a part of the imaginative world [Herbert] ... create[s] that the issue of didacticism never arises" (*Frank Herbert* vii). There are no explicit references to Heidegger or Jaspers in the *Dune* series, but their ideas infuse the novels. Most critics examine the ecological aspects of the *Dune* series and its meditation on the hero mystique.[6] Critics including Mark Bould and Sherryl Vint note that emerging environmentalist concerns and the countercultural attitudes of the 1960s contribute to the themes present in *Dune* (120). However, with the notable exception of O'Reilly's work, there has been limited critical engagement with Herbert's specific intellectual orientation. This chapter examines the treatment of gods and heroes in the series in relation to the ideas about authentic being that are articulated by Jaspers and Heidegger. The *Dune* series is thus shown to critically examine established mythic systems while exploring ways humankind may achieve a self-conscious awareness of the nature of existence.

It is also of note that most studies treat *Dune* as a novel in isolation, without reference to its sequels.[7] Given that Herbert conceived of the first three novels in the sequence as one extended narrative (Herbert, "Dangers" 97), the breadth of his vision cannot be fully appreciated without a consideration of at least the initial trilogy. Indeed, this chapter examines the representation of the hero myth in all six of the *Dune* novels: *Dune* (1965), *Dune Messiah* (1969), *Children of Dune* (1976), *God Emperor of Dune* (1981), *Heretics of Dune* (1984) and *Chapterhouse: Dune* (1985). In my view, Herbert's engagement with the hero narrative and the attempt, in his SF, to generate alternative myths cannot be adequately charted without considering *Heretics of Dune* and *Chapterhouse: Dune,* which are set after the deaths of the absolute rulers that rise in the preceding novels. It is in these final works that democratic myths are developed to replace the hero pattern that is critiqued in the first four novels. In undertaking to examine all six novels, the scope of this analysis will necessarily be limited to discussing the series' critique of humankind's reliance on heroes and gods and to identifying the alternative myths that are developed in the later *Dune* novels, which are as philosophically complex as those that precede them.[8]

Herbert undertook six years of research before writing *Dune* (Herbert, "When" v). He was inspired to invent a fictional desert world after preparing an article in 1957 about a U.S. Department of Agriculture project to control sand dunes in Florence, Oregon (Herbert, "Dangers" 99).[9] At the time, Herbert was also considering the impact of heroes on society. Herbert explains that he conceived of the first three books of the *Dune* series as "a long novel ... about the messianic convulsions that periodically overtake us. Demagogues, fanatics, con-game artists, the innocent and the not-so-innocent bystanders—all were to have a part in the drama" ("Dangers" 97). He adds that the idea grew "from [his] theory that superheroes are disastrous for humankind" (97).

Herbert's views on heroes can be attributed, at least in part, to his friendship with Ralph and Irene Slattery, a pair of psychologists Herbert met after moving to Santa Rosa, California in 1949. Herbert was working as a journalist for the *Press-Democrat* at the time and struck up a friendship with the couple after attending a lecture on psychology by Irene Slattery. Ralph Slattery had a background in philosophy and introduced Herbert to the works of Heidegger and Jaspers, while Irene Slattery gave Herbert access to class notes she had taken while studying under Carl Jung in Zurich in the 1930s (O'Reilly, *Frank Herbert* 18–19; Touponce 9). Herbert's son, Brian Herbert, comments in *Dreamer of Dune: The Biography of Frank Herbert* that Irene Slattery had been in Berlin in the 1930s and witnessed Hitler speak. He writes: "Hitler terrified [Irene Slattery] from the moment she first gazed upon him.... He was a hero to the German people, and terribly dangerous in that position, she felt, because of the way his people followed him slavishly, without questioning him, without thinking for themselves" (72). Brian Herbert reports that Irene Slattery related these views about Hitler to Herbert, who would later explore the dangers of hero worship in the *Dune* series (72).

Thus the Slatterys introduced Herbert to some of the core ideas that would be examined in his SF. Herbert frequently expresses fears that a desire for stability sees humans willingly forfeit their powers of critical thought to heroic leaders, who establish systems that become corrupt with the inevitable demise of the hero ("Listening" 9; "Dangers" 97). This notion that humans tend to submit to established systems and authority figures draws on Heideggerian philosophy, which posits that our existence is enacted within a specific social context and that we largely fail to recognize the structures that inform our selfhood. As discussed in Chapter 3,[10] Heidegger uses the term "Dasein" to describe human existence as "Being-in-the-world" (*Being and Time* 65). He writes: "Dasein is never ... free from Being-in" (84). In other words, our selfhood is generated and defined within the confines of human society; we have no individuality that exists outside the world we live in. This, naturally, makes us inclined to accept the systems that surround us as static.

However, Heidegger distinguishes between two different forms of Being-in: authentic Dasein and inauthentic Dasein. He describes authentic Dasein as a state of existence in which an individual understands the forces that enact their being and is thus able to take hold of their full potential for action (*Being and Time* 68; 184). On the other hand, inauthentic Dasein, also known as "everyday Dasein," "the they-self" or "Das Man," is the submersion of the individual within the mass of humanity and involves the unconscious acceptance of the systems that enact being and an engagement with the world and its cares (84; 164; 167). Heidegger writes: "The Self of everyday Dasein is the *they-self*, which we distinguish from the *authentic Self*—that is, from the Self which has been taken hold of in its own way.... As they-self, the particular Dasein has been *dispersed* into the 'they,' and must first find itself" (167).

Herbert describes the common state of inauthentic Dasein in a 1973 article, saying: "We peer myopically ... through the screens of 'consensus reality,' which [are] a summation of the most popular beliefs of our time" ("Listening" 10). Jaspers is also concerned about the propensity for modern humanity to submit to the dominant culture and accept the status quo. He writes of the possibility of transcendence, whereby the individual moves beyond blind acceptance of the world into an awareness of the historically constructed systems that surround them (*Philosophy* 81). It is this kind of self-awakening that is advocated in the *Dune* series. By becoming aware of how selfhood is influenced by external forces and grasping their potential for action, characters in the series resist entrenched systems and seek to reshape traditional myths.

The *Dune* series highlights messiah myths as particularly common narratives in human culture. It suggests that a desire to conceive of the universe as a place where leaders rise and guide humankind hampers the achievement of authentic Dasein in the general populace. In the first four novels of the series we see the personal and social consequences of the ascension of godlike leaders to positions of power. The final two novels, *Heretics of Dune* and *Chapterhouse: Dune*, go on to chart the social turmoil that follows in the wake of a failed power structure and explore avenues for the positive evolution of humanity.

Importantly, Herbert's SF does not overtly critique any particular religious creed. It targets, instead, the savior or hero myth that recurs in both religious and secular worldviews. This makes Herbert's SF distinct from those texts written by other twentieth-century authors, including H. G. Wells, which decry Christianity only to present alternative redeemer myths. From the perspective of the *Dune* series, the inclusion of spiritual myths in SF is a symptom of the wider social compulsion toward reality models that remove the need for human self-determination and posit the existence of a divine guiding force. The illumination of problematic aspects of the hero myth in the *Dune* novels represents a trend that became common in mid-twentieth-century SF. Other notable works that deal skeptically with savior figures include Robert A. Heinlein's *Stranger in a Strange Land* (1961), Roger Zelazny's *Lord of Light* (1967) and Michael Moorcock's *Behold the Man* (1969).[11] Herbert's *Dune* series thus represents a form of SF that consciously resists the spiritual myths that tend to be espoused by both SF and society at large.

To understand this movement in SF toward a deliberate resistance to hero myths, this chapter examines the *Dune* series in relation to Herbert's intellectual context and personal philosophical orientation. This chapter charts the engagement with ideas about Dasein in the *Dune* novels and consider the new myths generated over the course of the series. In the later novels of Herbert's *Dune* series there is a clear illustration of the power of education as a means of promoting authentic Dasein among the masses. In contrast to the hero figures of the early novels, who achieve enlightenment and become godlike leaders of the slavish masses, *Chapterhouse: Dune* conveys myths of democratic mobilization. Thus Herbert's series presents the restoration of critical awareness and powers of conscious resistance to the masses as the only way to break away from traditional myths and face the reality of the changing universe.

Human Ecology

Of *Dune*, Herbert writes: "It was to be an ecological novel ... with many overtones" ("When" v). While *Dune* is consistently recognized as a novel about desert ecology, it is just as invested in exploring the mechanisms of human ecology.[12] Herbert regards "ecology [as] the science of understanding consequences" ("The Sparks" 104).[13] As O'Reilly notes, Herbert draws this definition of ecology from the writing of American ecologist Paul B. Sears (*The Maker* 104). In his 1962 work *Where There Is Life*, Sears writes: "the highest function of science is to give us an understanding of consequences" (128). He further argues that "There is an ecology of ideas and values, as well as one of substantial living organisms. Patterns of thought and preference develop ... as a result of process[es] in the past" (89). Thus, ecology encompasses the interactions and consequences of the total systems at work in the universe, including both organic processes and human systems.

Herbert views human social structures, and the thought patterns that underlie them, as particularly inflexible, problematic aspects of the world ecology. Of human structures he writes: "the systems themselves ... [are] dangerous. ... [they] originate with human creators. ... [then] take over and grind on and on. They are like a flood tide that picks up everything in its path" ("Dangers" 97–98). For Herbert, then, the ecology of human society has a major impact on the total environment. Social structures, and the mythic systems that inform them, become a key focus in the *Dune* series.

Although *Dune* is set in a distant future, its political setting reflects aspects of Herbert's Cold War context. Jaspers describes Cold War ecology in his 1958 work *The Future of Mankind*, saying that "the over-all aspect remains the same: either the sudden outbreak of nuclear war in a matter of years or decades, or the establishment of world peace" (vii). We encounter a similar context in *Dune*: rival "Great Houses," controlling fiefdoms on planets across the universe, enact covert designs against one another without being able to commit open acts of war because each House has the atomic capacity to destroy the planetary bases of at least fifty of its rivals (Herbert, *Dunne Messiah* 49). The outbreak of hostilities between the family of protagonist Paul Atreides[14] and the Harkonnen clan makes the search for peace a primary concern in all six *Dune* novels. The correlation of the political setting of the series with Cold War Earth means that Herbert's SF is positioned to explore the future consequences of mid-twentieth-century society.

The representation of warring families in the *Dune* series signals the inherited nature of human systems. *Dune* poses the question: "*What is the son but an extension of the father?*" (56). While Paul achieves greater power than any of his forebears, his moral orientation, loyalties and rivalries are inherited from his father. By extension, we can surmise that the whole breadth of human ecology, with its complex matrix of political, economic, social and religious institutions, is inherited and passed down by each new generation so that Dasein is always constructed by historical forms. Heidegger points this out in *Being and Time*. He writes: "[the] fundamental structure in Dasein. ... is ... 'a priori' ... [it] is primordially and constantly a whole" (65). Thus, selfhood is not defined by individual inclinations but is formed by pre-existing systems. According to Heidegger, the public life of humanity "proximally controls every way in which the world and Dasein gets interpreted" (165) so that "Everyone is the other, and no one is himself. ... every Dasein has already surrendered itself in Being-among-one-another" (165–66). If selfhood is thus embedded within, and determined by, inherited structures, humanity must be regarded as trapped within its own constructs.

Paul discovers the fixity of established systems in *Dune Messiah*. Having seized political power, Paul seeks to reshape society but is thwarted by the overwhelming power of entrenched social, political and religious systems. Although Paul initially views himself as "an inventor of government" (160) he ultimately realizes that his government has "fallen into the old patterns" (160). He laments that any attempt at social reform is "like some hideous contrivance with plastic memory" (160–61) that inevitably "snap[s] into the ancient forms" (161). Paul recognizes that social resistance to change is the result of ingrained traditions: "forces beyond his reach in human breasts [that elude] and [defy] him" (160). This illustrates Heidegger's statement that "Dasein is inclined to fall back upon its world ... [and] falls prey to ... tradition" (*Being and Time* 42).

Heidegger further notes that "tradition keeps [Dasein] from providing its own guidance, whether in inquiring or in choosing" (*Being and Time* 42–43). In this sense, each individual is simply a nexus of the traditional behaviors and beliefs that construct consensus reality. Thus, any real attempt at radical social change from within the political arena clashes with the essential Being of the mass populace, for whom "tradition [has become] master" (Heidegger, *Being and Time* 43). Complicating this dilemma further is Heidegger's suggestion that the mass of humanity remains completely unaware of their social conditioning. According to Heidegger, the traditions that inform each individual's selfhood prevent the development of any self-conscious understanding of the nature of existence (43). He explains: "Tradition takes what has come down to us and delivers it over to self-evidence; it blocks our access to those primordial 'sources' from which the categories and concepts handed down to us have been ... drawn" (43). Thus, consensus reality becomes accepted as unquestionable, absolute truth. Therefore, as Heidegger puts it, the "elemental historicality of Dasein ... remain[s] hidden from Dasein itself" (41).

Herbert similarly argues that "We are disposed to perceive things as they appear, filtering the appearance through our preconceptions and fitting it into ... past forms (including all the outright mistakes, illusions, and myths of the past forms)" ("Listening" 9). This automatic subscription to traditional systems of thought is also described in *Heretics of Dune*, which presents the idea that "Forces that we cannot understand permeate the universe. We see the shadows of those forces ... but understand them we do not" (51). This representation of hidden influences guiding our lives reflects Herbert's personal beliefs about consensus reality. In his twenties, Herbert began to suspect that his life was under the direction of external forces ("Doll" 202–03). He concluded that the set of ideas that construct our understanding lodge "somewhere in [our] consciousness [and carry] major influence over what [we perceive] as reality" (203). Herbert explains that these traditional ideas constantly reaffirm the status quo, preventing us from absorbing data that does not coincide with established systems by suppressing one's "critical sense of disbelief" (203).

Alfred Korzybski also argues that perceived reality is constructed by tradition. He asserts in *Science and Sanity* (1941) that, from birth, our perceptions are distorted by parents and teachers who seek to induct us into the consensus reality (xv). Korzybski states that this distortion occurs at the level of language, which is the means by which humankind represents reality (xv; 76). He further writes that the semantic systems that we use to articulate our understanding of the world do not necessarily reflect empirical facts (63). Herbert echoes Korzybski's position, saying that, although language is essential for the articulation of ideas, "Language is like a tar pit which has accumulated the fossils of our past" ("Dangers" 100) so that "Language programs us, decides what we see and how we see it" ("Science Fiction and a World" 38). Language thus ensures that traditional myths endure.

Importantly, the *Dune* series suggests that entrenched myths have not evolved organically to suit the needs of human culture. Rather, it is implied that particular ways of viewing the world are encouraged by those in power to preserve the authority of the ruling class. This notion relates to the theories articulated by psychiatrist Thomas Szasz (1920–2012).[15] Szasz argues that "Rulers have always conspired against their subjects and sought to keep them in bondage ... [using] force and fraud" (5). We see this comment reflected in *Dune Messiah* when we learn that Paul and his sister, Alia, have been "taught to govern" (151) by being "imbued with a shrewd grasp of politics and a deep understanding of the uses of war and ritual" (151). Logistician Duncan Idaho declares in *Dune Messiah* that there is no such thing as natural law at work in human society (151). Instead, the authority of the ruling class is perpetuated by their promotion of the systems that first placed them in power. This notion is also propounded by Korzybski, who comments that "The affairs of man are conducted by our own, man-made rules" (*Science* 76), which are articulated using language and symbols (76). Furthermore, Korzybski argues that humanity "shall always be ruled by those who rule symbols" (77). This is the case with Paul and Alia in *Dune Messiah*.

In contrast, Jaspers writes that the utilization of linguistic structures by the ruling class is always accompanied by oppression. He argues that "In its reality ... every human order is founded on force. States maintain themselves by force or by the threat of force" (*The Future* 32). Thus, traditional systems are also maintained by the disempowerment of the populace. In *Children of Dune*, Idaho observes that "Good subjects must feel guilty" (352) so the "good" ruler "provides many opportunities for failure in the populace" (352). Poor educational standards and the discouragement of critical thought facilitate such failure.

In a 1985 interview, Herbert expresses fears that meaningful, critical education is being phased out altogether in bureaucratic modernity ("Conversations" 230). He argues that "modern education tends to put blinders on students and channelize them" (232). Herbert's concerns reflect Jasper's observation that, when intelligence testing became widespread at the start of the twentieth century, experts were appalled by the general ignorance and lack of critical faculties displayed by the masses (*The Future* 305). Jaspers worries that democratic society will fail if "the majority is neither sufficiently gifted for critical thought nor sufficiently well educated and informed for independent judgement" (305) because under such circumstances the populace will respond only momentarily to the political maneuvers of power seekers and will generally remain in a state of "political lethargy" (305).

Herbert's *Dune* series further suggests that governments deliberately limit the educational opportunities granted to the populace to prevent any threat to established power. In *Chapterhouse: Dune* the Bene Gesserit, a powerful all-female movement, are threatened by another all-female society, the Honored Matres, who seek to establish their bureaucratic government as the sole power in the known universe. The Honored Matres constitute a "Power-closed government intent on making all potential challengers ineffectual" (347). They ensure their own continued authority by "Screen[ing] out ... bright [individuals]" (347) to "Blunt [the] intelligence" (347) of the population. Lucilla, a Bene Gesserit, observes that the bureaucracy of the Honored Matres "*elevates conformity*" (100) or, rather, "*elevates 'fatal stupidity'*" (100) in the populace. For bureaucracies, education is simply "*regurgitat[ion] [of facts] on demand*" (Herbert, *Chapterhouse* 115): students memorize absolutes and conform to established patterns of behavior. In this way, "Educational bureaucracies dull a child's questing sensitivity" (115). By discouraging independent thought and creativity, rulers ensure the masses remain reliant on politicians and blind to the machinations of the ruling class.

Furthermore, Odrade, another Bene Gesserit, accuses adults, in general, of being hostile to developing genius. She argues that "the conventional teacher feels threatened by emerging talents and squelches them because of a deep-seated desire to feel superior and safe in a safe environment" (*Chapterhouse* 116). Herbert echoes this sentiment, stating that "most teachers ... tend to be threatened by the really gifted student and ... react against [them]" ("Conversations" 233). Thus, for Herbert, the effective education of the masses is hampered by authority figures on both the microcosmic and macrocosmic level so that, at every stage, emerging talent is stifled and the status quo is preserved.

In contrast to the methods of the educational bureaucracy, Szasz explains in 1967 that true education should promote independent, critical thought and encourage the gifted to reach their full potential (142). However, like Herbert, he recognizes that "critical teaching ... fosters many qualities and values antagonistic to those of simple socialization" (141–42). According to Szasz, socialization promotes qualities that are "noncompetitive, and institutional" (142) and encourages "the acceptance of culturally shared myths" (142). Hence, entrenched power structures endorse systems that privilege socialization over learning by "discouraging idiosyncratic behavior and exploration, and ... encouraging conduct favoring group solidarity" (Szasz 142). Szasz's assertions are echoed in *Heretics of Dune*: "*holders of power wish to suppress wild research [because] [u]nrestricted questing after knowledge ... produc[es] unwanted competition*" (201). Furthermore, it is stated that "*The powerful want 'safe ... investigations,' which ... develop only those products and ideas that can be controlled*" (201). This, of course, perpetuates existing systems and prevents developments or discoveries that might destabilize established ways of understanding the universe.

Importantly, Herbert does not describe the mass populace as struggling against repressive power structures. Rather, the *Dune* series suggests that humankind is not only limited by corrupt governments but is also held back by its own refusal to acknowledge the falsity of traditional mythic patterns. This reflects Korzybski's assertion that "The majority ... [prefer] to have their thinking done for them; they accept ready-made ... doctrines ... and follow them more or less blindly. Every generation looks upon its own creeds as true and permanent" (*Manhood* 11). Similarly, in a 1973 article, Herbert comments that human society has historically generated linear, spiritual narratives to explain life, even though such narratives are incongruous with the chaotic nature of the universe ("Listening" 9). He writes: "Humans want beginnings and nice anthropomorphic motives and happy endings. But.... Infinity does not require beginnings or endings.... Without ends, there can be no ultimate (absolute) goals, no judgements, and the whole concept of sin and guilt ... falls apart" ("Science Fiction and a World" 32).

Herbert's identification of religious myth as overlaying a finite structure on the universe is supported by Jaspers, who states: "the Christian ideal ... ha[s] an incomparable grip upon the individual" (*Man* 12). Jaspers explains that the Christian conception of the universe posits that events are contributing to "a historical process that [is] mov[ing] towards the fulfilment of a plan of salvation" (12). He further points out that, with the development of scientific conceptions of the universe in the sixteenth century, the idea of progress began to dominate Western myths. This meant that, by the eighteenth century, "Whereas hitherto when men had looked forward it had been towards the end of the world and Judgement Day, they now contemplated the perfectionment of the civilisation" (Jaspers, *Man* 13).[16]

Heidegger also regards Western thought as moving from "The Christian-theological interpretation of the world" ("The Self" 32) to "the later mathematical-technical thinking of the modern age" (32). According to Heidegger, both these philosophies reduce the universe to a linear, mappable structure. He writes that, with the advent of science, "Nature and history [became] the objects of a representing that explains" (*The Question* 127).[17] Herbert similarly declares: "Western culture is particularly obsessed with ... absolutism. We have been taught to believe that for every problem there is a scientific answer" ("Men" 73). Thus, the modern age has seen both religious and scientific worldviews produce linear narratives that seek to overlay a sense of progress and control onto the chaos of the universe. As is observed by Paul in *Dune*: "*The concept of progress acts as a protective mechanism to shield us from the terrors of the future*" (371).

Herbert is aware that twentieth-century science has illustrated the unquantifiable nature of the universe and is, therefore, incompatible with linear and absolutist myths. He writes, "no theory be it ever so grand can have unlimited applicability; a single law will not explain anything forever" ("Science Fiction and You" 1).[18] Herbert regards absolutist myths as problematic because they prevent humankind from recognizing the possibilities of an endless universe. He writes: "To accept a universe where anything can happen ... is to accept a hellish insecurity" ("Science Fiction and a World" 32). Therefore, Herbert postulates that "we strive for the illusion of all-knowing. ... [and] seek that basic law to explain [the] never-ending All which stands as a seething backdrop" (32–33) to human life. Similarly, Paul notes that "*Deep in the human unconscious is a pervasive need for a logical universe that makes sense. But the real universe is always one step beyond logic*" (*Dune* 430).

Herbert sees the need for absolutes as limiting humanity's positive evolution. He writes, "The old patterns of thinking ... continue to hamstring us" ("Listening" 19), explaining that the "linear orientation of our perceptions ... makes it extremely difficult to break away from the belief that we occupy a universe where there are straightforward linked cause-and-effect events" (14). According to Herbert, this false understanding of the universe endangers humanity's ability to adapt and change by erroneously suggesting that the status quo can be maintained without reference to the ever-changing state of the universe (17). The *Dune* series goes so far as to represent the inflexibility of human worldviews as evidence of primitive animalism in the species.

From the opening of *Dune*, when Paul faces the gom jabbar to test his humanity, we are confronted with what it means to be human. The answer is plainly given: a human being is one who is able to make decisions for the long-term benefit of humankind, even if this means individual suffering in the present.[19] This reflects Korzybski's definition of humanity. He writes, "a human being is a time-binder" (*Manhood* 11) in that, unlike animals, "each generation of humans, at least potentially, can start where the former generation left off" (*Science* 39). In other words, humankind is capable of making long-term plans for the positive evolution of the species. According to Korzybski, however, humankind's time-binding potential can only be realized if humanity resists traditional patterns. He writes that the persistence of traditional systems means that human affairs are in danger of falling victim of a "vicious circle ... of ... un-sanity" (41). Korzybski further explains that each new generation suffers maladjustment under a constant cycle of "rulers ... [who] impose their own infantilism on ... institutions, educational methods, and doctrines" (41) so that human development is consistently hampered by "old animalistic limitations" (41).

In the *Dune* series, it is revealed that the only way to escape animalism and make effective long-term decisions is to recognize and adapt to the ever-changing nature of the universe. As Paul's son, Leto II, observes, the capacity to "make truly long-term decisions" (*God* 66) is dependent on the "ability to change your mind" (66). However, the vast system of traditions that inform civilization stifles humanity's ability to change and adapt by perpetuating a belief in absolutes. It therefore becomes essential that humankind achieve an authentic understanding of the historical forces that influence their Being so that they can resist absolutist myths and recognize the changing state of the universe. Leto II observes that "*The life of ... an entire people, persists as memory.... Humankind [should] ... call upon this material ... [to adapt to] a changing universe*" (*Children* 119). However, as Leto II points out, "*The* species *can forget!*" (119) so that vital information fails to be integrated into evolutionary knowledge. According to the *Dune* series, it is this forgetfulness that turns humankind into animalistic slaves to tradition because it prevents them from remembering that human systems are simply historical constructs.

The act of moving beyond animalistic existence into an awakened understanding of Being is described by Heidegger. He first explains that, by immersing itself within the social group, Dasein is "disburden[ed] ... of its Being" (*Being and Time* 165). In other words, to exist in a state of inauthentic Dasein is to take an "easy" (165) approach to existence, allowing oneself to be enacted and guided by tradition. Under such circumstances the individual fails to recognize the systems that influence their Being. According to Heidegger, it is only when the individual becomes aware of the historically-constructed nature of Being, by achieving authentic Dasein, that they can reach their full potential (184).

Heidegger writes that "If ... Being is to have its own history made transparent, then ... hardened tradition must be loosened up, and the concealments which it has brought about must be dissolved" (*Being and Time* 44). Under such circumstances, Heidegger argues that "there is a way by which [the elemental historicality of Dasein] can be discovered and given proper attention" (41) so that "Dasein can discover tradition, preserve it, and study it explicitly" (41). By thus recognizing the traditions that construct Being, it is possible for humankind to examine "what [tradition] 'transmits' and how [it] is transmitted" (Heidegger, *Being and Time* 41) and move into a state of existence that consists of conscious inquiry (41). This is not to say that Dasein will ever escape its essential characteristic of being-in-the-world but that the individual may exist in a purposeful, self-aware state (Heidegger, *Being and Time* 344).

This heightened awareness is achieved by certain characters in the *Dune* series, including the siblings Paul and Alia, and Paul's son, Leto II. With the aid of a spice drug, they gain mental access to the memories of their ancestors and thus become intimately aware of the historical circumstances that shape their present reality. Known as "Kwisatz Haderach" these individuals are able to "be two places simultaneously" (*Dune* 579), in that they carry knowledge of the past and the present. Unlike the ignorant masses, "*the Kwisatz Haderach cannot forget*" (*Children* 119) and are, therefore, conscious of the historical forces at work in their society. Similarly, the Bene Gesserit are able to mentally access their female ancestral line. Leto II explains that "*If you know all of your ancestors, you [are] a personal witness to the events which created the myths and religions of our past*" (*God* 247). Thus, through an understanding of the historicality of Dasein, human ecology becomes recognizable as a man-made construct.

The Kwisatz Haderach and the Bene Gesserit are also equipped with powers of prescience. Paul explains, "One discovers the future in the past, and both are part of the whole" (*Children* 84). The ability to see the whole of Being from a timeless perspective is a notion that is also explored by Heidegger, who regards clock-time as an arbitrary human framework (*The Concept* 4E). He argues that authentic Dasein is achieved through the anticipation of the end of Being. He writes: "*anticipation [of death] reveals to Dasein its lostness in the they-self, and brings it face to face with the possibility of being itself*" (*Being and Time* 311). By confronting death, or as Heidegger puts it, by "running up against its most extreme possibility" (*The Concept* 13E), Dasein moves beyond the entrapments of the now and can look critically upon its entire existence (12E–13E).

Similarly, Jaspers writes that an authentic understanding of reality can only be achieved from a position that transcends the present. He writes, "It is only in retrospect, from a transcending standpoint, that my finite existence comes clearly into view" (*Philosophy* 77). Jaspers describes the moment of transcendence thus: "when our disquiet ceases ... [and] existence becomes transparent. Time stands still.... The knowledge of what was makes the past an eternal present" (78). Paul echoes Jaspers' emphasis on an escape from Time, saying, "*Anyone can rip aside the veil of Time*" (*Children* 377) and, in doing so, "*discover the future in the past*" (377). In recognizing that the future is determined by history, the individual is able to identify the human structures that perpetuate the status quo. Jaspers argues that, to transcend the present moment, "means that instead of being in the world naively [one is] there knowingly" (*Philosophy* 81). Thus, whereas inauthentic existence is characterized by "seeking stability" (Jaspers, *Philosophy* 89), transcendence allows the individual to recognize the arbitrary nature of established social systems and the "infinite possibilities" (89) of the universe. Furthermore, Jaspers states that, transcendence allows for effective reflection on "what *should be done in the present*" (*Way* 124). Thus transcendence, or authentic Dasein, results in an awareness of the traditional systems at work in human society and an ability to resist cultural norms and enact change in the present.

In *God Emperor of Dune*, Leto II, having achieved authentic Dasein, attempts to resist established social structures by reshaping the myths that underpin dominant worldviews. He names himself both a "mythkiller" (41) and a "*mythmaker*" (247), signaling his power to resist traditional narratives and formulate new ways of understanding the universe. Importantly, in becoming a mythmaker, Leto II also becomes a tyrant. He hopes to alter social systems, and the myths that inform them, to ensure the positive evolution of the species. However, by becoming "God Emperor" and forcing his will on a populace that remains in a state of inauthentic Dasein, he becomes a dictator. Jaspers argues that this in an inherent problem with individual transcendence. He writes: "A total knowledge of history would permit total planning, and man would become material for man, to be shaped and transformed to suit his purposes. Humanity would be at man's disposal" (*Philosophical* 2). Jaspers concludes that, although the will to reshape humankind may spring from a positive place of transcended awareness, any attempt by a privileged few to manipulate humanity will "be the end of man" (2).

This notion that those who achieve authentic Dasein will, even in attempting to serve the species, impose on the liberty of others is echoed by Szasz. He writes: "an important limitation [on] man's freedom ... [is] the freedom of other men. The external conditions man seeks to control include other people and social institutions" (1). Thus, in attempting to reshape established systems and create new myths, the transcended individual inevitably impinges on the freedom of others. We see this dilemma represented in the *Dune* series. Characters who achieve authentic Dasein gain great political influence. Paul and Leto II in particular rise above the masses and are regarded, respectively, as a messiah and a god. The populace relinquishes all powers of critical thought and submits to their rule. Leto II declares, "*I am God because I am the only one who really knows his heredity*" (*God* 60). In other words, when only one individual achieves authentic Dasein they surpass all others and the rest of society becomes servile before them. This maintains the traditional system in which rulers shape and encourage cultural myths while the populace remains in a state of inauthentic Dasein. In this way, the absolute ruler, or elite ruling class, ensures the continued passivity of the masses by perpetuating the entrenched "pharaonic disease" (*God* 41) whereby the populace surrenders their liberty to a "god."

Thus, Herbert's *Dune* novels signal the importance of an authentic understanding of, and resistance against, the traditional systems that construct consensus reality. However, the act of transcendence is problematized in the series, which illustrates that, if only achieved by a privileged few, authentic Dasein merely perpetuates unfair social structures. Herbert's series suggests that the myths that facilitate the ascendance of an absolute ruler, particularly in the form of a religious figure-head or messiah, are particularly pervasive in human culture and cause problems for those who achieve authentic Dasein and seek to reshape civilization.

Gods and Heroes

The *Dune* series suggests that the general population delights in the ascendance of a messianic or godlike ruler. According to Herbert, mid-twentieth-century society longs for a leader onto whom they can pin traditional hero myths. In a 1974 article Herbert writes that humankind fears the vastness of the universe and so sets limits by projecting gods, governments and professional experts against the backdrop of infinity ("Science Fiction and a World" 32). He regards such behavior as dangerous, declaring: "Certain pitfalls exist in our tendency toward overdependence upon the professional expert, the specialist. When we turn toward such counsel, we begin by admitting we are helpless and require *superior* guidance" (27). The *Dune* series suggests that, regardless of the expert's good intentions, deferral to a higher intelligence leads to the intellectual stagnation of the supplicant, who no longer seeks their own transcendence and, instead, relies on the expert for leadership. This is commented on by Idaho in *God Emperor of Dune*, who observes that "liberties all vanish when you look up to any absolute ruler" (296).

Herbert argues that the human desire for an absolute ruler is apparent in twentieth-century politics. He writes, "in the power arena of politics … people tend to give over every decision-making capacity to any leader who can wrap himself in the myth fabric of the society. Hitler did it. Churchill did it. Franklin D. Roosevelt did it. Lenin did it" ("Dangers" 98).

He cites one of his favorite examples of such political maneuvering as that displayed by John F. Kennedy. Herbert explains that, by "fitt[ing] ... into the flamboyant Camelot pattern, [and] consciously assuming a bigger-than-life appearance" (98), Kennedy invoked established mythic patterns to solidify his authority.[20] By highlighting the correlation, in the public mind, between Kennedy and King Arthur, a savior who was and is to come, Herbert indicates that humankind is particularly interested in venerating messiah figures.

O'Reilly notes that Herbert draws on the "traditional messianic pattern" (*Frank Herbert* 48) to examine "how society functions with built-in expectations of who will lead and who will follow" (48). Pivotal to these expectations are the mythic narratives by which we understand the world and with which we seek to reconcile current events. Just as Kennedy successfully invoked the Camelot myth, Paul recognizes that he must fit into the myth fabric of society to be accepted as a leader. He states, "*Greatness ... depends ... upon the myth-making imagination of humankind. The person who experiences greatness must have a feeling for the myth he is in*" (*Dune* 151). Upon Paul's arrival on Arrakis, Fremen nomads call out to him, naming him "'*Mahdi*'" (119) in the "*hope [that] he [is] the one foretold as the Lisan al-Gaib, the Voice from the Outer World*" (119).[21] Paul knows that he "*must reflect what is projected on him*" (151) in order to gain authority and realizes that the society of Arrakis is primed to seek out a savior because their traditional myths conform to "the familiar messiah pattern" (122).

The messiah myth thus works cyclically: those with leadership potential recognize the expectations of their constituents and shape their own behavior accordingly, further perpetuating traditional patterns. This cycle is shown to be disastrous for human society in the *Dune* series. Paul soon realizes that, while he is a "*seed*" (*Dune* 233) fallen in the "fertile ... ground" (233) of Fremen culture, his adoption of the prophesied role of Mahdi exposes him to the "terrible purpose" (233) that attaches itself to messiah figures. Paul's prescient abilities tell him that his ascension to godhood will result in a militant religion that will carry a jihad across the universe. This future is repugnant to Paul but, having played into the messiah myth of his people, he is unable to "deflect the juggernaut" (*Dune* 366) of mass culture. Although Paul achieves authentic Dasein and recognizes the traditional systems that inform his society, his acceptance of a role that conforms to entrenched patterns prevents him from enacting change. We learn that "When godhead's given, that's the one thing the so-called god no longer controls" (*Dune Messiah* 44) because the prophet gets locked into pre-existing systems.

Herbert describes Kennedy as an example of a savior figure who was trapped by traditional expectations. In an interview with O'Reilly, Herbert argues that

> Kennedy deliberately set out to create that charismatic image and surrounded himself with the knights of the round table. And then ... society ... projected back ... expectations of certain kinds of behaviour and certain kinds of decision-making which they absolutely demanded ["Conversations" 231].

Herbert argues that this entrapment within social expectations "did as much to kill [Kennedy] as anything" (231). Paul finds himself similarly caught by traditional patterns in *Dune Messiah*. He desperately seeks a way to "disengage" (38) himself from the disastrous messianic pattern he is trapped in but his attempts to assert his individual agency and escape godhood are ultimately doomed. He explains, "*I [want] ... to look back and say: 'There! There's an existence which couldn't hold me.... No restraint or net of human devising can trap me again. I renounce my religion.... I'm free!*'" (46). Paul finally realizes, however, that he cannot escape the systems that enact his Dasein and ensured his ascendency.

Thus, just as Jaspers states that humankind "exists in ... a historically determined ... situation" (*Man* 10), Herbert's *Dune* series illustrates that all human individuals, including absolute rulers, exist within entrenched systems. Indeed, having observed the vilification of Richard Nixon in the 1970s, Herbert writes: "Nixon did *not* invent the system of consensus reality within which he made his choices" ("Introduction" 163). For Herbert, political leaders are trapped, like their citizens, within negative, traditional systems. As Brian Herbert states, the dangers of absolute rulers "is less obvious ... with men who are not deranged or evil in and of themselves. Such a man was Paul Muad'Dib, whose danger lay in the myth structure around him" (192). Paul himself recognizes this dilemma, declaring: "I've heard enough sad histories of gods and messiahs. Why should I need special powers to forecast ruins of my own" (*Dune Messiah* 164).

According to Herbert, any system that facilitates the rise of an absolute leader jeopardizes the positive evolution of humankind because "Beneath the hero's façade, you will find a human being who makes human mistakes" ("Dangers" 98). Paul becomes such a figure in *Dune Messiah*. Having experienced a prescient vision of his civilization fall, he becomes fixated on a particular element of the vision: the death of his lover, Chani (158; 165).[22] Paul becomes willing to jeopardize the welfare of his society for extra time with Chani. He knows that by privileging his personal desires he will become a bad leader but he cannot acquire the inhumanity necessary to become the selfless god demanded by messianic myth (*Children* 349). He therefore sacrifices social stability for his personal needs. Herbert thus highlights how "Enormous problems arise when human mistakes are made on the grand scale available to a superhero" ("Dangers" 98).[23]

Despite the clear dangers of absolute rulers, resisting the messiah myth is shown to be very difficult in the *Dune* series because entrenched systems of belief hamper change. Leto II observes: "There's always a prevailing mystique in any civilization.... It builds itself as a barrier against change ... leav[ing] future generations unprepared for the universe's treachery" (*Children* 404). Leto II identifies a range of mystiques, stating: "All mystiques are the same in building ... barriers—the religious mystique, the hero-leader mystique, the messiah mystique, the mystique of science/technology" (404). He further argues that the danger of such patterns lies in the fact that people fail to distinguish between the mystique and the reality of the changing universe (404). In this way, Leto II argues that "the mystique is like demon possession; it tends to take over the consciousness, becoming all things to the observer" (404). The concept of psychic possession is a recurring thematic in the *Dune* series. Those characters that hold the accumulated memories of their ancestors in their minds are in danger of being possessed by one of their forebears. To be possessed is to become an "Abomination," lost within your own psyche and controlled by the dead. According to Leto II's analogy, when a society is overwhelmed by traditional mystiques, it becomes Abomination: possessed by the worldviews of the past and powerless to resist entrenched systems.

The narrative structure of the *Dune* series works to illustrate how vulnerable we are to possession by traditional myths. The depiction of Paul in *Dune* as a stereotypical hero activates the reader's awareness of the hero schema before the dangers of absolute rule are illuminated in the sequels.[24] Herbert explains: "*Dune* was set up to imprint on you the reader, a superhero. I wanted you ... totally involved with that superhero.... And then I wanted to show what happens" ("The Sparks" 108). *Dune* subtly maneuvers the reader into a sympathetic alignment with Paul. Paul frequently acts as focalizer; however, some of his most impressive deeds, including his duel with the Fremen, Jamis, are focalized by onlookers whose awe infects the reader (*Dune* 347–53).[25] Regardless of the successfulness of Herbert's strategy, the intention of the *Dune* series is clearly to develop Paul as a heroic figure and then undermine the hero myth in *Dune Messiah* and *Children of Dune*.

Indeed, Paul's downfall in *Dune Messiah* precipitated editor John Campbell's refusal to serialize the narrative in his magazine, *Analog*. Campbell had published *Dune* under the titles "Dune World" and "The

Prophet of Dune" between December 1963 and May 1965. However, he was uncomfortable with Herbert's manuscript for *Dune Messiah*. In explaining Campbell's rejection of the narrative, Herbert states: "His argument was that I had created an anti-hero in Paul in the sequel, and he had built his magazine ... on the hero" ("The Sparks" 108). In a letter to Herbert regarding *Dune Messiah*, Campbell observes: "The reactions of science-fictioneers ... over the past few decades have persistently and quite explicitly been that they want *heroes*—not anti-heroes" (Herbert, Herbert, and Anderson 234). This popular reliance on hero narratives is exactly what Herbert's *Dune* series seeks to illuminate and critique. Campbell's response to *Dune Messiah* illustrates the saturation of twentieth-century SF by traditional schemata. The production of spiritual myths in SF by Wells, Arthur C. Clarke and Philip K. Dick is further evidence of the genre's engagement with entrenched modes of thought and raises questions about the ability of SF to offer new ways of understanding the world.

The prevalent redeemer myth is presented in the *Dune* novels as particularly damaging to human society because of its tendency to produce institutionalized religions. Numerous SF writers, including Wells and Clarke, have criticized traditional religion while simultaneously expounding spiritual myths. Herbert's series, however, resists all elements of religion, particularly the redeemer myth. Herbert observes that messiah figures and heroes are disastrous for humankind because "even if we find a real hero ... eventually fallible mortals take over the power structure" ("Dangers" 97) established by the hero and transform it into a corrupt bureaucracy. Similarly, the *Dune* series suggests that humans are predisposed, to their detriment, to seek out absolute leaders, whose philosophies are transformed into rigid institutions by the power-hungry and corrupt. The hero thus becomes the root cause of oppressive systems, religious and otherwise.

Even during Paul's lifetime, the religious government that grows around him becomes a means by which "Men learn to gain and hold personal power" (*Dune Messiah* 188). This situation only worsens with Paul's disappearance. His government becomes a "bureaucratic monster which [sits] astride human affairs" (*Children* 5). In *Children of Dune* it is argued that "*Good government never depends upon laws, but upon the personal qualities of those who govern [because the] machinery of government is always subordinate to the will of those who administer that machinery*" (148). Given that Herbert's series posits that "*Power attracts pathological personalities*" (*Chapterhouse* 59) it becomes clear that, even if the originator of a regime has good intentions, power structures will ultimately be controlled by those least fit to rule.

The *Dune* series represents institutionalized religion as being particularly prone to corruption. Herbert himself observes that "Religion can be both an amplifier and a suppressant of consciousness" ("Conversations" 242) but explains that he is wary of religion because "Organized religions have a managerial bureaucracy aspect to them" (242) and are therefore vulnerable to exploitation. This reflects Jaspers' conflicting views on religion. In *The Future of Mankind*, Jaspers notes the positive influence of the Church on education (256) and argues that Protestant philosophy is democratic in principle because it offers "universal priesthood" (259) so that the truth is not mediated by a ruling body. He hopes that Protestant religion will guide politics to salvation through its ability to promote knowledge, confidence, good will and an awareness of transcendence (251; 252).[26] However, Jaspers also recognizes that, historically, the Church has tended to "proclaim dogmatic beliefs and exclude those who hold [other views]" (256) and has thus discredited itself by becoming absorbed in internecine struggles and political maneuvering (256). For Jaspers, despite its positive potential, the Church has traditionally been an institution that has "help[ed] [its] own, always limited circles, rather than mankind at large" (256).

It is this narrow use of religion that we see exhibited in the early *Dune* novels by the Bene Gesserit Sisterhood. The Bene Gesserit recognize religion as "*a source of energy*" (*Chapterhouse* 317) that "*can be directed for [their] purposes*" (317). Their Missionaria Protectiva deliberately sows "*implant-legends*" (*Dune* 62) in civilizations across the universe to spawn religions based on symbols the Sisterhood controls. Instead of utilizing religion to promote learning, the Missionaria seeks to benefit Bene Gesserit interests by seeding religions that will protect their personnel and allow them to easily attain powerful positions in foreign societies (*Dune* 62). It is this scheme that allows Paul and his Bene Gesserit mother, Jessica, to gain influence among the Fremen: by knowing the prophecy pattern planted on Arrakis by the Missionaria centuries earlier, they are able to adopt the characteristics of the long-awaited messiah and his priestess mother and soon take control of the Fremen government. This reflects Jaspers' comment that religions tend to become a front for individuals who seek power. He writes that in theocratic governance "The human will to power is disguised as God's will" (*Philosophical* 44).

The overwhelming effectiveness of the Bene Gesserit implant legends highlights humanity's desire for spiritual myths and illustrates the tendency for humankind to become dependent on religious leadership. Odrade eventually realizes that "the Missionaria Protectiva's teachings [destroy] human independence.... Mak[ing] [humankind] followers, obedient to [Bene Gesserit] needs" (*Heretics* 312). Indeed, one Bene Gesserit Credo reads: "*Religion is the encystment of past beliefs.... And always the ultimate unspoken commandment is 'Thou shalt not question!'*" (*Children* 285). Leto II reiterates this view in his comment: "*Religion suppresses curiosity*" (*God* 198). Similarly, Jaspers argues that the Church "becalm[s] man's reason, diminish[es] his responsibility and foster[s] passivity with reference to divine Providence" (*The Future* 257). Paul goes further, stating that all religious "institution[s] [move humanity] toward cowardice ... mediocrity, inertia, and self-satisfaction" (*Children* 224). Thus, according to the *Dune* series, "Religious institutions perpetuate a ... master-servant relationship. ... [and] create an arena which attracts prideful human power-seekers with all their nearsighted prejudices!" (*God* 306).

Importantly, the legends planted by the Bene Gesserit move beyond the control of their creators once an institutionalized religion grows up around them. This is what we see in the case of Paul, who attempts to commandeer Bene Gesserit myths but is ensnared by the institutions they generate. Furthermore, once a bureaucratic religion has developed around a hero figure, neither the hero's actions in life, nor their death, hold the "antidote" (*Dune Messiah* 187) for the "mental epidemic" (187) spawned by religious myth. There is no "death-as-surcease" (*Children* 343) for the messiah figure, only martyrdom, which, ironically, reinvigorates entrenched beliefs. The *Dune* series thus represents heroes, and the myths that develop around them, as deleterious to humankind's positive evolution because they inspire passive acceptance of external guidance, resulting in a populace that exists in a state of Das Man, unconsciously accepting the, often corrupt, systems that control their lives.

Although absolute rulers are shown to be dangerous for human society in the *Dune* series, Leto II offers an interesting exception to this rule. He becomes God Emperor and reigns as a tyrant for over three thousand years, guiding humankind onto the Golden Path that will ensure the survival of the species. However, that Leto II only manages to guide humanity on to the beginnings of the Golden Path by transforming into a human-sandworm hybrid and living for thousands of years illustrates yet again the inability of human heroes to enact effective, long-term change. We also see, in the tragic life of Leto II, the cost of a life dedicated to guiding humankind toward knowledge and self-determination.

By the conclusion of *Children of Dune*, Paul's institutionalized theocracy has been subsumed by Leto II's ascension to the Imperial throne as God Emperor and it appears that the messiah pattern is set to repeat again. However, it becomes clear that Leto II is not like Paul: he has no personal stake in assuming leadership and only accepts the mantle of God-king because his prescient abilities tell him that humanity will become extinct if he does not interfere in the species' evolution (*Children* 346). In recognizing that "*[he does] not have to be what [his] father was*" (*Children* 384), Leto II grasps "*man's most unique capability*" (*Children* 384): the power of authentic Dasein and self-determination. In becoming God Emperor, Leto II recognizes the mythic patterns that are at work in his society and begins a long-term battle to eliminate humankind's reliance on hero myths. With "the cruelty of [a] husbandman" (*Children* 405), Leto II takes the "human universe [as his] farm" (405). He deliberately becomes a tyrant and seeks to stifle the initiative of his subjects to force the populace to recognize the stagnation that is imposed on them by absolute rulers and institutionalized religion. Leto II thus makes "freedom ... more precious everyday" (*God* 238) in the minds of his people. By encouraging the populace to hate him as a tyrant, Leto II hopes to taint the hero mystique and imprint on humankind the dangers of submitting to absolute rule.[27]

Leto II realizes that his attempt at "ultimate control of the universe" (*Children* 343) will result in his destruction but seeks to ensure that his death leads to the positive evolution of human society. He manipulates human genetics to make the species less susceptible to control and, by holding a monopoly of power in his bureaucratic government, he guarantees that his death will bring social collapse, and, subsequently, the growth of humankind.[28] Bene Gesserit Taraza explains, "[Leto II] was a key log.... He created the jam and he released it" (*Heretics* 119). Furthermore, Leto II observes that "*Without absolute monarchs patterned after the Old Gods ... Liberty and Freedom would never have gained their present meaning*" (*Heretics* 190). He thus deliberately becomes an oppressive force to facilitate the achievement of authentic Dasein, and an accompanying desire for freedom, in his subjects.

Leto II's use of violence and tyranny to force humanity into recognizing the limiting systems they have historically subscribed to reflects the impartation of knowledge described through the cave allegory in Plato's *Republic*. In this sequence, Plato writes that it is the duty of those who have achieved enlightenment to share their knowledge with those who remain in the darkened cave of ignorance (246). According to Heidegger's interpretation of Plato's allegory, the one who liberates the species from the cave commits an act of violence against those who have lived in ignorant darkness. He writes:

> The liberator is ... someone who has become free in that he looks into the light, has the illuminating view, and thus has a surer footing in the ground of human-historical Dasein. Only then does he gain power to the violence he must employ in liberation. This violence is no blind caprice, but the dragging of others out into the light which already fills and blinds his whole view [*The Essence* 60].

Heidegger further notes that Plato's allegory ends with the death of the liberator (59–60). He writes: "As liberator of the prisoners, the philosopher exposes himself to the fate of death in the cave. ... this is death ... at the hands of cave-dwellers" (61). This is precisely what we see, both literally and figuratively, in the case of Leto II. His subjects, recognizing the tyranny of the absolute leader, finally rebel against him and he is assassinated. He dies in a shadowy cave (*God* 415–20).

Leto II's ability to submit to death for the good of humankind differentiates him from other heroes in the series, most notably his father, Paul. Leto II deliberately eschews human impulses and desires, accepting his transformation into a sandworm and sacrificing human relationships, to ensure that he lives long enough to see his plans fulfilled. In doing so, Leto II dooms himself to a life without love, a choice Paul could not make.[29] Leto II rids himself of the human flaws that, according to Herbert, cause the downfall of absolute rulers. Leto II does feel human emotions and struggles with his desires, particularly his love for Ambassador Hwi Noree. However, he knows that pursuing such "selfish goals" (*God* 181) will jeopardize humanity's survival on the Golden Path. Leto II therefore chooses to sacrifice his short-term happiness for the good of humankind. He thus becomes the ultimate human by Bene Gesserit standards. He lives the trial of the gom jabbar daily: choosing personal pain for the long-term benefit of the species. Leto II is, in actuality "a selfless servant of the people" (*God* 61). Only when his plans have been completed does he allow himself to fraternize with Hwi Noree, knowing that such an exposure of human weakness will afford his enemies an opportunity to kill him and thus complete his design.

Leto II's sacrifice, and its power to shape human society, is reminiscent of Jaspers' description of suprapolitical action in *The Future of Mankind*. Jaspers sees "*conscious* sacrifice" (42), including actions that pose great personal risk to the agent but are performed in service of a greater cause, as evidence of the sublime in humankind and argues that "only a suprapolitical force can bring political salvation" (39) to humanity. He describes self-sacrificial acts as the "unconditioned imperative" (*Way* 52), stating: "When we obey the unconditional imperative, our empirical existence becomes ... raw material.... It is encompassed in an eternal aim" (52). He further writes: "as opposed to passive acceptance of things as they are, the unconditional attitude implies a decision.... It means to partake in the eternal, in being" (56). Jaspers recognizes the potential for unconditional, suprapolitical action in humanity and sees it as a means by which entrenched systems can be resisted.

However, Jaspers laments that "suprapolitical sacrifice ... seems to vanish in the contagion of a mass movement" (*The Future* 41–42). He further concedes that, because human life is always immersed within existing political systems, suprapolitical action may never be possible at all (249). While the unconditional imperative allows for individuals to grasp their authentic self and subordinate their lives to a long-term goal, Jaspers notes that unconditional action tends to only occur under extreme circumstances, such as when one is in love or in battle (*Way* 52). Thus the kind of sustained sacrifice performed by Leto II in *God Emperor of Dune* is, in reality, impossible for mortals. This suggests that it is only when absolute rulers overcome human nature and acquire genuine godhood that they are capable of successfully guiding humankind toward a better future. In other words, no mortal who succumbs to the hero pattern can provide long-term benefits to humanity. Furthermore, despite Leto II's best efforts at defeating the messiah myth, the society of the Dune universe remains susceptible to the hero mystique after Leto II's death.[30]

Thus the hero myth, as represented in the *Dune* series, is an entrenched pattern that is tremendously dangerous for the human psyche. The actions of Leto II serve to highlight the inability of absolute rulers to completely dispel established myths. However, the series also illustrates that, without recognizing the limitations imposed by absolute rulers, humankind cannot understand what it means to be free. We thus return to the importance of an authentic understanding of being-in-the-world. Traditional forms, if recognized, can become a map of what to avoid in the future. The final two novels of the *Dune* series, set after the deaths of both Leto II and Paul, examine how the species can evolve positively, unhampered by hero myths.

Democracy, Education and Authentic Dasein in the *Dune* Series

While religion is shown to offer the potential for enlightened thinking in the *Dune* series, it tends to be exploited by those who seek power. As we have seen, the Bene Gesserit Missionaria schemes produce the messianic religion of Paul Muad'Dib and the tyranny of Leto II's rule. The Bene Gesserit are therefore forced to re-examine their goals and methods in the final two novels of the *Dune* series: *Heretics of Dune* and *Chapterhouse: Dune*. Odrade, who becomes mother superior at the end of *Heretics of Dune*, realizes that the Bene Gesserit attempts to control humankind through the manipulation of pre-existing symbols and mythic patterns has done nothing more than create a *"dogmatic stink"* (*Heretics* 313) in the universe by promoting passivity and stagnation among the populace. She concludes that the Bene Gesserit mission must follow Leto II's Golden Path by seeking the survival and positive evolution of the species as their *"noble purpose"* (313). It becomes increasingly apparent in the *Dune* series that traditional systems can only be successfully combated by a united population. A democratic society, formed of individuals who have achieved authentic Dasein, becomes the only hope for the future growth of humankind.

A critical understanding of the systems that underlie human society is promoted by Korzybski in *Science and Sanity*. He argues that, to build a social system that is free from objectionable myths, the assumptions that underpin the current system must first be discovered, challenged and rejected (lxiii). The authentic Dasein of the Bene Gesserit affords them a clear understanding of the principles that construct consensus reality. However, as we have seen, inequalities arise when only a few individuals achieve transcendence and attempt to manipulate the unenlightened masses. It is under such circumstances that heroes emerge.

In Friedrich Nietzsche's *Thus Spoke Zarathustra* the heroic protagonist cautions against the idolization of the Superman, or Übermensch, saying, "You respect me; but how if one day your respect should tumble? Take care that a falling statue does not strike you dead!" (103). It is proposed in Nietzsche's work that "Man is a rope, fastened between animal and Superman—a rope over an abyss" (43). The evolution from human to Superman is fraught. Leto II feels the burden of acting as the bridge toward the positive evolution of the species, reflecting that, to manage the future is to "balance on a single, thin thread—playing God on a high tightwire" (*Children* 343). Such a role is a dangerous burden for any single individual. Just as Nietzsche's Zarathustra urges humankind to ignore the hero and collectively grasp their own potential for greatness (103), the Bene Gesserit in the *Dune* series come to recognize democracy as a means by which the whole species may develop, free from the tyranny of hero figures.[31]

Like Thomas Carlyle, the Bene Gesserit recognize that, when the populace lacks the critical faculties necessary to make effective electoral decisions, democracy is "demagogue-prone" (*Chapterhouse* 156).[32] However, as Jaspers argues, in a true democracy "every individual has a chance to think and act" (*The Future* 292). Of course, for these thoughts and actions to be meaningful, "Democracy ... requires the whole people should be educated" (Jaspers, *The Future* 292). It is this form of democracy that is promoted in Herbert's *Dune* series. In *Chapterhouse: Dune*, the Bene Gesserit seek to open their sect to new members so that, in time, all of humanity will achieve the authentic Dasein needed for effective social participation.

Unlike the Honored Matres, who tame the population by stifling talent, the Bene Gesserit eventually learn to promote "*Candor and honesty*" (*Chapterhouse* 116) as the "Basic tools for learning" (116). As logistician Miles Teg observes in *Heretics of Dune*, the methods used by the Honored Matres seek to "increase the dependency of those who support them" (122), a method described as "an addict's dead-end street" (122) because it allows for the maintenance of power for a time but leads to the eventual downward evolution of human civilization. In contrast, the Bene Gesserit ensure that education provides the faculties for creative thinking, a method that is particularly apparent in their education of the former Honored Matre Murbella in *Chapterhouse: Dune*. Such education is shown to be essential for the positive development of the individual. This reflects Jaspers assertion that, unlike animals, "Man cannot merely exist" (*Philosophy* 78) without the faculty of choice but must either "transcend and soar or go down, bereft of transcendence" (78). By genuinely educating their students, the Bene Gesserit abandon their former attempts at domination and control and accept democracy as the best way to promote transcendence and prevent fatal dependency in the population.

Of course, the Bene Gesserit cannot entirely eliminate the entrenched patterns that lead to the rise of heroes. Throughout the *Dune* series, we see heroic figures emerge, particularly within the Bene Gesserit ranks. However, in the final novel of the series, we see a deliberate attempt by the Sisterhood to prevent these individuals from rising to absolute power. Indeed, Sheeana, a Bene Gesserit and female descendent of Leto II, deliberately flees beyond the known universe at the conclusion of *Chapterhouse: Dune* to escape deification. Sheeana's departure from the human universe opens up the future to new "*interesting patterns*" (*Chapterhouse* 430), free from entrenched systems. This attempt to suppress the hero mystique and the religious institutions that grow up around such figures reflects the increasing democratization of the Dune universe. As Jaspers explains, "Democracy does not permit us to assume that rulers are, or could or should be, superhuman. It insists that ... every challenge faces human beings" (*The Future* 298) as a collective group.

In the *Dune* series, we discover that the challenges faced by humans in the ever-changing universe can only be met by a coordinated, educated community. The planetologist Liet Kynes' father recognizes this early in *Dune*, stating: "We must depend not so much on the bravery of individuals ... as upon the bravery of [the] whole population" (318). This, again, echoes Jaspers, who argues that "it would be folly to expect the world to be put right by a few reasonable men" (*The Future* 291). Heroes are not the means by which humanity will escape traditional systems. Rather, Jaspers explains, "To become effective and durable, reason must pervade the nations. This is why we need democracy, the system in which the people are meant to 'reason together'" (291). For the Bene Gesserit, this communal striving requires that they relinquish their emotionless self-possession and embrace the compromise that comes with loving cooperation (*Chapterhouse* 421).

This emphasis on compromise reflects Szasz's comment that true liberty not only involves freedom from arbitrary political and interpersonal control and the self-confidence necessary to display one's own creative potential, but also requires self-control (1). A Bene Gesserit tenet echoes this notion, stating: "*Seek freedom and become captive of your desires. Seek discipline and find your liberty*" (*Chapterhouse* 344). It is thus through self-discipline that compromise and equality can be achieved. Odrade reflects that democracy fails when it is "overthrown by its own excesses or eaten away by bureaucracy" (332). Effective social growth is therefore achieved by striking a balance, through compromise, between these two fates by promoting creative freedom and resisting the entrenchment of mythic patterns.

The level of human transformation necessary to create a truly democratic community is, of course, significant. As Jaspers argues in his appraisal of Cold War Earth, social rejuvenation calls for humanity to "transform ... in [its] moral, rational, [and] political aspects" (*The Future* 4) in "a transformation so extensive that it [will] become the turning point of history" (4). It is this kind of transformation that is imagined in the *Dune* series, which advocates the achievement of authentic Dasein across the community. According to Jaspers, modern society is in a unique position because "Man to-day has been uprooted, having become aware that he exists in what is but a historically determined and changing situation" (*Man* 10). This recognition of reality as a human construct offers humanity a chance to resist established patterns and create new myths (Jaspers, *Man* 10). Authentic Dasein thus offers the opportunity for humankind to generate positive evolutionary paths. Herbert argues in a 1985 interview that "human beings are not through evolving. And ... if we are going to survive ... we're going to have to do things which allow us to go on evolving" ("The Sparks" 110). The *Dune* series posits that a recognition of the patterns that have historically enacted our selfhood and a deliberate attempt to reshape human culture in response to the chaotic universe we inhabit will allow for the positive evolution of humankind.

According to Jaspers, the development of a positive civilization requires that knowledge "progress endlessly" (*Philosophical* vii) and enter every aspect of human life. Herbert's *Dune* series similarly calls for recognition of the impossibility of ever gaining complete knowledge of the universe. It is stated in *Children of Dune* that "nothing [is] durable in all the universe ... nothing remains in its state ... each day ... brings change" (267). Such a worldview prohibits the formulation of absolute myths or predictions. For Herbert, an acceptance of the chaotic nature of the universe provides freedom to continually search for knowledge, to generate ever-changing myths and adapt to new discoveries. Indeed, he confides in a 1963 letter to John Campbell that he "find[s] ... the chaos reassuring [because it] means that there are no walls, no limits, no boundaries except those man himself creates" (O'Reilly, *Frank Herbert* 175).

Thus, Herbert utilizes SF to articulate his personal convictions about the universe. However, instead of rejecting established myths only to produce narratives that reinscribe traditional ideas, Herbert's *Dune* series articulates a myth of democratic resistance, which promotes an authentic awareness of the social structures that limit being and a rejection of absolutist myths. Absolute rulers and absolute myths are dismissed in the *Dune* novels, having been shown to cripple the evolutionary ascendance of the species. Instead, the reader is faced with a universe of infinite possibilities in which, through democratic striving, humankind may carve a positive future.

Frank Herbert and Science Fiction

As we have seen, Herbert's SF represents human civilization as constructed and limited by entrenched systems. In particular, humanity's susceptibility to the messiah myth and institutionalized religion is presented as deleterious to the positive evolution of the species. The dependency and subsequent social stagnation that accompany absolute rule are criticized in the *Dune* series, which presents the fundamental transformation of the mass consciousness as the only antidote for social degeneration. Herbert's *Dune* novels advocate the attainment of authentic Dasein as the means by which traditional myths can be recognized, resisted and reshaped. Herbert's use of SF to propound such a view is particularly adroit, given the genre's investment in modern myth creation. By breaking with the conventions of the hero narrative, the *Dune* series highlights that much twentieth-century SF has reinforced, rather than resisted, traditional patterns.

Writers such as Dick and Wells, who outline new spiritual myths of divine intervention in their SF are, by Herbert's standards, subscribing to the same messiah mystique that has dominated Western thought since the middle ages. He writes that SF tends to be "linked ... to all of the old myth strings we humans carry around" ("Men" 74). Although SF writers are often critical of traditional religion, they tend to return to religious frameworks when devising alternative myths. This is something Herbert's SF deliberately avoids. His SF illuminates the entrenched mythic patterns that determine our understanding of the universe without constructing an alternative religious myth. Instead, the *Dune* series presents a narrative of conscious resistance. It outlines a myth of human self-determination whereby, through effective education and social cooperation, humanity can achieve transcendence and resist limiting traditions.

Herbert notes that, by constructing imaginative worlds that incorporate and build on existing thought patterns, SF can act to sensitize the reader to the impact of current myths ("Science Fiction and a World" 22). Of course, this potential is somewhat impeded by those SF works that reinscribe traditional myths. Herbert's *Dune* series, however, is invested in sensitizing the reader to humankind's overdependence on absolute, often religious, myths. Herbert argues that the universe is constantly changing and evolving while humanity scrambles to construct myths that articulate comforting absolutes ("Listening" 9; "Science Fiction and a World" 28; "Introduction" 166). The *Dune* series highlights the need for humankind to evolve perpetually to meet the challenging circumstances of life. According to Herbert, this evolution demands that humanity retain, or regain, its critical faculties, strive for knowledge and resist the urge to defer to entrenched systems. Herbert's series thus seeks the same goal as the Bene Gesserit in *Chapterhouse: Dune*: the awakening of the individual into authentic Dasein and the democratic reshaping of the myth patterns that inform our existence.

Of course, the key difficulty in producing new myths is that the very language we use enforces traditional structures. Korzybski argues that the Aristotelian structural characteristics of language, which verbally split "mind" and "body," "emotion" and "intellect," and "space" and "time" are dangerous for civilization because they do not reflect empirical reality (xxx). However, because of the entrenched nature of the linguistic structures that construct consensus reality, humankind remains ensnared by traditional modes of expressing and understanding. Herbert observes: "The conditioning of most cultures on the planet tends to set up absolute categories ... good-bad, beautiful-ugly ... sacred-profane. Western culture is particularly obsessed with this absolutism" ("Men" 73). He further notes that "Language opens up the reflection of thought, but by its very nature it also creates boundaries which appear insurmountable.... It is the root of prejudice and a limiter of perceptions as the embodiment of previous experiences which have been judged and catalogued" ("Science Fiction and a World" 38).

However, as Herbert exclaims, "Without language there would be no science fiction. What a crisis that would be!" ("Science Fiction and a World" 38). According to Herbert, SF offers a vehicle for appraising traditional myths and articulating new ones. Describing the process of SF writing he asserts that it "allows you to generate your own values.... It permits you to go beyond those cultural norms that are prohibited by your society and enforced by unconscious (and conscious) literary censorship" ("Men" 82). However, it cannot be denied that the ability of SF to resist pre-existing systems is jeopardized by the fact that it must utilize linguistic structures that are saturated by traditional patterns.

Korzybski states, "language ... can be somewhat altered from within, but cannot be *revised structurally* without going *outside* the former system" (xiii). We see this observation borne out in the *Dune* series with regard to traditional myth patterns. In adopting the role of messiah, Paul realizes too late that he cannot alter existing systems from within. So too, the Bene Gesserit Missionaria Protectiva perpetuates existing systems by working with established religious discourses. We learn from Heidegger that our Dasein is always immersed in existing systems. The question of how humanity can escape tradition and reshape the myth fabric of society to reflect contemporary knowledge forms a key question in Herbert's *Dune* series. Indeed, SF, as a genre engaged in mythmaking, is fundamentally concerned with negotiating the coexistence of traditional mythic systems and the contemporary realization that humanity needs to be liberated from entrenched thought patterns.

Herbert's SF is engaged with the struggle between traditional, absolutist myths and the modern recognition of the infinity of the universe. Herbert rails not only against the limitations of institutionalized religion and bureaucratic social systems but also against the belief that science will provide absolute knowledge. Jaspers articulates a similar view, writing: "Scientific knowledge and technological skills are admirable. ... [but] They imperil man and his existence" (*Philosophical* vii) because "their light obscures the essence" (vii). That is, science can give the false impression that humankind has uncovered the full store of knowledge available, generating "a sophistica[ted] delusion" (Jaspers, *Philosophical* vii) that enslaves us to a fictitious worldview. Thus all absolutist myths are regarded by Herbert as dangerous for humankind. As Leto II observes, "reality—or the belief that you know a reality, which is the same thing—always sets up a ferment in the universe" (*God* 145).

What Herbert's *Dune* series illustrates is that "*humankind is still evolving, in a process that will never end*" (*Children* 1) and so must discover "*a philosophy with which a human can meet problems arising from an ever-changing universe*" (1). The *Dune* series suggests that, for such a philosophy to be devised, humankind must first achieve an authentic understanding of the forces that construct consensus reality and learn to resist traditional myths. In illustrating the deleterious influence of absolute rulers on humankind, the *Dune* series suggests that humankind must function as a democratic collective to adapt to their dynamic environment. However, although Herbert's series identifies authentic Dasein as the first step toward positive evolution, it offers no definite explanation of how human democracy will achieve liberation from entrenched patterns.

Naturally, Herbert refuses to fully explain the complex interplay of themes in his novels, declaring: "I refuse ... to provide further answers.... You find your own answers; don't look to me as your leader" ("Dangers" 101). This challenge illustrates the fundamental goal of his *Dune* series: to empower the reader to explore the diverse social problems faced by humanity. Herbert's series thus supports Jaspers' assertion that "To make us free, enlightenment must ... enter every horizon, must never be complete" (*Philosophical* vii). Herbert's SF sees the endless change of the chaotic universe as reassuring because it offers a limitless scope for human development. All absolute myths must be resisted in such a universe. Thus, in the *Dune* series, we see SF resist entrenched narrative patterns and articulate an awareness of the traditional myths that hamper the genre's potential for modern myth creation. In particular, the religious narratives that influence human society come under attack in Herbert's writing, highlighting the tendency for other SF texts to defer to traditional frameworks.

Conclusion

According to Arthur C. Clarke, "science fiction writer[s] can do a great service to the community" (*Greetings* 249) by encouraging readers to achieve the "flexibility of mind" (249) that will allow them to adapt to change. Indeed, as we have seen, the novels of Clarke, H. G. Wells, Philip K. Dick and Frank Herbert all demonstrate an openness toward change and seek to resist entrenched social systems and dogmatic ways of thinking. These writers directly utilize SF as a vehicle for reconsidering the systems that inform human understanding. They recognize the power of SF to convey social commentary, resist traditional beliefs and generate new myths that reflect changes in our understanding of the universe and offer hope for humanity's future evolution.

Rather than articulating worldviews based solely on modern science, the myths presented in SF are amalgamative because SF engages with the range of discourses, both ancient and modern, that coexist in contemporary thought. This means that SF myths tend to simultaneously resist and reinscribe traditional systems of thought and, in so doing, reflect the discordant philosophies of contemporary culture. In Wells' early writing we see SF established as a sociological mode. Wells deliberately seeks to construct myths that reflect the findings of evolutionary science and articulate the moral values essential to human civilization. This use of SF to explore scientific discoveries and examine human society illustrates the all-inclusive nature of SF myth, which, in Wells' case, articulates faith in a transcendental God. Of course, the incorporation of sociological and scientific concerns in SF illustrates that the myriad discourses that inform human reality interact and intermingle to create contemporary knowledge.

Indeed, as illustrated in Chapter 2, spiritual notions even feature in twentieth-century biology so that science itself cannot be considered a purely materialist discourse. We see the juxtaposition of vitalist and materialist theories in the writings of scientists such as J. B. S. Haldane, Alfred

Russel Wallace and Lawrence J. Henderson. This incorporation of materialist and spiritual theories in biology is reflected in contradictory representations of life in the SF myths of Clarke's *Space Odyssey* series. Clarke uses his SF to advocate the scientific point of view, which emphasizes the importance of mental flexibility and openness to change, as opposed to the staid dogma of some traditional religions. However, the inclusion of vitalist notions in Clarke's most influential novels has resulted in a reinscribing of spiritual myths of transcendence and suprahuman guidance.

In contrast to Clarke, who attempts, in his later fictions, to repudiate the spiritual myths of his early SF, Dick's novels become increasingly religious over the course of his career. Like Wells, Dick uses SF as a vehicle for social commentary. Drawing on the works of Herbert Marcuse and from ancient philosophy, Dick seeks to resist consumer capitalist ideologies and uncover the latent structure of the universe. Just as Wells draws from the writings of Plato to discover a pre–Christian alternative to modern social systems, Dick invokes the Presocratics to resist contemporary ideologies and speculate about the nature of reality. In rejecting contemporary worldviews, Dick's late work draws from Gnostic religion, Platonic philosophy and Greek myth to construct alternative myths of divine salvation, making his SF largely spiritual, rather than materialist.

Conversely, we see in Herbert's *Dune* series a conscious reaction against the spiritual myths produced so often in twentieth-century SF. Herbert regards human society as reliant on the hero myth. He depicts humankind as constantly seeking to relinquish responsibility to a higher authority and refusing to recognize that the chaotic universe is not manifesting a divine plan for human salvation. Drawing on Heideggerian philosophy, Herbert attempts to reject the hero narrative and produce myths that promote the achievement of authentic Dasein in a collectively-striving, democratic populace.

We continue to see the works of Wells, Dick, Clarke and Herbert influencing current SF and being adapted for visual media. Indeed, films and television series based on the SF of Wells, Dick and Herbert have appeared on screen in recent years and Clarke's *Childhood's End* was released as a television miniseries in 2015.[1] Ironically, despite Clarke's attempts to articulate materialist myths in his later fictions, it is his early, quasi-spiritual narratives that have gained the greatest cultural currency. Clarke's representation of Overminds controlling humanity's evolution in *2001: A Space Odyssey* and *Childhood's End*, and his depiction of the transcendent evolution of Dave Bowman constitute the most well-known aspects of his corpus. Similarly, adaptations of the *Dune* series tend to reshape Herbert's vision to fit conventional narrative patterns. Further, the disproportionate notoriety of *Dune* compared to its sequels means that Herbert's SF tends to be popularly associated with the ascendance of a superhuman messiah.[2]

The adaptation of the works of Wells, Clarke, Dick and Herbert for film and television is the result of the proliferation of SF into non-print media, which occurred in the second half of the twentieth century. Adam Roberts argues that the expansion of SF into visual modes has allowed the genre to achieve "a much deeper cultural penetration" (*The History* 264), noting that, when figures are adjusted for inflation, four out of the five top-grossing films of the twentieth century are SF (293). He further observes that late-twentieth-century SF films such as George Lucas' *Star Wars* (1977) and Ridley Scott's *Blade Runner* (1982), based on Dick's *Do Androids Dream of Electric Sheep?*, maintain a cultural relevance that other genres of the period do not (282). This is particularly true for the *Star Wars* franchise, which was acquired by The Walt Disney Company in 2012 and has been re-energized across television and print media ahead of a new set of films. Here we see the enduring legacy of Herbert's *Dune*, which acts as an intertext for *Star Wars*.

Brian Herbert writes in *Dreamer of Dune: The Biography of Frank Herbert* that he found *Star Wars* "shocking … for all the similarities between it and [Frank Herbert's] book, *Dune*" (288). He writes that, when Frank Herbert saw the film, "he picked out sixteen points of what he called 'absolute identity' between his book and the movie" (289). It is not difficult to recognize some of these points of similarity. Like Herbert's novel, *Star Wars* involves a desert planet, complete with Dune Sea, where a worm species holds power. We further see the *Star Wars* saga represent a prophesied messiah who is trained by a mysterious sect of individuals seeking to protect society. Like Herbert's Bene Gesserit, the Jedi have powers that afford them great mental and physical acuity, equipping them with psychic abilities and the power to manipulate others using only their voice.[3]

An important point of difference between *Dune* and *Star Wars* is the representation, in Lucas' series, of an all-pervading, mysterious force at work in the universe. The Bene Gesserit's skills are gained from physical training, knowledge of human history and drug use; the Jedi gain their powers from connection with a spiritual force. Lucas thus presents a more spiritual and less materialistic universe than Herbert does, in which heroes are born with powers beyond the grasp of the mass populace. The emphasis on suprahuman hero-figures and the dismissal of scientific principles in the *Star Wars* films reflects a movement in SF toward more spiritual conceptions of the universe and the increased production of traditional narrative patterns in which heroes rise to guide humankind.[4]

Mark Bould and Sherryl Vint note that the twenty-first-century proliferation of SF in visual media has seen a rise in franchises and "remak[es] [of] formerly successful titles" (182). Of course, financial conservatism and risk aversion underlie decisions to remake existing narratives and create franchises.[5] However, franchising also means that a particular set of SF narratives, and their associated myths, are being retold for contemporary audiences. This has meant that the blending of religious and scientific discourses that characterizes nineteenth-and-twentieth-century SF is being reflected in twenty-first-century narratives such as the *Star Wars* prequel trilogy and film adaptations of comic book stories.

Furthermore, original works set in outer space often explore spiritual themes. For example, in Alfonso Cuarón's *Gravity* (2013) religious icons placed within the seemingly incongruous setting of Earth orbit raise questions about the nature of human life and faith. Further investigation of twenty-first-century SF is needed to establish the relative influence of contemporary cultural discourses, compared to intertextuality, on the myths being articulated in SF today. The cultural saturation of SF in contemporary society makes a study of the myths it embodies crucial to understanding the underlying philosophy of our culture and the way literature is contributing to and reflecting twenty-first-century worldviews.

In twenty-first-century SF we are seeing a major emphasis on suprahuman savior figures and hero myths in adaptations of Marvel and DC comic book stories. These narratives tend to consistently reaffirm the hero myth pattern and thus reinscribe traditional ways of understanding humanity's place in the universe. Whether the heroes in these narratives are aliens, gods or men, there is a general suggestion, particularly in the Marvel films, that the mass populace should defer to heroes in times of crisis. Interestingly, like *Star Wars*, Marvel is now owned by Disney so that the most prolific producer of SF films today is a company that has traditionally been a creator of children's and young adult literature.

Disney's recent production of the children's cartoons *Avengers Assemble, Hulk and the Agents of S.M.A.S.H., Ultimate Spiderman* and *Star Wars Rebels* demonstrates the company's commitment to marketing their SF acquisitions to both children and adults. Given the mythic potential of SF, the genre is particularly suited to inculcate culturally dominant thought systems in young viewers. A shift in Disney's output from fantasy and fairy tale toward SF will in all likelihood have far-reaching implications for the study of children's literature. The representation of hero myths in

Marvel and *Star Wars* narratives aimed at children will become of interest to the field, which has tended to focus on the appropriation of traditional fairy tales and folk tales in contemporary fiction for children.

Wells established SF as a genre for the critical examination of the thought patterns that underlie human life. However, the power of the genre to reflect on contemporary reality and produce new myths is jeopardized when writers seek simply to capitalize on the success of established texts or reproduce traditional, expected narratives. The myths of social mobilization that Wells, Herbert and Clarke regard as essential for the positive evolution of humankind are no less relevant today. Yet, just as we have seen entrenched linguistic and social systems influence the myths produced by Wells, Clarke, Dick and Herbert, we can still see traditional beliefs and conventional narrative patterns influencing contemporary SF. It is those texts inspired by Dick's fictions, including Christopher Nolan's *Inception* (2010), The Wachowski Brothers' *The Matrix* (1999), Duncan Jones' *Source Code* (2011), Joseph Kosinski's *Oblivion* (2013), Doug Liman's *Edge of Tomorrow* (2014) and Rian Johnson's *Looper* (2012), that tend to be most effective in questioning consensus reality.[6] However, beyond their mind-bending narrative structures, these films, with perhaps the exception *The Matrix*, tend not to embody new myths, as Dick's fictions do.

Further study of the intertextual influence of the myths produced by successful SF authors of the twentieth century is needed to illuminate mythic trends in the genre and to determined whether twenty-first-century SF continues to offer the same potential for sociological commentary and modern myth production as its predecessors. The ever-increasing proliferation and popularity of SF in the twenty-first century illustrates the power of SF myth in modern society. However, the cultural dominance of narratives that privilege myths of messiahs and heroes may indicate a degree of complacency in a culture that looks to external forces for salvation. Such an attitude is exactly what writers like Wells, Clarke and Herbert sought to resist with their SF and is more closely aligned to those myths produced by Dick. The potential for contemporary SF to live up to the legacy of these SF progenitors and to create new myths, rather than reproducing established patterns, is yet to be determined.

Chapter Notes

Introduction

1. For instance, critic and SF author Adam Roberts' argument in *The History of Science Fiction* is based on the proposition that SF developed during the Protestant Reformation and, therefore, still articulates the "cultural dialectic between 'Protestant' rationalist ... science ... and 'Catholic' theology" (3) that dominated social discourse at the time of its birth. See also David Seed and Isaac Asimov who both posit that the persistent emphasis on technology in SF is a result of the genre's emergence in the nineteenth century (Seed, *Science* 3; 47; Asimov, "Social" 61).

2. This point is also made by Brian Aldiss and David Wingrove in their comprehensive study *Trillion Year Spree: The History of Science Fiction* (1986). They write that scholars often forget that SF "writers write in the flux of life going on about them" (28) rather than solely drawing on earlier SF for inspiration.

3. In analyzing the discourses that influence the writings of Wells, Clarke, Dick and Herbert this work identifies correlations between the ideas explored in their SF novels and the notions articulated in the published, public utterances of prominent writers, scientists and philosophers. Such an approach allows for the identification and analysis of the relationship between the myths produced in SF and dominant social discourses. We may expect, however, that there are always other, unseen factors that contribute to the myths presented in the works of SF authors. Wherever possible, this study incorporates information about the personal lives and experiences of its chosen authors but it cannot encompass all the influences that inform SF myth production. Instead, this work presents an argument based on a thorough examination of those public, verifiable sources that most obviously influence SF myth creation in the works of Wells, Clarke, Dick and Herbert.

4. Wells and Clarke each produced novels for close to half a century, Wells writing novels from 1895 to the 1940s and Clarke publishing novels from 1953 to 2007.

5. Critics Mark Bould and Sherryl Vint also define SF in relation to science. They emphasize the role of applied science in SF, stating that the genre is concerned with the social and cultural changes that arise from new technologies (39). Likewise, David Seed writes that "One of the most recurrent themes in science fiction is its examination of humanity's relation to its own material constructions" (*Science* 47). For similar definitions see George Slusser's argument that "SF is all about science" (28); Vint's comment that "The relationship between science and sf is sometimes considered as a defining characteristic of the genre" ("Science" 413); and Gary Westfahl's point that "In its very name, science fiction announces a special concern for, and a special connection to, science" (187).

6. See also, Karlheinz Steinmüller who regards SF as a genre that incorporates a range of discourses and, in doing so, acts as a bridge between science and the humanities (339). Gabriel Mckee echoes this viewpoint, describing SF as the "middle ground" (*The Gospel* xiv) between science and religion. Similarly, Adam Roberts describes SF as a mode in which "art and science connect" (*The History* 5).

7. In a similar vein, Roberts writes that SF tends to incorporate a "proliferation of [scientific] theories" (*The History* 18), rather than adopting a "notional uniformity or 'truth'" (18). In describing SF this way, Roberts is drawing on Paul Feyerabend's definition of science, described below.

8. Indeed, Steinmüller goes so far as to describe SF as "an unexplored source of the history of science" (339) because it reflects "pivotal [scientific] themes and achievements" (339).

9. This stance is also adopted by critics such as McConnell in his 1981 work *The Science Fiction of H. G. Wells* (4).

10. Of course, there are critics who oppose this view and argue that SF is strictly concerned with materialist science. For instance, in his 1979 work *Metamorphoses of Science Fiction*, Darko Suvin argues that "*SF is ... a metaempirical and ... estranged ... genre ... which is not ... metaphysical*" (20). However, while Suvin describes SF as adhering to a cognitive approach, he recognizes that it also exhibits a "tendency toward mystifying escapism" (ix). Suvin attempts to suggest that fantastic elements are only characteristic of "second-rate SF" (ix). However, he acknowledges that masterpieces of SF, including Mary Shelley's *Frankenstein* (1818) and the works of H. G. Wells, incorporate the fantastic and the spiritual (ix). Suvin also notes that many of Philip K. Dick's most successful novels display an ontological, metaphysical orientation ("P. K." 15).

11. For a more detailed discussion of the distinctions between the different fictional genres see H. Bruce Franklin's *Future Perfect: American Science Fiction of the Nineteenth Century* (3).

12. For further reading on the ancient texts that are commonly recognized as at least distantly related to modern SF, see Aldiss and Wingrove (29; 68); Roberts (*The History* vii); Brian M. Stableford ("Proto SF"); and Robert Lambourne, Michael Shallis and Michael Shortland's *Close Encounters? Science and Science Fiction* (1).

13. Also titled *A Voyage to the Moon.*

14. Steinmüller also dates the genre to the seventeenth century but does not emphasize religion in his discussion of SF (340). See also Mark R. Hillegas (2).

15. Indeed, as Roberts observes, the majority of critics subscribe to the short history model ("The Copernican" 3). The text most frequently discussed as the starting point for SF is Mary Shelley's *Frankenstein* (1818). Aldiss convincingly presents this novel as the first true SF work (3) and is cited frequently in other SF histories and definitions, including those written by Stableford, Clute and Nicholls; Slusser (27); Fred Botting (113); Asimov (*Asimov* 19); and Lambourne, Shallis and Shortland (5).

16. Other writers that use this rationale to justify their subscription to the short history include Asimov, who regards SF as a genre that responds to the changes wrought on society by developments in science and technology. He writes: "Until modern times, the rate of change [in society] was so slow as to make the process unnoticeable in the course of any one person's lifetime" (*Asimov* 81). However, the technological advancements of the Industrial Revolution meant that people began to witness rapid social change and SF grew up as a literary response to these developments (Asimov, *Asimov* 82). Similarly, Seed, who favors a slightly later starting date for the genre, argues that, as the nineteenth century progressed, the expansion of education and, subsequently, the growth of the commercial market provided a growing consumer base for SF (*Science* 3).

17. Chernyshova asserts that the everyday consciousness cannot incorporate the technical data and mathematical calculations that construct exact scientific knowledge ("Science" 352). She suggests, therefore, that when science is popularized, it is simplified to the point of becoming inexact knowledge. She writes that, when it enters the public consciousness, science is stripped of the calculations that make it exact and is shaped to fit in with popular systems of thought (352).

18. Of course, this is only one among many definitions of myth. A thorough overview of the varying approaches to myth that have developed since the nineteenth century cannot be accommodated here. However, there are numerous studies on the subject. For some of the more comprehensive, historical overviews of the study of myth, see Doty's *Mythography: The Study of Myths and Rituals*; Robert A. Segal's *Myth: A Very Short Introduction* (2004) and *Theorizing about Myth* (1999); David Bidney's "Myth, Symbolism, and Truth" (1972); and G. S. Kirk's *Myth: Its Meaning and Functions in Ancient and Other Cultures* (1970).

19. James Frazer was an influential proponent of this notion. In his famous work *The Golden Bough* (1890) he writes: "From the earliest times man has been engaged in a search for general rules whereby to turn the order of natural phenomena to his own advantage" (50). Frazer argues that myths, particularly those produced by fertility cults, are attempts to understand and control nature. He argues that "magic, religion, and science are ... theories of thought; and ... science has supplanted its predecessors" (712). This view of religious myth as outmoded in the scientific world is belied by the fact that religion

has not disappeared at all and, instead, continues to inform contemporary worldviews. Nevertheless, Frazer's views were particularly influential in the early twentieth century.

20. Like SF and myth, religion is challenging to define. This definition draws on a 2006 study by Corine Hyman and Paul J. Handal, which seeks to define religion and spirituality by surveying different religious professionals. The study reveals that the majority of practitioners questioned regard religion as the "search for the sacred that can be viewed objectively, occurs externally and involves a commitment to organizational practices, rituals and beliefs" (278) that guide behavior (270). John Headley Brooke adopts a similar definition in *Science and Religion: Some Historical Perspectives* (1991). He writes: "*Religion* has been defined in terms of belief in supernatural beings or in terms of a commitment to some transcendent 'other,' which serves to integrate one's life. It may refer to organized institutions that, through creed and ritual, claim to give coherent answers to questions of human destiny" (6).

21. Wertheim's 1997 work *Pythagoras' Trousers: God, Physics and the Gender Wars* is a detailed, chronological study of Western physics. It emphasizes the role of religious notions in the theories of numerous scientists including Descartes, Isaac Newton, Albert Einstein and Stephen Hawking (154; 122; 186; 219).

22. In this work, references to and discussions of religion are limited to Abrahamic faiths, particularly Christianity. There is an emphasis on spiritual narratives that involve a messianic figure and envisage a divine entity guiding humanity.

23. It can therefore be assumed that the SF of Clarke, Dick and Herbert is also informed by the changing norms and innovations of SF as a genre. However, this work focuses on the outward influence of these key writers on genre norms.

Chapter 1

1. Similarly, Tatiana Chernyshova identifies a range of folktale elements in Wells' narratives. She asserts that, in novels such as *The Invisible Man, The Island of Doctor Moreau* and *The Food of the Gods*, "the folktale tradition prove[s] artistically more valuable to Wells than scientific cognitions" ("The Folktale" 39) and argues that Wells established a new literary tradition that saw folktale themes, motifs and images enter increasingly into SF (39).

2. Wells' use of Darwinian science to contradict biblical doctrines represents one of the many reactions to evolutionary theory that helped define the age. Although Darwin's theory destabilized Pauline Christianity and caused much debate, many thinkers sought to reconcile the teachings of the Church with the findings of biological science. Huxley's "Mr. Darwin's Critics" (1871) offers an illustration of the diverse views held by scientists at the time. In the article, Huxley argues against the statements about evolutionary theory made by the influential biologists George Jackson Mivart and Alfred Russel Wallace. Huxley observes that these scientists seek to reconcile Darwin's theory with existing spiritual beliefs. Huxley provides an account of Wallace's belief in a divine creator and Mivart's assertion that evolution is consistent with orthodox Catholic theology ("Mr. Darwin's" 124; 122). Huxley is particularly dismissive of Mivart's view, writing "the [Catholic] belief that the universe was created in six natural days is hopelessly inconsistent with the doctrine of evolution" (138). He further argues, with reference to the inconsistencies between the biblical account of creation and the geological record, that "the contradiction between Catholic verity and Scientific verity is complete and absolute, quite independently of the truth or falsehood of the doctrine of evolution" (146). Also see James C. Livingston's 2006 work *Religious Thought in the Victorian Age: Challenges and Reconceptions*, which offers a historical analysis of the influence of Darwin's theory on Victorian religion (156–60). For an analysis of the treatment of Darwin's theory in nineteenth-century literature, see Gillian Beer's *Darwin's Plots: Evolutionary Narratives in Darwin, George Eliot and Nineteenth-Century Fiction* (2009).

3. For works that specifically examine the relation between "Evolution and Ethics" and Wells' writings, see David Y. Hughes, Patrick Parrinder and Christopher Rolfe (123), Parrinder (*H. G.* 8–9; *Shadows* 52), Krishnan Kumar (204), J. P. Vernier (71), John S. Partington (97–98), John Huntington (*The Logic* xii; 1–16), Norman Mackenzie and Jeanne Mackenzie (55–56); and John R. Reed (*The Natural* 3; 31; 34). For more general discussions of Huxley's influence on Wells see Darko Suvin ("Introduction" 10), Adam Roberts (*The History* 143), David C. Smith (11), John Batchelor (2), Kenneth Young (7) and Richard Hauer Costa (21).

4. See also John R. Reed, who writes: "Like Huxley, Wells put[s] no faith in Nature, which

he view[s] as a hostile force to be controlled" (*The Natural* 31).

5. *A Modern Utopia* is treated as SF here. Critics Brian M. Stableford and David Langford note that, in general, "those utopias which embody some notion of scientific advancement qualify as sf." The protagonist of *A Modern Utopia* differentiates his utopia from those of literary tradition, which he asserts fail to consider the role of technology in society. He observes that "Plato commenced the tradition of Utopias without machinery, a tradition we find Morris still loyally following" (72). In contrast, Wells' utopia is an industrial society that understands and utilizes modern science. Furthermore, the protagonist of *A Modern Utopia* dismisses William Morris' *News from Nowhere* (1890) as a fantastic paradise that does not consider the realities of human nature, whereas *A Modern Utopia* is based on human possibilities (12). Wells' novel thus aligns with Wells' desire as a writer to examine social realities and correlates with definitions of SF that stress the genre's engagement with contemporary human systems. See also Darko Suvin, who regards Wells' utopian novels as a subgenre of SF because they engage with the same social, political, scientific and ideological issues addressed in Wells' other SF novels ("Introduction" 15–16).

6. Beer also notes that social Darwinism uses elements of Darwin's theory to "serve as confirming metaphors for beliefs politically at odds with those of Darwin himself" (13).

7. As a liberal Christian, Arnold's views do not always align with Huxley's agnostic, scientific outlook. In particular, they held differences of opinion over education and have been presented, at times, as adversaries. However, they maintained an amicable friendship and shared a desire for a moral society. For further information on their independent beliefs, relationship and correspondence see W. H. G. Armytage's article "Matthew Arnold and T. H. Huxley: Some New Letters 1870–80," David R. Roos' "Matthew Arnold and Thomas Henry Huxley: Two Speeches at the Royal Academy" and James Woelfel's "Victorian Agnosticism and Liberal Theology: T. H. Huxley and Matthew Arnold."

8. Huxley's dismissal of science as a vehicle for the transmission of moral codes is also noted by Mackenzie and Mackenzie. They write: "Evolution had destroyed conventional theology. Could it provide an alternative basis for morality and say whether human life had any meaning? It took courage to ask that question, and it took more courage to give the negative answer, as ... Huxley did in ... 'Evolution and Ethics'" (55).

9. For works that dismiss *God the Invisible King* and Wells' religious non–SF, see Batchelor (156) and Kenneth Young (10).

10. It is generally agreed among critics that Wells' most skillful and influential contributions to SF were written during the first ten to twenty years of his writing career (Parrinder, *Shadows* ix; Parrinder and Rolfe 63; McConnell 32; Scholes and Rabkin 19; Roberts, *The History* 144; Suvin, "Introduction" 18).

11. Bennett and Wells were friends and shared a mutual respect for one another's writing. They carried on a written correspondence between September 1897 and Bennett's death in 1931. A record of this correspondence can be found in Harris Wilson's *Arnold Bennett and H. G. Wells: A Record of a Personal and a Literary Friendship* (1960).

12. Alternatively, Parrinder argues in *H. G. Wells* (1970) that, at the outset of his career at least, Wells was concerned with the preservation of imaginative standards, citing as evidence of this Wells' early book reviews (Parrinder, *H. G.* 87–88).

13. The focus on sociological change, rather than aesthetic concerns, in Wells' writing has been noted by critics. For instance, McConnell observes in relation to *A Modern Utopia* and *The Food of the Gods* that "Wells' passion for social reform could overweigh his instincts as a storyteller" (5). See also Raknem (422; 426).

14. For further reading on the disagreement between Wells and James see Gloria McMillan's article "The Invisible Friends: The Lost Worlds of Henry James and H. G. Wells" (2006). McMillan regards the conflict between Wells and James as stemming from differences of class and education and notes that "Wells was the explorer of *outer worlds*, Henry James mapped the *interior of the personality*" (136; 137). See also E. K. Brown, "Two Formulas for Fiction: Henry James and H. G. Wells." Furthermore, Smith's biography of Wells offers an account of Wells' relationship with James and numerous other writers, including George Gissing, Frank Swinnerton, Arnold Bennett and Joseph Conrad (151–76). Critic John Batchelor defends Wells' stance, declaring that "Wells had a coherent and intellectually defensible theory of the novel which he could have pressed much more vigorously and aggressively, and that he was outwitted by the patrician dignity and elaborate courtesy of his adversary" (113).

15. See Wells' autobiography in which he

writes that, between the ages of eighteen and twenty-one, he endeavored to learn as much as he could of the opinions of such "exalted names" (*Experiment* 1: 240) as Carlyle. The protagonist of *In the Days of the Comet* is also an avid reader, admirer and imitator of Carlyle (15).

16. In *The Time Traveller: The Life of H. G. Wells* (1973) Mackenzie and Mackenzie provide further discussion of the role of religion in Wells' early life, noting that the Church had opposed the education reforms that had led to Wells' admittance to the Normal School of Science in 1884 (53–54).

17. Although Darwin's theory emerged in 1859, there is a temporal lag between the advent of his scientific breakthrough and the incorporation of his theory into dominant worldviews. It is not until the late nineteenth century that we see evolutionary theory beginning to have a major influence on the popular consciousness.

18. Robert M. Philmus and David Y. Hughes also note that Wells rejects "religious and theological commonplaces" (17) in *The Island of Doctor Moreau*. Similarly, McConnell observes that the novel draws on Darwinian science to illustrate the bestial origins of humanity (89; 93).

19. The value judgment implied in any statement about "positive evolution" is inconsistent with Darwinian science because, according to Darwin's theory, evolution is simply change. However, early-twentieth-century thinkers and SF writers in particular tend to regard human evolution in terms of a movement "upward" toward a more intelligent, civilized form or "downward" toward unintelligence, barbarity and extinction. We observe a tendency in SF and twentieth-century philosophy to regard humankind as capable of controlling the social and biological evolution of the species through applied science and the formulation of myths that encourage behavior conducive to the preservation and advancement of human society. Discussions of "positive evolution," "upward evolution," "downward evolution," "evolutionary decline" and human control over evolution in this work refer to this popular conception of evolution in terms of a movement either toward a more advanced civilization or toward social degeneration and extinction.

20. The representation of the Morlocks as foul carnivores leads McConnell to read *The Time Machine* as an expression of Wells' mistrust of the laboring class (46–49).

21. Luckhurst offers an analysis of the Time Traveller's various theories and considers the social critique inherent in each hypothesis (*Science* 36–39). See also Bergonzi (51–52).

22. For critical works that read *The Time Machine* as a prophecy on the effects of industrialization and class conflict see McConnell (3) and Bergonzi (52).

23. Originally titled *When the Sleeper Wakes*, this work was initially serialized in 1898–1899 and was titled *The Sleeper Awakes* upon republication as a novel in 1910.

24. See also Parrinder's *Shadows of the Future: H. G. Wells, Science Fiction and Prophecy* (1995) and Luckhurst's *Science Fiction*. Both Parrinder and Luckhurst note that *The Time Machine* reflects the ideas about evolution presented in Wells' "Zoological Retrogression" (Parrinder, *Shadows* 58; Luckhurst, *Science* 37). Parrinder points out that *The Island of Doctor Moreau* can also be read as a representation of the realities of downward evolution (58).

25. For a discussion of Wells' treatment of social Darwinism in other novels, including *The First Men in the Moon* (1901), see Suvin ("Introduction" 25–27).

26. See also Wells' earlier non-fiction work *The Outline of History* in which he presents his negative views on socialism in a section entitled "Shortcomings of Socialism as a Scheme of Human Society" (612–14).

27. This has led McConnell to observe that "Wells ... was impelled to a version of revolution much quieter ... than many which were abroad in his time" (49).

28. W. Warren Wagar also argues that Wells consistently rejects "both Fabian permeation and Marxian revolution in favor of a broadly conceived program of research, education, and propaganda" (42).

29. This provides a contrast to later twentieth-century SF in which writers often represent humankind manipulating their own biological evolution through surgical intervention. We see this, for instance, in Olaf Stapledon's *Last and First Men* (1930) and Clarke's *The City and the Stars* (1956). Other writers that canvas the possibility of surgically altering human biology include J. B. S. Haldane and J. D. Bernal in their respective works *Possible Worlds and Other Essays* (1927) and *The World, The Flesh and the Devil: An Inquiry into the Future of the Three Enemies of the Rational Soul* (1929).

30. For further examinations of the critique of applied science offered in *The Island of Doctor Moreau*, see Sherryl Vint's article "Animals and Animality from the Island of

Doctor Moreau to the Uplift Universe" (2007). Vint examines the novel from an animal studies perspective, arguing that "focusing on the animals in *The Island of Doctor Moreau* ... enables us to see the centrality of the category of the animal to our conceptions of human subjectivity, and the relationship between this concept of the human and the practice of science" (95). She also asserts that Wells' novel anticipates feminist critiques of science (89). Other critics that observe an ambivalent or even negative attitude toward science in the novel include MacKenzie and MacKenzie (126) and McConnell (144). Bergonzi argues that Prendick, a former student of Huxley (Wells, *The Island* 35–36), is set up as a "humane scientist" (Bergonzi 106) in contrast to Moreau.

31. Although there is a broad consensus that Wells' views on civilization align with Huxley's, critic Leon Stover argues that the intellectual correlation between Wells and Huxley has been exaggerated. He states, "Huxley would combat the cosmic process and Wells ride it. The one says that cosmic nature must be overcome, the other that it must be harnessed" (131–32). I suggest that this is an oversimplification of the attitudes expressed by Wells and Huxley. Both Wells and Huxley argue that humankind's response to nature should vary according to the myriad needs of society. For instance, while Huxley argues that individual self-assertion should be curtailed to ensure social harmony, he also notes that self-assertion is a trait that will allow humans to maintain society against the state of nature ("Prolegomena" 31). Similarly, a range of responses to nature are outlined in Wells' *A Modern Utopia*. The protagonist initially argues that an ideal civilization "do[es] not resist and overcome the great stream of things, but rather float[s] upon it" (11). However, Wells later has him outline genetics programs whereby nature is combated and controlled (96; 99–101; 125). Therefore, both Huxley and Wells require that the aspects of nature that are detrimental to civilization be combated but recognize that nature may otherwise be harnessed for human benefit.

32. Huntington notes that *The Food of the Gods* also depicts the emergence of an elite ruling class (*The Logic* 129).

33. Such pronouncements later led to the association of Carlyle with Fascism (Schapiro 97). There has also been an association of Wells with both fascism and socialism. In his 1934 autobiography he observes a correlation between the social organization of his Modern Utopia and some aspects of Soviet Communism and Italian Fascism, noting the success of both systems (*Experiment* 2: 659). As critic Francis Wheen notes, "Wells had strong ideological objections to both Marxism and Fascism, but his tribute to some of the organizational methods of the Soviet Communist Party and the Italian Fascist Party ... explains why his political writings have been out of fashion (and out of print) for so long" (xxiv). See also Roberts, who notes that "Wells was by no means alone in [his] belief [in a ruling elite] in the early years of the twentieth century; but many of the people who believed this converted to fascism in Europe of the 1930s" (*The History* 152). Wells is not a fascist but his engagement with eugenics and depictions of elite ruling classes in his writings has led to him being criticized as such. In his article "The Death of the Static: H. G. Wells and the Kinetic Utopia" (2000) Partington offers an appraisal and dismissal of critics who seek to describe Wells as a eugenicist and a racist.

34. Roberts also notes the religious overtones of *The Sleeper Awakes* (*The History* 149).

35. Adapted from John's gospel (*Authorized King James Version,* John 11: 50).

36. Reed also offers a discussion of Wells' representation of language as that which distinguishes humankind from all other life forms (*The Natural* 179–83).

37. Roberts also argues that "As a novum the beast-men enable Wells to write fluently about the balance between civilisation and bestiality in humankind" (*The History* 147). He further asserts that the connection, in *The Island of Doctor Moreau*, between bestiality and humanity represents a broader dichotomy between the material and spiritual realms (147).

38. We know that Wells was familiar with Nietzsche's writings. In *The Sleeper Awakes* (1899) Nietzsche's concept of the Übermensch is represented in a negative light when Ostrog, a corrupt rebel leader, declares to an incredulous Graham: "The hope of mankind. ... [is that] some day the Over-man may come, that some day the inferior, the weak and the bestial may be ... eliminated" (551). Patrick Bridgwater describes the influence of Nietzsche on English writers between 1896 and 1914 in "English Writers and Nietzsche." He asserts that "It was in Wells's *When the Sleeper Wakes* ... that the superman arrived on the English literary scene" (245). Further, Mackenzie and Mackenzie note Nietzschean elements in *The War of the Worlds* (128–29) and Bergonzi comments on

the influence of Nietzsche on *The Island of Doctor Moreau* (107).

39. The protagonist of *In the Days of the Comet* is a self-professed disciple of Nietzsche. Although he has never actually read Nietzsche's works, Leadford ironically declares himself "Nietzsche's Over-man already come" (92). Leadford's immature, belligerent and violent attempts to combat social inequality are far removed from the image of the Over-man presented by Nietzsche in *Thus Spoke Zarathustra: A Book for Everyone and No One* (1883–85). Wells' representation of Nietzsche as having inspired such an ineffectual, immoral revolutionary may suggest a certain disdain for Nietzsche's optimistic suggestion that the Church will be easily supplanted by a more successful system.

40. Despite this correlation in their ideas about religion and morality, Wells is critical of Comte's Positivist approach to sociology. Comte founded the discipline of sociology, which was further developed by Spencer. Wells' 1906 paper "The So-Called Science of Sociology" argues that Comte and Spencer erred in attempting to approach the study of society via the "scientific method" (192) and advocates a more inclusive approach, stating that utopian literature and ancient Greek philosophy should be brought within the scope of sociology (192–93; 204–05). Wells writes: "sociology must be neither art simply, nor science ... but knowledge rendered imaginatively, and with an element of personality; that is to say, in the highest sense of the term, literature" (202). In his autobiography, Wells concedes that his criticisms of Comte were unjustly motivated by his "personal dislike" (*Experiment* 2:658) for the man. For further discussion of Wells' response to Comte and other Positivists see Martha S. Vogeler's "Wells and Positivism," Wagar's "Science and the World State" (45) and Kumar's "Wells and 'The So-Called Science of Sociology.'"

41. Wells directly discusses James' *The Varieties of Religious Experience* in his nonfiction work *God the Invisible King* (10). Wells also refers to William James as Henry James' "wonderful brother" (103) in his 1915 novel *Boon*.

42. See also Schlossberg, who explains that, although religion in the West had previously been exclusively associated with Christianity, the start of the twentieth century saw a rise in alternate theologies, while the influence of Christianity waned (298).

43. Reed notes that Spencer's suggestion that there is a divine purpose at work in the universe complicates his attempts to champion scientifically objective worldviews ("The Vanity" 137).

44. Wells is familiar with Frazer's work. In 1889 he describes *The Golden Bough* as a "most valuable and unreadable book" ("On Comparative" 43).

45. These novels include *Mr. Britling Sees it Through* (1916), *The Soul of a Bishop* (1917), *Joan and Peter* (1918) and *The Undying Fire* (1919). Given that these titles are not SF novels, they are not examined here. In his autobiography Wells provides a commentary on his religious writing and includes excerpts from *Mr. Britling* and *The Undying Fire* that illuminate the religious ideas propounded in these novels (*Experiment* 2: 670–77).

46. Furthermore, Vogeler notes that, despite Wells' insistence that he returned to atheism after 1922, he ordered a quasi-religious funeral service for his wife in 1927 (187).

Chapter 2

1. As Peter Nicholls explains, the term "hard SF" is used to describe SF that "seek[s] to provide natural rather than supernatural or transcendental explanations for the events and phenomena it describes" ("Hard SF"). By contrast, "soft SF" is a term applied to SF that deals with social science and sociological issues, or that does not deal with any recognizable science at all (Seed, *Science* 50; Nicholls, "Soft SF"). Nicholls points out that the distinction between "hard" and "soft" SF is, at times, arbitrary because we can often observe a blending of hard extrapolation and social science in SF ("Soft SF"). This is certainly the case in Clarke's works, despite the fact that critics, including Gary Westfahl, have named him a writer of hard SF (Westfahl 189). For further discussion of hard SF, see Westfahl and David N. Samuelson.

2. J. S. Haldane is not to be confused with J. B. S. Haldane. J. S. Haldane is J. B. S. Haldane's father. Henceforth, the full name, including initials, is used for J. S. Haldane while his son is referred to by surname only. Haldane admits that his views coincide with those of his father's, at least up until 1932 when Haldane writes: "our opinions differ mainly on questions of emphasis and terminology rather than of fact" (*The Inequality* vi). The similarity of their names has led to the father and son being mistaken for a single individual by some readers. Haldane uses the preface of *The Inequality of Man* (1932) to formally declare his non-identity with his father after an American writer accused them,

in their joint capacity, of "flagrant inconsistency" (*The Inequality* vi).

3. Henderson also offers an appraisal of Bergson's views on the debate (293).

4. See Edward James (434–35), David N. Samuelson (496), Peter Brigg (15; 27; 35) and John Huntington ("From" 211; 213).

5. For other critics that regard Clarke's SF as primarily atheistic, see Edward James (435) and David Sless (99).

6. Indeed, in a 1964 letter to Clarke, Haldane comments on Clarke's incorporation of religious material into his writing. Haldane writes: "I would like to see you awarded a prize for theology, as you are one of the very few living persons who has written anything original about God. You have in fact, written several mutually incompatible things" (Clarke, *Greetings* 359). For further information on their correspondence, see McAleer (331).

7. See also Clarke's *Greetings Carbon-Based Bipeds!* (295) and his 1986 interview for *Playboy* ("Playboy" 65).

8. John Huntington notes that Clarke's nonfiction writings, by comparison, focus on speculating about technological advancements, rather than exploring the possibility of transcendent evolution ("From" 211–12).

9. Critics have often described Clarke's SF as mythic but in a different sense than is meant here. For instance Sless identifies aspects of the hero monomyth and allusions to Greek myth in Clarke's works (95) while Betty Harfst identifies Jungian archetypes, monomyths and elements of Hinduism in Clarke's SF (87–88; 103). Such works highlight the often self-contradictory treatment of myth in SF scholarship. Writers tend to conflate Jungian archetypes with classical myth and with religion even though these discourses rely on different definitions of myth. Kenneth L. Golden's *Science Fiction, Myth, and Jungian Psychology* goes to greater lengths to define myth and provides a predominantly Jungian analysis of *Childhood's End* and *2001* (151–62; 181–89).

10. Aside from the clear correlation between Turing's theories and Clarke's depiction of artificial intelligences, Clarke also directly refers to Turing in the *Space Odyssey* series (*2001* 99; *2010* 34).

11. As with evolutionary theory, we can observe a temporal disjunction between the emergence of vitalism and its incorporation into SF narratives. Vitalist notions appear in Clarke's writings in the middle of the twentieth century, decades after the advent of the theory in the early twentieth century.

12. Bergson also favors vitalist conceptions of life. He acknowledges that there is a material relation between the mind and the body (*Mind-Energy* 35) but argues that "There is infinitely more, in a human consciousness, than in the corresponding brain" (40).

13. Rabkin similarly notes the link between Well's *The Time Machine* and Clarke's *The City and the Stars* (*Arthur* 31).

14. Clarke later reflects in a 1979 interview that the moment in Stanley Kubrick's film version of *2001* when the man-ape uses a bone as a club is "one of the most emotionally vivid things in the movie" ("At the" 130) because it symbolizes the inception of human intelligence and "also the beginning of war" (130).

15. This interview formed part of a series of broadcasts and interviews documenting the Apollo 11 mission for CBS News. The interview in question, featuring Cronkite, Clarke, Robert A. Heinlein and Bill Stout, aired on July 20, 1969. A brief excerpt from the conversation can be found in CBS News' *10:56:20 PM EDT, 7/20/69: The Historic Conquest of the Moon as Reported to the American People by the CBS News over the CBS Television Network* (107). The full interview, from which these quotations come, has been posted on YouTube by J. Neil Schulman for the online magazine *Mondo Cult*. Further discussion of Clarke's participation in the CBS coverage of the lunar landing can be found in McAleer's *Arthur C. Clarke: The Authorized Biography* (222–31).

16. In 1943, this point of view led Clarke into a correspondence with C. S. Lewis, who feared that humankind would simply transpose their petty rivalries and imperialist tendencies into space and inflict their failings on alien societies. A record of this correspondence can be found in Ryder W. Miller's *From Narnia to a Space Odyssey* (2003). While Clarke writes: "I have never encountered a single science-fiction enthusiast ... who regard[s] the idea of conquest of other races with anything but disgust" (Clarke and Lewis 37), Lewis responds that "a race devoted to the increase of its own forces [and] technology ... seem[s] to me a cancer of the universe" (40). Lewis also expounds his concerns about humankind entering space in *Out of a Silent Planet* (1938), the first novel of his *Cosmic Trilogy* (156; 171; 175).

17. Rabkin also notes Clarke's engagement with Bernal's writings (*Arthur* 17).

18. Huntington also notes that *The City and the Stars* implies that technological achievements are insufficient to achieve positive evolution ("From" 213), particularly when

"Technology ... tries to preclude higher realities" ("From" 215). Alternatively, Ryder W. Miller regards Clarke's short story "The Nine Billion Names of God" (1953) as indicating that "Clarke view[s] technology as a ... means to bring [humankind] closer to 'God'" (18).

19. Alan B. Howes describes three stages of evolution in *Childhood's End*: the social and technological change brought by the Overlords, the creation of the social utopia of New Athens and the absorption of all human children into the Overmind (162; 164; 166).

20. Rabkin also regards *Childhood's End* as "indulg[ing] in the Christian fantasy of the descent of Grace" ("Genre" 98) in its representation of human evolution.

21. For further comments on the unscientific representation of evolution in *Childhood's End* see Rabkin's "Genre Criticism: Science Fiction and the Fantastic." He observes that *Childhood's End* "throws [evolutionary theory] to the winds" (98) and that "science is spiritualized in Clarke" (98).

22. Robert Lambourne, Michael Shallis and Michael Shortland also observe that "*2001* ... does not present a Darwinian account of evolution" (135).

23. For other works that recognize the influence of Stapledon on Clarke's writing see Rabkin ("Clarke" 142; *Arthur* 10; 13), McAleer (19) and Brigg (36).

24. See McAleer for further discussion of Clarke's personal religious views (43–44; 99–100; 236).

25. Clarke's claim that "religion is a byproduct of malnutrition" is echoed verbatim in *The Fountains of Paradise* (68).

26. This quote is, of course, an allusion to Hamlet's statement following his encounter with the Ghost (Shakespeare, *Hamlet* 1.5.166–67).

27. There is a correlation between this sentiment and the criticisms of atheism articulated by Wells in *God the Invisible King*. See Chapter 1.

28. Lambourne, Shallis and Shortland also note the representation of human evolution as guided by a "superior, mysterious and external agency" (135) or "God" (135) in *2001*.

29. The article Clarke is referring to here is Louis K. Scheffer's "Machine Intelligence, the Cost of Interstellar Travel and Fermi's Paradox."

Chapter 3

1. See Chapter 1.
2. This trait is noted by Simon Critchley in an annotation in *The Exegesis of Philip K. Dick*, edited by Pamela Jackson and Jonathan Lethem. When examining Dick's use of Heidegger, Critchley observes that "Dick's reading of Heidegger is singular, to say the least" (548) in that it links Heidegger's ideas with Hebrew doctrines, an approach that, according to Critchley, would have "alarmed Heidegger" (548).

3. Also see Aldiss and Wingrove, who observe that, when read in isolation, many of Dick's novels "seem like lumber-rooms of ideas, cluttered and over-complex, as if attempting too much at once" (334). Furthermore, John Huntington criticizes Dick's SF, writing: "Dick, like [A. E] van Vogt ... learned how to give the impression of deep understanding simply by contradicting himself" ("Philip" 154).

4. For other works that focus on Dick's early writings and favor political readings of his SF see Carl Freedman's "Towards a Theory of Paranoia: The Science Fiction of Philip K. Dick" and Roger Luckhurst's *Science Fiction* (106–09). Also see Peter Fitting, who examines Dick's novels in relation to the social and political contexts in which they were written. He writes that, until his final novels, Dick demonstrates an "uneasiness and ambivalence towards ... metaphysical solution[s]" (222). Further, Eric S. Rabkin disregards Dick's later novels, including *VALIS*, as completely aberrant. He asks: "Why did Dick really write the *VALIS* trilogy? ... Frankly, I think he [went] ... insane" ("Irrational" 170).

5. For other works that identify a level of philosophical continuity throughout Dick's corpus see Anthony Enns (69), Lorenzo DiTommaso ("Gnosticism" 51), Christopher Palmer ("Philip" 390) and Scott Durham (174).

6. Although Darko Suvin argues that metaphysical speculation becomes apparent in Dick's SF starting with *The Three Stigmata* ("P. K." 15), recent scholarship has demonstrated that theological notions permeate Dick's SF far earlier than 1964. DiTommaso argues in "Gnosticism and Dualism in the Early Fiction of Philip K. Dick" (2001) that Dick's "pre–*Stigmata* novels" (49) also embody religious themes. He writes that, although "Dick did not publish systematic theology until *VALIS*" (49), "dualistic philosophies" (49) that draw on Platonic, Pauline and Gnostic notions are present in his works as early as 1952 (52; 55). While DiTommaso acknowledges that "Philip K. Dick's later writings find their first manifestation in his early fiction" (62), he writes that "When

compared to the complexities of [*The Man in the High Castle, The Three Stigmata* and *VALIS*], the philosophical discussion in [Dick's] early fiction is highly unpolished and not always well-integrated" (50). It is for this reason that I focus on selected works from *The Three Stigmata* to the end of Dick's career as representative of the culmination of his ever-evolving philosophy.

7. There is a strong correlation between the ideas expressed by Marcuse and those articulated in Dick's writing. Eric Davis also notes the similarity between the Marxist notions articulated in Dick's private notes in 1979 and those expressed by Marcuse (Jackson and Lethem 506).

8. For other works that identify Presocratic notions in Dick's SF see Robert Galbreath ("Redemption"106) and Roger J. Stilling (91).

9. Charles H. Khan's translation of Heraclitus is used in this chapter. It does not employ the conventional Diels-Kranz numbering system. For quotations taken from Khan's translation, both the Diels-Kranz numbering and Khan's system are provided. The conventional numeration is preceded by "D." and Khan's numbering is in Roman numerals.

10. Aldiss and Wingrove also assert that although "Dick professed himself not to be a Christian ... his work is heavily permeated with Christian theological thought" (333).

11. See also Jean-Noël Dumont, Danièle Chatelain and George Slusser's article "Between Faith and Melancholy: Irony and the Gnostic Meaning of Dick's 'Divine Trilogy'" (1988). Further, DiTommaso identifies Gnostic notions and Pauline theology in Dick's *Time out of Joint* ("A λόγος") and Andrew M. Butler points out that the religious contexts of Dick's novels tend to be "bitheistic rather than ... monotheistic" (21).

12. Consequently, Dick, like Wells, is also relatively unconcerned with the artistic limitations of some SF works. In response to a 1969 symposium question about the relationship between SF and "mainstream" literature, Dick writes: "SF fails to explore the depths of interpersonal relationships, and this is its lack; however on a purely intellectual level it possesses more conceptual ideas ... and hence in this respect is superior to mainstream or quality fiction" ("The *Double*" 64).

13. For instance George Orwell's *1984* (1949), Walter M. Miller's *A Canticle for Leibowitz* (1959) and Ray Bradbury's *Fahrenheit 451* (1953).

14. Throughout *VALIS*, Fat argues theology with a character named Phil Dick, who initially seems to be one of Fat's friends. In these discussions, Phil takes a secular, logical perspective that contrasts with Fat's mystical philosophy. It is eventually revealed that Phil is actually suffering from a split-personality disorder and that Fat is the spiritually questing, potentially insane aspect of Phil's personality (188). Fat's strange name is explained thus: "'Philip' means 'Horselover' in Greek, lover of horses. 'Fat' is the German translation of 'Dick'" (188). Thus Horselover Fat is simply another version of Phil Dick. Throughout the novel, Fat writes a tractate containing his attempts to create a plausible theology. The observations in the tractate and the accounts of Fat's visionary experiences in *VALIS* often correlate with Dick's real life visions and his private, theological writings.

15. Such reflections on American culture illustrate that *VALIS* is centrally concerned with socio-political critique. For other works that examine *VALIS* as a commentary on contemporary politics see Canaan ("Time" 336), Rossi ("Illuminating" 463; "Holy" 154) and James Burton (268).

16. Can-D is manufactured and distributed by a subsidiary of the company that produces the Perky Pat layouts. This company thus holds a commercial monopoly on Mars.

17. For further discussion of the mood organ, see Enns who considers how the "Penfield mood organ," named after neuroscientist Wilder Penfield, in *Do Androids Dream* represents a "conflation of media technologies and psychic states" (69).

18. For further discussion of Dick's representation of the saturation of modern life by consumer items see Freedman (18), who also considers the role of militarization in consumer capitalist societies (19). Also see Suvin ("P. K." 16).

19. Donald Palumbo describes Mercerism as conflating "the passion of Christ with the eternal torment of Sisyphus, who is condemned forever to roll uphill a rock that always rolls back down" ("Faith" 1284) and argues that Mercer's cycle simultaneously illuminates the futility of post-apocalyptic existence and offers the hope of resurrection (1284).

20. Note that I am only referring here to Mercerism as offered by the state-mediated empathy box. The existence of Mercer as an independent, divine being is discussed below.

21. For further commentary on Mercerism as a government-sponsored means of social control see Palumbo ("Faith" 1284).

22. Also see Burton who examines the "de-humanizing tendency" (266) of "industrialization and modern technology" (266), as represented in Dick's SF.

23. See also Fitting, who writes that, in *The Three Stigmata*, "The liberatory potential of the media and new technologies has been completely debased" (227) and that "new technologies are developed and exploited solely for commercial purposes (227–228).

24. For an alternative interpretation of the android in Dick's novel, see Galvan's article "Entering the Posthuman Collective in Philip K. Dick's *Do Androids Dream of Electric Sheep?*" Galvan argues that *Do Androids Dream* "interrogates a fixed definition of the human subject ... acknowledg[ing] him as only one component of the living scene" (414). She posits that the novel envisions a community of the posthuman where humans and machines coexist (414). Deckard's conclusion that "electric things have ... lives, too" (211) does lend itself to Galvan's interpretation. However, despite Deckard's empathic responses, I contend that there is ultimately a clear denigration of the androids as emotionally inferior, albeit biologically alive.

25. Suvin also points out that a central tenet of Dick's SF is that social pressures have alienated modern humankind from the "*authentic core*" ("P. K." 18) that houses their humanity (18). According to Suvin's reading, Dick's novels also suggest that, within each individual, there is an inner resistance which seeks to reject repressive capitalist forces by building genuine empathic connections (18).

26. For a discussion of how Dick's earlier, 1950s works critique permanent war economy and examine human life under conditions of perpetual war see Luckhurst (*Science* 106).

27. Dick further writes that "Any lying language creates at once in a single stroke a pseudo-reality, contaminating reality, until the Lie is undone" (*The Exegesis* 20). His novel *Time Out of Joint* (1959) represents an earlier meditation on this idea. In it, the protagonist Ragle Gumm asks himself: "what is a word? Arbitrary sign. But we live in words. Our reality [is] among words not things. No such thing as a thing anyhow.... Thingness ... [is an] illusion" (45). For further discussion of *Time Out of Joint* see David Seed (*Science* 89), DiTommaso ("Α λόγος") and Rossi ("Just").

28. Georg Wilhelm Friedrich Hegel also recognizes the centrality of ancient Greek philosophy in Western thought. He writes: "all our science and art ... has either emanated directly from Greece or come to us from Greece in a roundabout way via the Romans" (10).

29. Fat is quoting page 35 of Hussey's *The Presocratics*.

30. In his private writings after 2-3-74, Dick examines his SF as a means of interpreting his visions and formulating a new philosophy. In 1974 he reflects: "In ... *Ubik* certain anomalies occur which prove to the characters that their environment is not real. Those same anomalies are now happening to me. By my own logic in the novel I must conclude that my or perhaps our collective environment is only a pseudo-environment" (*The Exegesis* 22).

31. Hussey's translation of fragment 54 differs from Khan's. Khan translates the fragment: "The hidden attunement (*harmoniē*) is better than the obvious one" (202; LXXX). However, Khan comments that "*harmoniē*" could be translated "hidden structure" instead of "attunement" and acknowledges Hussey's translation as valid (203). It is Hussey's translation that Dick is familiar with.

32. In his discussion of *The Man in the High Castle*, Palmer similarly asserts that Dick's SF represents some things that are truly real ("Postmodernism" 334). Alternatively, other critics, including Adam Roberts (*The History* 240) and Burton (279), argue that Dick's SF consistently questions all the realities it depicts.

33. For further discussion of the ultimate authenticity of Mercer see Roberts (*The History* 241) and Palmer ("Philip" 393). Alternatively, Palumbo maintains that all manifestations of Mercer are unreal, being either government-sponsored or hallucinatory ("Faith" 1284; 1286).

34. According to Dick's foreword to the novel, the theology of *A Maze of Death* is a "logical system of religious thought, based on the arbitrary postulate that God exists." The theology was devised by Dick and his friend William Sarill. They were furnished with theological material by Bishop James A. Pike. Pike served as coadjutor bishop of California from 1958 to 1966, when he was censored for rejecting central Christian tenets. His life and death form the inspiration for the character Timothy Archer in Dick's final novel *The Transmigration of Timothy Archer* (1982).

35. Mckee also takes this view. He argues: "In Dick's stories, amid all the anxiety over disintegrating universes and unstable realities, there is always a sense of an ultimate

reality underlying the fakery. The absolute shines through the cracks in the walls of the universe, and the hand of God—or Ubik, or the Walker-on-Earth, or Wilbur Mercer—reaches through to help us. This is Dick's basic ontological faith: contrary to appearances, *something* is actually real" (Jackson and Lethem 73–74). Mckee argues in *Pink Beams of Light from the God in the Gutter: The Science-Fictional Religion of Philip K. Dick* (2004) that the spiritual realities represented in Dick's SF are primarily influenced by Christian doctrines (31).

36. This second quote, "all things are wrapped in *appearances*," from fragment 34 comes from Hussey's translation, with which Dick was familiar. In contrast, J. H. Lesher translates the same segment of the fragment as "But opinion is allotted at all" (39).

37. We know that Dick read Eliade's work. Eliade's *Myth and Reality* (1963), which explores the belief that time can be conquered, is heavily referenced in *VALIS* (45; 52; 136; 233). Historian of religions, Jeffrey J. Kripal also notes Dick's engagement with Eliade's *Shamanism: Archaic Techniques of Ecstasy* (1951) in his private writing (Jackson and Lethem 491).

38. In 1968 Dick writes, "*The Three Stigmata* ... deals with absolute evil" ("Self Portrait" 17) and was written during "a great crisis in [his] religious beliefs" (17). See also Dick's 1970 letter to the Australian fanzine *SF Commentary* in which he writes that the failure of "Anglo-Catholic [theology] ... [to] include ... a real, active, evil power who has control ... of the earth" ("Letter" 32) made him skeptical of the Church.

39. Hussey notes that "among gods and men" is just a turn of phrase and does not indicate a belief in more than one god (13). Xenophanes is outlining the existence of a single divinity in fragment 23 (31).

40. For a historicized account of Xenophanes' writing, see Hussey (11–31). He notes that, while Xenophanes was probably not an original thinker, the surviving fragments of his works contain the first statements of a monotheistic theology in Greece (13). Hussey cites evidence from Aristotle's *Physics* to suggest that other Milesian Presocratics, particularly Anaximander, also posit the existence of a single, all-powerful, immortal divinity that encompasses and controls the universe (16).

41. Khan notes that, while it is clear that Heraclitus is describing god in fragment 67, the subject of fragment 10 is more ambiguous. However, he concedes that "Both in form and content these two fragments serve as complements to one another, providing a ... summary of Heraclitus' thought" (281). The two fragments have, therefore, been linked here as both articulating a description of one, boundless god.

42. *Logos*, as used by Heraclitus, is an ambiguous term. Although it generally means "speech," "report" or "account" (Khan 29; 97), it signifies something more in Heraclitus' writing and is associated with the divine. See Khan for further commentary on the translation of this term and its use to denote a universal, divine principle (97–98). See also Warren (63) and Hussey (39). For additional discussion of Dick's use of the term see DiTommaso ("Gnosticism" 50; "Α λόγος" 289) and Rossi ("Just" 205–08).

43. Critchley notes that monistic and dualistic philosophies also vie for dominance in Dick's *Exegesis*. He argues that Gnostic views are ultimately favored by Dick.

44. For a discussion of the difficulties associated with classifying and defining Gnosticism see Karen L. King's *What Is Gnosticism?* (2003). King argues that "There was and is no such thing as Gnosticism, if we mean by that some kind of ancient religious entity with a single origin and a distinct set of characteristics" (1).

45. For a commentary on and translations of numerous Gnostic texts, including the Nag Hammadi codices, see Kurt Rudolf's *Gnosis: The Nature and History of Gnosticism* (1977).

46. Erik Davis notes that Dick's *Exegesis* also incorporates ideas espoused by Walter Benjamin (Jackson and Lethem 506).

47. Of *VALIS*, Dick writes: "it has to do with the mysterious religions of the first century B. C. and what they ... discovered about restoring the faculties that man possessed before the Fall" ("The Short" 35).

48. See John Calvin's *Institutes of the Christian Religion* (244). Mckee notes that, although Calvin attributes this idea to Augustine, Dick believes that Calvin is the primary proponent of this concept (Jackson and Lethem 58).

49. Mckee notes that "Dick's use of 'occlusion' in [his *Exegesis*] ... directly correlates with the concept of rebellion against God" (Jackson and Lethem 432), indicating that Dick is using the term to illustrate that the Black Iron Prison has been created by the sins of humanity (432). This observation supports Mckee's Pauline reading of Dick (*Pink* 3) and contrasts with Critchley's interpretation of Dick's SF as espousing Gnostic

views, which regard external forces as responsible for the fallen nature of the world.

50. Zagreus, a Greek god often associated with Dionysus, is the son of Zeus and Persephone. In response to Zeus' intention to make Zagreus his heir, the jealous Hera persuades the Titans to murder Zagreus, who Zeus had sent to Earth.

51. Peter Fitting notes that Fat never actually finds Zebra. Although Fat becomes convinced that the child Sophia is the divinity reborn, her sudden death destroys this theory. Fitting thus points out that the novel concludes with a "restrained mix of expectation and despair" (231). This conclusion reflects the emotional fluctuations in Dick's own private writings. See also Rossi ("The Shunts" 256) and Galbreath ("Redemption" 111).

52. Dick is making this statement in response to Arthur C. Clarke's *Childhood's End* (1953). Dick had been looking forward to reading the novel and comparing it to his 2-3-74 experience. He clearly regards Clarke's SF as representing truths about reality. Indeed, Dick describes Clarke's work as "philosophy disguised as a novel" (*The Exegesis* 177). Dick ultimately concludes that, although there is no specific resemblance between the details of *Childhood's End* and his own visions, the essence of "[Clarke's] story is compatible with [his] experience" (177). Contrary to my own reading of *Childhood's End*, in Chapter 2, Dick regards Clarke as ultimately subsuming religious symbolism with typical "S-F 'non-terrestrial' explanations" (177). He does, however, note the overwhelming presence of a controlling spiritual force in the novel, which is camouflaged from the majority of the population, and uses humankind for its own ends (177).

Chapter 4

1. In "Men on Other Planets" Herbert discusses the craft of SF writing and, in particular, the way that traditional myths are incorporated into SF narratives (74).

2. Timothy O'Reilly explains that Herbert worked as a ghost writer for S. I. Hayakawa, an expert in general semantics, at around the same time that he was writing *Dune* (*Frank Herbert* 59–60). O'Reilly examines the incorporation of ideas from general semantics, and Korzybski's works in particular, in the representation of the Bene Gesserit, an all-female order in the *Dune* series (59–63). Roger Luckhurst also notes the use of Korzybski in *Dune* (*Science* 161).

3. O'Reilly's *Frank Herbert* (1981) remains the most comprehensive critical work on Herbert's SF. It examines the content and themes of Herbert's major works, up to 1981, and draws on extensive interviews that O'Reilly conducted with Herbert. One obvious limitation of this work is that it was produced prior to the publication of the final three novels of the *Dune* series, a fact that is commented on by Walter E. Meyers in his review of *Frank Herbert* (106). For other sources that acknowledge, albeit in less detail, the incorporation of Heidegger's and Jaspers' philosophies in *The Santaroga Barrier*, see Roger Luckhurst (*Science* 161), Kristian Lund (151) and Brian Herbert (216–17).

4. In "Wiping Finite Answers from an Infinite Universe" Lund references Heidegger's phenomenological view of technology as a framework for analyzing the representation of technology in the *Dune* series (151–60). Heidegger's views on technology are not canvassed in this chapter, which focuses on his ideas about Being.

5. The protagonist Dr. Gilbert Dasein, named using Heidegger's term for "Being-in-the-world" (*Being and Time* 83), is in love with Jenny Sorge, whose surname is the German word for "care." Heidegger writes: "Dasein ... is care" (84) in that existence is defined by one's relationship of concern toward the world. In the novel, Dasein is torn between his desire to escape from the mysterious town of Santaroga, where the townspeople ingest a mind-altering substance called "Jaspers," and his love for Jenny, who wants him to become part of the Santaroga community. Both Heidegger and Jaspers are further discussed below.

6. Lorenzo DiTommaso notes that *Dune* explores ecology and the social dangers posed by a hero ("History" 317). David Langford also notes that *Dune* "offers a heady mixture of desert Ecology ... galactic Politics and the making of a Messiah" ("Dune"). For further discussion of the ecological themes in *Dune*, see Susan Stratton, R. J. Ellis and Mark Siegel. Alternatively, Julia List examines the critique of the messiah figure that is offered in *Dune* and other mid-twentieth-century SF.

7. This is the case in the works of Stratton, DiTommaso ("History"), Ellis and Siegel. For works that canvas all six Dune novels, see *Frank Herbert* by William F. Touponce, Donald Palumbo's article "The Monomyth as Fractal Pattern in Frank Herbert's *Dune* Novels" and Aldiss and Wingrove's *Trillion Year Spree: The History of Science Fiction* (396–

400). Works that focus on the first four novels of the series include John L. Grigsby's "Herbert's Reversal of Asimov's Vision Reassessed: *Foundation's Edge* and *God Emperor of Dune*" and Leonard M. Scigaj's "*Prana* and the Presbyterian Fixation: Ecology and Technology in Frank Herbert's *Dune* Tetralogy."

8. Aldiss and Wingrove also note that *Heretics of Dune*, in particular, offers a continuation of the dense philosophical notions introduced in the earlier novels (398). They observe that "The later novels are less spontaneous, if far more clever" (398) than the early works of the *Dune* series and state that *Heretics of Dune* and *Chapterhouse: Dune* offer a more expansive view of human life by moving beyond narratives of individual heroes and toward a representation of the intergenerational life of the species (398; 399). While Aldiss and Wingrove assert that the last two novels of the series are, "perhaps, over-cerebral" (399), Adam Roberts flatly dismisses them, saying: "The significance of [*Heretics of Dune* and *Chapterhouse: Dune*] is not intrinsic, for they are not good novels" ("Frank" 103). This chapter demonstrates that all six novels of the series are equally invested in the examination of human discourses and the production of myths designed to ensure the positive evolution of humankind.

9. Also see O'Reilly (*Frank Herbert* 39). Herbert's article about the Florence sand dunes, titled "They Stopped the Moving Sands," was never published (Herbert, Herbert, and Anderson 205). For a more detailed account of Herbert's article see *The Road to Dune* by Frank Herbert, Brian Herbert and Kevin J. Anderson. It contains correspondence between Herbert and his agent Lurton Blassingame regarding the article (205-09).

10. See Chapter 3.

11. It is beyond the scope of this chapter to engage with these other works. However, an examination of the messiah figure In *Dune*, *Stranger in a Strange Land* and *Lord of Light* is offered in Julia List's article "'Call Me a Protestant': Liberal Christianity, Individualism, and the Messiah in *Stranger in a Strange Land*, *Dune*, and *Lord of Light*." See also Adam Roberts' *The History of Science Fiction*, which contrasts the representations of messiah figures in *Stranger in a Strange Land*; *Dune*; John Barth's *Giles Goat-Boy, or The Revised New Syllabus of George Giles Our Grand Tutor*; and Moorcock's SF (233-40).

12. Although it is beyond the scope of this chapter, there is no doubt that Herbert is also very invested in exploring environmentalist issues in *Dune*. He writes: "I wrote in the mid-sixties what I hoped would be an environmental awareness handbook. The book is called *Dune*" (*New* 5). Some scholars view the positioning of desert ecology alongside the hero myth in *Dune* as a strange pairing. Stratton, in her article comparing environmental action in *Dune* and Kim Stanley Robinson's *Pacific Edge*, writes: "Paul's heroic-combative story clashes with the ecological story of Arrakis" (309). Similarly, Luckhurst terms *Dune* a "hybrid form" (*Science* 160), noting that "Herbert's ecological science is rigorous ... yet the plot of *Dune* uses all the apparatus of heroic fantasy" (*Science* 160). In contrast, Ellis argues that the "structural tension" (104) in *Dune* between the ecological narrative about a desert planet and the story of a hero is "constitutive and revelatory" (104–05). I suggest that the narrative's dual focus on desert ecology and human systems of thought can be seen as evidence of the novel's engagement with all aspects of ecology.

13. This definition of ecology is echoed in *Dune* (570).

14. Later referred to as Paul Muad'Dib.

15. There is a striking similarity between Szasz's writings and the notions articulated in Herbert's *Dune* series. Further, O'Reilly notes the correlation between Szasz's work and Herbert's 1956 novel *Under Pressure*, also known as *The Dragon in the Sea* (*Frank Herbert* 36; 197).

16. Jaspers does acknowledge that Christian doctrines continue to coexist with scientific conceptions of the world. He writes that, while there are those who have abandoned traditional religious beliefs, many modern views draw on Christian notions (*Man* 12).

17. Timothy Clark explores, in detail, the outline of Western philosophy that is presented across Heidegger's works, noting, in particular, Heidegger's illustration of the modern drive toward technical and objectifying modes of knowledge at the expense of more reverential kinds of existence (32–40).

18. Herbert also draws on the work of physicist, Werner Heisenberg, stating, "As ... Heisenberg warned us, the inherent abstracting process of science creates a chasm between the world which inflicts itself upon your flesh and the abstracted physical theories" ("Science Fiction and You" 1). Additionally, in "Men on Other Planets," Herbert declares: "There can be more than one reality. You see, Dr. Einstein, we heard you" (74). For

a detailed explanation of the scientific theories Herbert is responding to, see O'Reilly (*Frank Herbert* 6). O'Reilly points to Einstein's theory of relativity as having established that there is no absolute reference point for our observations (6). He also discusses Gödel's theorem and Heisenberg's uncertainty principle in connection with Herbert's worldview (6).

19. See the gom jabbar test (*Dune* 20). To pass, Paul must submit to torture knowing that if he flinches he will be put to death. On passing the test, he receives the following explanation: "You've heard of animals chewing off a leg to escape a trap? There's an animal kind of trick. A human would remain in the trap, endure the pain, feigning death that he might kill the trapper and remove the threat to his kind" (20). By sacrificing his hand to torture to ensure his long-term survival, Paul proves that he is a human being, that is, a creature capable of forward planning rather than an animal that only acts instinctually to preserve its own comfort in the moment.

20. See also Brian Herbert's *The Dreamer of Dune*. He notes: "Among the dangerous leaders of human history, my father sometimes mentioned General George S. Patton, because of his charismatic qualities—but more often his example was President John F. Kennedy. Around Kennedy a myth of kingship formed, and of Camelot. His followers did not question him, and would have gone with him virtually anywhere" (191–92).

21. The use here of *Mahdi*, the Muslim term for the one who will restore justice and religion before the end of the world, works to highlight that the messiah pattern is prevalent in numerous religions including Islam, Christianity, Hinduism and Judaism.

22. Indeed, Paul is initially unable to discern whether his vision reveals the downfall of Fremen culture or Chani's death (*Dune Messiah* 158–65). When he experiences a vision of a falling moon, he is distressed and wonders if it portends the fall of civilization before realizing that the "moon has a name" (165) and represents Chani. Thus, for Paul, the destruction of civilization and the loss of his lover are equally appalling.

23. See also *Chapterhouse: Dune*: "Leaders [make] mistakes. And those mistakes, amplified by the numbers who [follow] without questioning, [move] ... inevitably toward great disasters" (137).

24. O'Reilly identifies aspects of *Dune* that fulfill the hero myth pattern, or monomyth, as described by Joseph Campbell (*The Hero*), Lord Raglan and Otto Rank (*Frank Herbert* 80–82). He notes, however, that "*Dune* is not an *imitation* of myth, but an illustration of ... the pervasiveness of the 'monomyth'" (82). Similarly, Norman Spinrad argues that, while much SF presents formulaic reproductions of the hero's journey narrative, the first three novels of the *Dune* series present "a mordant commentary on the story of the Hero with a Thousand Faces" (155). Spinrad further notes that Paul fails as a hero, writing: "the superficially triumphant denouement of *Dune* is really a tragedy. The Hero ... cannot place the scepter of enlightenment and power in the hands of Everyone ... nor can he escape the dire consequences of his own godhood" (155). See also Palumbo's "The Monomyth as Fractal Pattern in Frank Herbert's *Dune* Novels," which explores aspects of the hero monomyth in all six *Dune* novels.

25. Touponce argues that the hero mystique only infects those reading *Dune* for "its entertainment value alone" (121). Given that the narrative was composed as entertainment, this criticism hardly seems fair. Herbert identifies audience engagement as a key goal of his novels, writing "If someone enters a bookstore and sets down ... money for your book, you owe that person some entertainment and as much more as you can give" ("When" vi). Touponce asserts that identification with Paul is hampered by an "underlying system of indeterminacies in the text, which introduce negations into our image of Paul at crucial points" (121–22). His work offers a fascinating Bahktinian reading of *Dune* and its sequels as polyphonic novels.

26. Jaspers is careful to note that the spiritual influence of the Church can only be firmly established if it relinquishes those tenets that are exclusive to Christianity. He declares that such doctrines are "no longer ... believed" (*The Future* 258) and that the Church should adhere only to those basic symbols that are shared across numerous religions (258). He sees such traditional symbols as providing a "freedom ... of meaning" (252) that allows individuals to create their own understanding of reality.

27. Aldiss and Wingrove thus term Leto II "a predator with a conscience" (397).

28. For a discussion of eugenics in the *Dune* series, see Stephanie Semler's "The Golden Path of Eugenics."

29. For an alternative argument that suggests that Paul does succeed in sacrificing his humanity, see Jeffery Nichols' "Facing the Gom Jabbar Test" (5–6).

30. For further discussion of Leto II's

character and long-term plans, see Grigsby. He argues that Herbert's series "parodies and reverses" (174) Isaac Asimov's *Foundation* series. He writes that Leto II ultimately fails to reorder society, citing the final pages of *God Emperor of Dune* as evidence that the Dune universe is still hampered by political manipulation (178–79). Written in 1984, Grigsby's article does not encompass the final two novels of the series, published in 1984 and 1985. These novels reveal that, although human society is still drawn to the hero mystique, Leto II's Golden Path is the most effective evolutionary avenue for humanity.

31. For a more detailed examination of the correlations between Nietzsche's writings and the ideas expressed in Herbert's *Dune* series see Roy Jackson's "Paul Atreides the Nietzschean Hero." See also Brook W.R. Pearson's "Friedrich Nietzsche Goes to Space," which argues that "Herbert's *Dune* saga is a work of philosophy that interacts primarily with the ideas of Friedrich Nietzsche" (189).

32. See Chapter 1 for further discussion of Carlyle's ideas.

Conclusion

1. The five episode series was broadcast on Syfy in December 2015 and was directed by Nick Hurran, who had previous experience with SF directing *Doctor Who*.

2. For instance, David Lynch's 1984 film, *Dune*, adapts only the first novel of Herbert's series and, subsequently, conforms to the traditional hero narrative. The film concludes with Paul being named the "Kwisatz Haderach," the foretold messiah, and ascending to the Imperial throne. John Harrison's television miniseries *Frank Herbert's Dune* (2000) reflects more of the nuances of Herbert's commentary on the dangers of hero worship while still depicting the emergence of Paul as a messianic hero. Similarly, Harrison's sequel *Frank Herbert's Children of Dune* (2003), based on *Dune Messiah* and *Children of Dune*, also addresses some of Herbert's key concerns. However, the choice to adapt only the first three novels, which conclude with Leto II's ascendance as God Emperor, results in the reinscribing of the traditional narrative patterns that Herbert resists in his novels. Furthermore, although all of the *Dune* novels were commercially successful on initial publication, they tend not to be marketed as a series. At present, no publisher offers a matching set of Herbert's six *Dune* novels. Instead, *Dune* is published as either an independent work or as an omnibus grouped with *Dune Messiah* and *Children of Dune*. Contemporary audiences are accustomed to narratives that activate the hero schema and this is what publishers and producers have sought to transform *Dune* into through the selective adaptation and publication of Herbert's series.

3. For other works that note the similarities between *Star Wars* and the *Dune* series see Aldiss and Wingrove (273) and Peter Wright (92). Furthermore, the documentary film *Jodorowsky's Dune* (2013), directed by Frank Pavich, argues that the storyboards and concept art created in the 1970s for Alejandro Jodorowsky's unmade film adaptation of *Dune* have greatly influenced subsequent Hollywood SF films, including *Star Wars*.

4. Isaac Asimov remarks on the lack of scientific plausibility in *Star Wars*, writing: "*Star Wars*. ... is utterly brainless, but the special effects are fun and it is restful sometimes to park one's brain outside" (*Asimov* 270).

5. Jodorowsky and director Richard Stanley discuss this aspect of Hollywood explicitly in *Jodorowsky's Dune* when describing the rejection of Jodorowsky's *Dune* script by American production companies.

6. For additional examples of recent Dickian films see Bould and Vint (183).

Works Cited

Aldiss, Brian. *Billion Year Spree: The History of Science Fiction.* London: Weidenfeld, 1973. Print.

Aldiss, Brian, and David Wingrove. *Trillion Year Spree: The History of Science Fiction.* New York: Atheneum, 1986. Print.

Alexander, S. *Space, Time and Deity: The Gifford Lectures at Glasgow 1916–1918.* Vol. 2. London: Macmillan, 1966. Print.

Aristotle. *Physics.* Trans. Robin Waterfield. Oxford: Oxford University Press, 2008. Print. Oxford World's Classics.

Armytage, W. H. G. "Matthew Arnold and T. H. Huxley: Some New Letters 1870–80." *Review of English Studies* 4.16 (1953): 346–353. Print.

Arnold, Matthew. *Culture and Anarchy.* Ed. Samuel Lipman. New Haven: Yale University Press, 1994. Print. Rethinking the Western Tradition. Print.

Arthur C. Clarke's World of Strange Powers. Dir. Peter Jones, Michael Weigall and Charles Flynn. 1985. TimeLife, 2009. DVD.

Asimov, Isaac. *Asimov on Science Fiction.* Garden City: Doubleday, 1981. Print.

———. "Social Science Fiction." Knight 29–61.

Authorized King James Version. London: Oxford University Press, 1977. Print.

Avengers Assemble. Disney. 26 July 2013–28 Sept. 2014. Television.

Barth, John. *Giles Goat-Boy or, The Revised New Syllabus.* London: Secker, 1967. Print.

Batchelor, John. *H. G. Wells.* Cambridge: Cambridge University Press, 1985. Print. British and Irish Authors Introductory Critical Studies.

Beer, Gillian. *Darwin's Plots: Evolutionary Narratives in Darwin, George Eliot and Nineteenth-Century Fiction.* 3rd ed. Cambridge: Cambridge University Press, 2009. Print.

Benjamin, Walter. *Illuminations.* Trans. Harry Zohn. Ed. Hannah Arendt. London: Jonathan Cape, 1970. Print.

Bergonzi, Bernard. *The Early H. G. Wells: A Study of the Scientific Romances.* Manchester: Manchester University Press, 1961. Print.

Bergson, Henri. *Creative Evolution.* Trans. Arthur Mitchell. Ed. Keith Ansell Pearson, Michael Kolkman and Michael Vaughan. Houndsmills: Palgrave, 2007. Print. Henri Bergson Centennial Series.

———. *Mind-Energy.* Trans. H. Wildon Carr. Ed. Keith Ansell Pearson and Michael Kolkman. Houndsmills: Palgrave, 2007. Print. Henri Bergson Centennial Series.

Bernal, J. D. *The World, The Flesh and the Devil: An Enquiry into the Future of the Three Enemies of the Rational Soul.* Bloomington: Indiana University Press, 1969. Print.

Bidney, David. "Myth, Symbolism, and Truth." *Myth: A Symposium.* Ed. Thomas A. Sebeok. Bloomington: Indiana University Press, 1972. 3–24. Print.

Blade Runner. Dir. Ridley Scott. Warner Bros., 1982. Film.

Botting, Fred. "'Monsters of the Imagination': Gothic, Science, Fiction." Seed, *A Companion to Science Fiction.* 111–26.

Bould, Mark, Andrew M. Butler, Adam Roberts, and Sherryl Vint, eds. *The Routledge Companion to Science Fiction.* London: Routledge, 2009. Print.

Bould, Mark, and Sherryl Vint. *The Routledge Concise History of Science Fiction.* New York: Routledge, 2001. Print.

Bowen, Roger. "Science, Myth, and Fiction in H. G. Wells's *Island of Doctor Moreau.*" *Studies in the Novel* 8.3 (1976): 318–35. Print.

Bradbury, Ray. *Fahrenheit 451.* 1953. New York: Del Rey-Ballentine-Random, 2009. Print.

Bridgwater, Patrick. "English Writers and Nietzsche." *Nietzsche: Imagery and Thought: A Collection of Essays.* Ed. Malcolm Pasley. Berkeley: University of California Press, 1978. 220–58. Print.

Brigg, Peter. "The Three Styles of Arthur C. Clarke: The Projector, the Wit, and the Mystic." Olander and Greenberg 15–51.

Brooke, John Hedley. *Science and Religion: Some Historical Perspectives.* Cambridge: Cambridge University Press, 1991. Print. The Cambridge Hist. of Science Ser.

Brown, E. K. "Two Formulas for Fiction: Henry James and H. G. Wells." *College English* 8.1 (1946): 7–17. Print.

Brown, Ivor. *H. G. Wells.* London: Nisbet, 1923. Print. Writers of the Day.

Burton, James. "Machines Making Gods: Philip K. Dick, Henri Bergson and Saint Paul." *Theory, Culture and Society* 25.7-8 (2008): 262–84. Print.

Butler, Andrew M. *Philip K. Dick.* Harpenden: Pocket Essentials, 2007. Print. Pocket Essentials.

Calvin, John. *Institutes of the Christian Religion.* Trans. John Allen. 6th ed. Vol. 1. Philadelphia: Presbyterian Board of Publication, 1813. Print.

Campbell, Joseph. *The Hero with a Thousand Faces.* 3rd ed. California: New World, 2008. Print.

———. *The Masks of God: Creative Mythology.* New York: Viking, 1968. Print.

Canaan, Howard. "Metafiction and the Gnostic Quest in *The Man in the High Castle*." *Journal of the Fantastic Arts* 12.4(48) (2002): 382–405. Print.

———. "Time and Gnosis in the Writings of Philip K. Dick. *Hungarian Journal of English and American Studies* 14.2 (2008): 335–55. Print.

Carlyle, Thomas. *Latter-Day Pamphlets.* London: Chapman, 1850. Print.

CBS News, CBS Television Network. *10:56:20 PM EDT, 7/20/69: The Historic Conquest of the Moon as Reported to the American People.* New York: Columbia Broadcasting System, 1970. Print.

Chernyshova, Tatiana. "The Folktale, Wells and Modern Science Fiction." Trans. Darko Suvin. Suvin and Philmus 35–47.

———. "Science Fiction and Myth Creation in Our Age." Trans. Istvan Csicsery-Ronay, Jr. *Science Fiction Studies* 31.3, Soviet Science Fiction: The Then and After (2004): 345–357. Print.

Clark, Timothy. *Martin Heidegger.* 2nd ed. London: Routledge, 2011. Print.

Clarke, Arthur C. "At the Interface: Technology and Mysticism—Dialog. .. Arthur C. Clarke and Alan Watts." *Playboy* Jan. 1972: 94+. Print.

———. "Author's Note." *2010: Odyssey Two.* By Clarke. London: Voyager-Harper, 1997. 11–15. Print.

———. "Back to 2001." *2001: A Space Odyssey.* By Clarke. London: Orbit, 2009. ix–xix. Print.

———. *Childhood's End.* 1953. London: Gollancz-Orion, 2009. Print. SF Masterworks.

———. *The City and the Stars.* 1956. London: Gollancz-Orion, 2001. Print. SF Masterworks.

———. *The Fountains of Paradise.* 1979. London: Gollancz-Orion, 2000. Print. SF Masterworks.

———. *Greetings Carbon-Based Bipeds! A Vision of the 20th Century as it Happened.* Ed. Ian T. Macauley. London: Harper, 1999. Print.

———. "The Nine Billion Names of God." *The Collected Stories.* London: Gollancz-Orion, 2000. 417–22. Print.

———. "Playboy Interview: Arthur C. Clarke—Candid Conversation." *Playboy* July 1986: 49–66. Print.

———. *Profiles of the Future: An Inquiry into the Limits of the Possible.* Rev. ed. London: Gollancz, 1974. Print.

———. "Sources." *3001: The Final Odyssey.* By Clarke. London: Voyager-Harper, 1997. 253–66. Print.

———. *3001: The Final Odyssey.* London: Voyager-Harper, 1997. Print.

———. *2001: A Space Odyssey.* 1968. London: Orbit-Little, Brown, 2009. Print.

———. *2061: Odyssey Three.* 1988. London: Voyager-Harper, 1997. Print.

———. *2010: Odyssey Two.* 1982. London: Voyager-Harper, 1997. Print.

Clarke, Arthur C., and C. S. Lewis. "The Clarke/Lewis Correspondence." *From Narnia to a Space Odyssey.* Ed. Ryder W. Miller. New York: ibooks, 2003. 35–52. Print.

Clarke, Arthur C., and Robert A. Heinlein. Interview by Walter Cronkite and Bill Stout. *CBS News.* CBS. WCBS, New York, 20 July 1969. Television.

Clarke, Stephen R. L. "Science Fiction and Religion." Seed, *A Companion to Science Fiction.* 95–110.

Clute, John, David Langford, Peter Nicholls, and Graham Sleight, eds. *The Encyclopedia of Science Fiction.* 3rd ed. Gollancz, 2011. Web.

Comte, Auguste. *A General View of Positivism.* 1848. Trans. J. H. Bridges. London:

New Universal Lib-Routledge; New York: Dutton, 1908. Print.

Conquest, Robert. "Science Fiction and Literature." Rose 30–45.

Copeland, B. Jack, ed. *The Essential Turing: Seminal Writings in Computer Logic, Philosophy, Artificial Intelligence, and Artificial Life Plus the Secrets of Enigma*. Oxford: Clarendon, 2001. Print.

Cornford, Francis Macdonald, trans. and ed. *Plato's Cosmology: The* Timaeus *of Plato Translated with a Running Commentary*. London: Routledge, 1966. Print. International Library of Psychology Philosophy and Scientific Method.

Costa, Richard Hauer. *H. G. Wells*. New York: Twayne, 1967. Print. Twayne's English Authors Ser.

Coupe, Laurence. *Myth*. 2nd ed. New York: Routledge, 2009. Print. The New Critical Idiom.

Critchley, Simon. "Philip K. Dick, Sci-Fi Philosopher. *The Opinion Pages: Opinionator*. New York Times, 20–22 May 2012. Web. 24 Nov. 2012.

Cyrano de Bergerac, Savinien de. *A Voyage to the Moon*. Trans. Archibald Lovell. New York: Doubleday, 1899. Print.

Darwin, Charles. *The Descent of Man and Selection in Relation to Sex*. 2 vols. London: Murray, 1871. Print.

_____. *The Origin of Species by Means of Natural Selection or the Preservation of Favoured Races in the Struggle for Life*. London: Oxford University Press, 1907. Print.

Descartes, René. "Description of the Human Body." Descartes, *The World* 170–205.

_____. *Discourse on Method and the Meditations*. Trans. F. E. Sutcliffe. Harmondsworth: Penguin, 1968. Print.

_____. "Discourse on the Method of Properly Conducting One's Reason and of Seeking the Truth in the Sciences." Descartes, *Discourse* 25–91.

_____. "Mediations on the First Philosophy in which the Existence of God and the Real Distinction Between the Soul and the Body of Man are Demonstrated." Descartes, *Discourse* 93–169.

_____. "Treatise on Man." Descartes, *The World* 99–169.

_____. *The World and Other Writings*. Trans. and ed. Stephen Gaukroger. Cambridge: Cambridge University Press, 1998. Print.

Dick, Philip K. "The Android and the Human." 1972. Sutin 183–210.

_____. "Author's Note." *A Scanner Darkly*. By Dick. Gollancz-Orion, 1999. Print. SF Masterworks.

_____. *Do Androids Dream of Electric Sheep?*. 1968. Gollancz-Orion, 2007. Print.

_____. "'The *Double: Bill* Symposium': Replies to 'A Questionnaire for Professional SF Writers and Editors.'" 1969. Sutin 63–67.

_____. "Drugs, Hallucinations, and the Quest for Reality." 1964. Sutin 167–74.

_____. *The Exegesis of Philip K. Dick*. Ed. Pamela Jackson and Jonathan Lethem. Boston: Houghton, 2011. Print.

_____. *Flow My Tears, the Policeman Said*. 1974. Gollancz-Orion, 2001. Print. SF Masterworks.

_____. Foreword. *A Maze of Death*. By Dick. London: Gollancz-Orion, 2005. Print. SF Masterworks.

_____. "How to Build a Universe that Doesn't Fall Apart Two Days Later." 1978. Sutin 259–80.

_____. "Letter of Comment." *SF Commentary* 9 (1970): 8–10. Rpt. in *Philip K. Dick: Electric Shepherd*. Ed. Bruce Gillespie. Melbourne: Norstrilia, 1975. 31–33. Print. The Best of SF Commentary.

_____. *A Maze of Death*. 1970. London: Gollancz-Orion, 2005. Print. SF Masterworks.

_____. "Notes on *Do Androids Dream of Electric Sheep?*." 1988. Sutin 155–61.

_____. "Pessimism in Science Fiction." 1955. Sutin 54–56.

_____. "Philip K. Dick on Philosophy: A Brief Interview." 1988. Sutin 44–47.

_____. *A Scanner Darkly*. 1977. Gollancz-Orion, 1999. Print. SF Masterworks.

_____. "The Short Happy Life of a Science Fiction Writer." 1976. Sutin 29–36.

_____. *The Three Stigmata of Palmer Eldritch*. 1964. Gollancz-Orion, 2003. Print. SF Masterworks.

_____. *Time Out of Joint*. 1959. London: Gollancz-Orion, 2003. Print. SF Masterworks.

_____. *The Transmigration of Timothy Archer*. London: Gollancz-Orion, 2011, Print.

_____. "Self Portrait." 1968. Sutin 11–17.

_____. *Ubik*. 1969. London: Gollancz-Orion, 2004. Print. SF Masterworks.

_____. *VALIS*. 1981. London: Gollancz-Orion, 2001. Print. SF Masterworks.

DiTommaso, Lorenzo. "Gnosticism and Dualism in the Early Fiction of Philip K. Dick." *Science Fiction Studies* 28.1 (2001): 49–65. Print.

_____. "History and Historical Effect in Frank Herbert's *Dune*." *Science Fiction Studies* 19.3 (1992): 311–325. Print.

_____. "A λόγος or Two Concerning the

λογοζ of Umberto Rossi and Philip K. Dick's *Time Out of Joint*." *Extrapolation* 39.4 (1998): 287–98. Print.

Doctor Who. BBC. 26 Mar. 2005–25 Dec. 2014. Television.

Doty, William G. *Mythography: The Study of Myths and Rituals*. 2nd ed. Tuscaloosa: University of Alabama Press, 2000. Print.

Dumont, Jean-Noël, Danièle Chatelain, and George Slusser. "Between Faith and Melancholy: Irony and the Gnostic Meaning of Dick's 'Divine Trilogy.'" *Science Fiction Studies* 15.2 (1988): 251–53. Print.

Dune. Dir. David Lynch. Universal Pictures, 1984. Film.

Durham, Scott. "P. K. Dick: From the Death of the Subject to a Theology of Late Capitalism." *Science Fiction Studies* 15.2 (1988): 173–86. Print.

Edge of Tomorrow. Dir. Doug Liman. Warner Bros., 2014. Film.

Eliade, Mircea. *Myth and Reality*. 1963. Trans. Willard R. Trask. New York: Harper, 1975. Print.

———. *Shamanism: Archaic Techniques of Ecstasy*. 1951. Trans. Willard R. Trask. Princeton: Princeton University Press, 1964. Print. Bollingen Series LXXVI.

Ellis, R. J. "Frank Herbert's *Dune* and the Discourse of Apocalyptic Ecologism in the United States." *Science Fiction Roots and Branches: Contemporary Critical Approaches*. Ed. Rhys Garnet and R. J. Ellis. Houndsmills: Macmillan, 1990. 104–124. Print.

Encyclopædia Britannica. 15th ed. 1974. Print.

Enns, Anthony. "Media, Drugs, and Schizophrenia in the Works of Philip K. Dick." *Science Fiction Studies* 33.1 (2006): 68–88. Print.

Feyerabend, Paul. *Against Method*. 3rd ed. London: Verso, 1993. Print.

Fitting, Peter. "Reality as Ideological Construct: A Reading of Five Novels by Philip K. Dick." *Science Fiction Studies* 10.2 (983): 219–36. Print.

Frank Herbert's Dune. Dir. John Harrison. Sci Fi Channel. 3–6 Dec. 2000. Television.

Frank Herbert's Children of Dune. Dir. Greg Yaitanes. Screenplay by John Harrison. Sci Fi Channel. 16–26 Mar. 2003. Television.

Franklin, H. Bruce. *Future Perfect: American Science Fiction of the Nineteenth Century*. New York: Oxford University Press, 1966. Print.

Frazer, James George. *The Golden Bough: A Study in Magic and Religion*. Abr. ed. London: Macmillan, 1929. Print.

Freedman, Carl. "Towards a Theory of Paranoia: The Science Fiction of Philip K. Dick." *Science Fiction Studies* 11.1 (1984): 15–24. Print.

Freud, Sigmund. *New Introductory Lecture on Psycho-Analysis*. Trans. and ed. James Strachey. London: Hogarth; Inst. of Psycho-Analysis, 1974. Print.

Galbreath, Robert. "Fantastic Literature as Gnosis." *Extrapolation* 29.4 (1988): 330–37. Print.

———. "Redemption and Doubt in Philip K. Dick's Valis Trilogy." *Extrapolation* 24.1 (1983): 105–15. Print.

Galvan, Jill. "Entering the Posthuman Collective in Philip K. Dick's *Do Androids Dream of Electric Sheep?*" *Science Fiction Studies* 24.3 (1997): 413–29. Print.

Godwin, Francis. *The Man in the Moone: or, A Discourse of a Voyage Thither by Domingo Gonsales, The Speedy Messenger*. London: Norton, 1638. Print.

Golden, Kenneth L. *Science Fiction, Myth, and Jungian Psychology*. Lewiston: Edwin Mellen Press, 1995. Print.

Gravity. Dir. Alfonso Cuarón. Warner Bros., 2013. Film.

Grigsby, John L. "Herbert's Reversal of Asimov's Vision Reassessed: *Foundation's Edge* and *God Emperor of Dune*." *Science Fiction Studies* 11.2 (1984): 174–180. Print.

Haldane, J. B. S. *Daedalus or Science and the Future: A Paper Read to the Heretics, Cambridge on February 4th, 1923*. New York: Dutton, 1924. Print.

———. *Fact and Faith*. London: Watts, 1936. Print. The Thinker's Library 44.

———. *The Inequality of Man and Other Essays*. London: Chatto, 1932. Print.

———. *Keeping it Cool and Other Essays*. London: Chatto, 1940. Print.

———. *Possible Worlds and Other Essays*. London: Chatto, 1928. Print.

Haldane, J. S. *Mechanism, Life and Personality: An Examination of the Mechanistic Theory of Life and Mind*. London: Murray, 1921. Print.

Harfst, Betsy. "Of Myths and Polyominoes: Mythological Content in Clarke's Fiction." Olander and Greenberg 87–120.

Hegel, Georg Wilhelm Friedrich. *Lectures on the History of Philosophy 1825–6*. Trans. R. F. Brown and J. M. Stewart. Ed. Robert F. Brown. Vol. II. Oxford: Clarendon, 2006. Print.

Heidegger, Martin. *Being and Time*. Trans. John Macquarrie and Edward Robinson. Oxford: Blackwell, 1978. Print.

———. *Being and Truth*. Trans. Gregory Fried

and Richard Polt. Bloomington: Indiana University Press, 2010. Print.
―――. *The Concept of Time: English-German Edition.* Trans. William McNeill. Oxford: Blackwell, 1992. Print.
―――. *Early Greek Thinking: The Dawn of Western Philosophy.* Trans. David Farrell Krell and Frank A. Capuzzi. San Francisco: Harper, 1984. Print.
―――. *The Essence of Truth: On Plato's Cave Allegory and Theaetetus.* Trans. Ted Sadler. London: Continuum, 2002. Print.
―――. *The Question Concerning Technology and Other Essays.* Trans. William Lovitt. New York: Garland, 1977. Print.
―――. "The Self-Assertion of the German University." *The Heidegger Controversy: A Critical Reader.* Ed. Richard Wolin. Cambridge: MIT Press, 1993. 29–39. Print.
Heinlein, Robert A. "Science Fiction: Its Nature, Faults and Virtues." 1959. Knight 3–28.
―――. *Stranger in a Strange Land.* London: Hodder, 1991. Print.
Henderson, Lawrence J. *The Fitness of the Environment: An Inquiry into the Biological Significance of the Properties of Matter.* 1913. Gloucester: Smith, 1970. Print.
Heraclitus. *The Art and Thought of Heraclitus: An Edition of the Fragments with Translation and Commentary.* Trans. Charles H. Khan. Cambridge: Cambridge University Press, 1979. Print.
Herbert, Brian. *Dreamer of Dune: The Biography of Frank Herbert.* New York: Tor, 2003. Print.
Herbert, Frank. *Chapterhouse: Dune.* 1985. New York: Ace-Penguin, 1987. Print.
―――. *Children of Dune.* 1976. New York: Ace-Penguin, 1987. Print.
―――. "Conversations in Port Townsend." O'Reilly, *The Maker* 230–48.
―――. "Dangers of the Superhero." O'Reilly, *The Maker* 97–101.
―――. "Doll Factory, Gun Factory." O'Reilly, *The Maker* 190–213.
―――. *The Dragon in the Sea.* 1956. New York: Tor, 2008. Print.
―――. *Dune.* 1965. London: Hodder, 2006. Print.
―――. *Dune Messiah.* 1969. New York: Ace-Penguin, 1987. Print.
―――. *God Emperor of Dune.* 1981. New York: Ace-Penguin, 1987. Print.
―――. *Heretics of Dune.* 1984. New York: Ace-Penguin, 1987. Print.
―――. "Introduction to *Saving Worlds*." O'Reilly, *The Maker* 160–168.
―――. "Listening to the Left Hand." O'Reilly, *The Maker* 8–19.
―――. "Men on Other Planets." O'Reilly, *The Maker* 71–87.
―――, ed. *New World or No World.* New York: Ace, 1970. Print.
―――. *The Santaroga Barrier.* 1968. New York: Tor, 2002. Print.
―――. "Science Fiction and a World in Crisis." O'Reilly, *The Maker* 20–46.
―――. "Science Fiction and You." *Tomorrow, and Tomorrow, and Tomorrow...* Ed. Bonnie L. Heintz, Frank Herbert, Donald A. Joos and Jane Agorn McGee. New York: Holt, 1974. 1–8. Print.
―――. "The Sparks Have Flown." O'Reilly, *The Maker* 102–10.
―――. "When I Was Writing Dune." *Heretics of Dune.* By Herbert. New York: Ace-Penguin, 1987. v–vi. Print.
Herbert, Frank, Brian Herbert, and Kevin J. Anderson. *The Road to Dune.* 2005. New York: Tor, 2006. Print.
Hillegas, Mark R. "Early Literary Background of Science Fiction." Parrinder, *Science* 2–17.
Homer. *The Odyssey.* Trans. Robert Fagles. London: Penguin, 1997. Print.
Howes, Alan B. "Expectation and Surprise in *Childhood's End*." Olander and Greenberg 149–71.
Hughes, David Y. "The Garden in Wells's Early Science Fiction." Suvin and Philmus 48–69.
Hulk and the Agents of S.M.A.S.H. Disney. 11 Aug. 2013–28 June 2015. Television.
Huntington, John. *The Logic of Fantasy: H. G. Wells and Science Fiction.* New York: Columbia University Press, 1982. Print.
―――. "From Man to Overmind: Arthur C. Clarke's Myth of Progress." Olander and Greenberg 211–22. Rpt. of "The Unity of *Childhood's End*." *Science Fiction Studies* 1.3 (1974): 154–64.
―――. "Philip K. Dick: Authenticity and Insincerity." *Science Fiction Studies* 15.2 (1988): 152–60. Print.
―――. "The Science Fiction of H. G. Wells." Parrinder, *Science* 34–50.
Hussey, Edward. *The Presocratics.* 1972. London: Duckworth; Indianapolis: Hackett, 1995. Print.
Huxley, Thomas H. *Darwiniana: Essays.* New York: Appleton, 1901. Print. Vol. 2 of *Collected Essays by Thomas H. Huxley.* 9 vols. 1893–1918.
―――. "Evolution and Ethics." 1893. Huxley, *Evolution and Ethics* 46–116.
―――. *Evolution and Ethics and Other Essays.* New York: Appleton, 1918. Print. Vol. 9 of *Collected Essays by Thomas H. Huxley.* 9 vols. 1893–1918.

———. "Letters to the *Times*." 1891. Huxley, *Evolution and Ethics* 237–311.

———. *Man's Place in Nature and Other Anthropological Essays*. London: Macmillan, 1894. Print. Vol. 7 of *Collected Essays by Thomas H. Huxley*. 9 vols. 1893–1918.

———. "Mr. Darwin's Critics." 1871. Huxley, *Darwiniana* 120–86.

———. "On Our Knowledge of the Causes of the Phenomena of Organic Nature." 1863. Huxley, *Darwiniana* 303–475.

———. "On the Relations of Man to the Lower Animals." 1863. Huxley, *Man's Place in Nature* 77–156.

———. "On the Study of Biology." 1876. Huxley, *Science and Education* 262–93.

———. "Prolegomena." 1894. Huxley, *Evolution and Ethics* 1–45.

———. "The School Boards: What They Can Do, and What They May Do." 1870. Huxley, *Science and Education* 377–403.

———. "Science and Culture." 1880. Huxley, *Science and Education* 134–59.

———. *Science and Education: Essays*. London: Macmillan, 1893. Print. Vol. 3 of *Collected Essays by Thomas H. Huxley*. 9 vols. 1893–1918.

Hyman Corine, and Paul J. Handal. "Definitions and Evaluation of Religion and Spirituality Items by Religious Professionals: A Pilot Study." *Journal of Religion and Health* 45.2 (2006): 264–282. Print.

Inception. Dir. Christopher Nolan. Warner Bros., 2010. Film.

Jackson, Pamela, and Jonathan Lethem, eds. *The Exegesis of Philip K. Dick*. Boston: Houghton, 2011. Print.

Jackson, Roy. "Paul Atreides the Nietzschean Hero." Nicholas 177–187.

James, Edward. "Arthur C. Clarke." Seed, *A Companion to Science Fiction* 431–40.

James, Henry. "The Younger Generation." 1914. James and Wells 178–215.

James, Henry, and H. G. Wells. *Henry James and H. G. Wells: A Record of Their Friendship, Their Debate on the Art of Fiction, and Their Quarrel*. Ed. Leon Edel and Gordon N. Ray. London: Rupert, 1959. Print.

James, William. *The Varieties of Religious Experience: A Study of Human Nature. Being the Gifford Lectures on Natural Religion Delivered at Edinburgh in 1901–1902*. London: Longmans, 1929. Print.

Jameson, Fredric. *Archaeologies of the Future: The Desire Called Utopia and Other Science Fictions*. London: Verso, 2005. Print.

Jaspers, Karl. *The Future of Mankind*. Trans. E. B. Ashton. 1958. Chicago: U of Chicago P, 1961. Print.

———. *Man in the Modern Age*. Trans. Eden Paul and Cedar Paul. 1933. London: Routledge, 1959. Print.

———. *Philosophical Faith and Revelation*. Trans. E. B. Ashton. 1962. London: Collins, 1967. Print.

———. *Philosophy*. Trans. E. B. Ashton. Vol. 1. 1932. Chicago: University of Chicago Press, 1969. Print.

———. *Way to Wisdom: An Introduction to Philosophy*. 1951. Trans. Ralph Manheim. 2nd ed. New Haven: Yale University Press, 2003. Print.

Jodorowsky's Dune. Dir. Frank Pavich. Sony Pictures Classics, 2013. Film.

Jung, C. G. *Flying Saucers: A Modern Myth of Things Seen in the Sky*. 1959. Trans. R. F. C. Hull. London: Ark-Routledge, 1987. Print.

———. "The Psychology of the Child Archetype." *Theories of Myth: From Ancient Israel and Greece to Freud, Jung, Campbell, and Lévi-Strauss*. Ed. Robert A. Segal. New York: Garland, 1996. 215–254. Print. A Garland Ser. 1. Psychology and Myth.

Kant, Immanuel. *Critique of Pure Reason*. Trans. Norman Kemp Smith. 2nd ed. Houndmills: Palgrave, 2007. Print.

———. "What is Enlightenment?" *Foundations of the Metaphysics of Morals*. Trans. Lewis White Beck. 2nd ed. New York: Macmillan; London: Collier, 1990. 83–90. Print. The Library of Liberal Arts.

Kepler, Johannes. *Somnium: The Dream or Posthumous Work on Lunar Astronomy*. Trans. Edward Rosen. Madison: University of Wisconsin Press, 1967. Print.

Khan, Charles H., trans. *The Art and Thought of Heraclitus: An Edition of the Fragments with Translation and Commentary*. Cambridge: Cambridge University Press, 1979. Print.

King, Karen. *What is Gnosticism?* Cambridge: Belknap-Harvard University Press, 2003. Print.

Kirk, G. S. *Myth: Its Meaning and Functions in Ancient and Other Cultures*. Cambridge: Cambridge University Press, 1970. Print.

Knight, Damon, ed. *Turning Points: Essays on the Art of Science Fiction*. New York: Harper, 1977. Print.

Korzybski, Alfred. *Manhood of Humanity: The Science and Art of Human Engineering*. New York: Dutton, 1921. Print.

———. *Science and Sanity: An Introduction to Non-Aristotelian Systems and General Semantics*. 2nd ed. Lancaster: International Non-Aristotelian Library, 1941. Print.

Kumar, Krishan. "Wells and 'The So-Called Science of Sociology.'" Parrinder and Rolfe 192–217.

Lambourne, Robert, Michael Shallis, and Michael Shortland. *Close Encounters? Science and Science Fiction*. Bristol: Hilger-IOP, 1990. Print.

Langford, David. "Dune [series]." John Clute, David Langford, Peter Nicholls and Graham Sleight. 17 Sept. 2013. Web. 14 June 2015.

Latham, R. E. Introduction. *On the Nature of the Universe*. By Lucretius. Trans. R. E. Latham. London: Penguin, 1951. 7–19. Print.

Lee, Desmond, trans. *The Republic*. By Plato. 2nd ed. London: Penguin, 2007. Print.

Lesher, J. H., trans. Xenophanes. *Xenophanes of Colophon: Fragments: A Text and Translation with a Commentary*. Toronto: Toronto University Press, 2001. Print.

Lewis, C. S. *Out of the Silent Planet*. 1938. London: Harper, 2005. Print.

_____. *Perelandra*. 1943. London: Harper, 2005. Print.

_____. *That Hideous Strength*. 1945. London: Harper, 2005. Print.

List, Julia. "'Call Me a Protestant': Liberal Christianity, Individualism, and the Messiah in *Stranger in a Strange Land*, *Dune*, and *Lord of Light*." *Science Fiction Studies* 36.1 (2009): 21–47. Print.

Livingston, James C. *Religious Thought in the Victorian Age: Challenges and Reconceptions*. New York: Clark-Continuum, 2006. Print.

Looper. Rian Johnson. TriStar Pictures; Film District, 2012. Film.

Luckhurst, Roger. "Pseudoscience." Bould, Butler, Roberts and Vint 403–12.

_____. *Science Fiction*. Cambridge: Polity, 2005. Print. Cultural History of Literature.

Lucretius. *On the Nature of the Universe*. Trans. R. E. Latham. London: Penguin, 1951. Print.

Lund, Kristian. "Wiping Finite Answers from an Infinite Universe." Nicholas 149–160.

MacKenzie, Norman, and Jeanne MacKenzie. *The Time Traveller: The Life of H. G. Wells*. London: Weidenfeld; 1973. Print.

Marcuse, Herbert. *Counterrevolution and Revolt*. London: Penguin; Boston: Beacon; Toronto: Saunders, 1972. Print.

_____. *Eros and Civilization: A Philosophical Inquiry into Freud*. 1955. London: Penguin, 1970. Print.

_____. *One Dimensional Man: Studies in the Ideology of Advanced Industrial Society*. 1964. London: Routledge, 1968. Print.

The Matrix. The Wachowski Brothers. Warner Bros.; Roadshow Entertainment, 1999. Film.

McAleer, Neil. *Arthur C. Clarke: The Authorized Biography*. Chicago: Contemporary, 1992. Print.

McConnell, Frank. *The Science Fiction of H. G. Wells*. New York: Oxford University Press, 1981. Print. Science-Fiction Writers 1.

McGrath, James F. *Religion and Science Fiction*. Eugene: Pickwick, 2001. Print.

Mckee, Gabriel. *The Gospel According to Science Fiction: From the Twilight Zone to the Final Frontier*. Louisville: Westminster, 2007. Print.

_____. *Pink Beams of Light from the God in the Gutter: The Science-Fictional Religion of Philip K. Dick*. Dallas: University Press of America, 2004. Print.

McMillan, Gloria. "The Invisible Friends: The Lost Worlds of Henry James and H. G. Wells." *Extrapolation* 47.1 (2006): 137–47. Print.

McWilliams, John C. *The 1960s Cultural Revolution*. Westport: Greenwood, 2000. Print.

Meyers, Walter E. "Problems with Herbert." Rev. of *Frank Herbert*, by Timothy O'Reilly and *Frank Herbert*, by David M. Miller. *Science Fiction Studies* 10.1 (1983): 106–8. Print.

Miller, Ryder W. *From Narnia to a Space Odyssey*. New York: ibooks, 2003. Print.

Miller, Walter M. *A Canticle for Leibowitz*. London: Gollancz-Orion, 2013. Print. SF Masterworks.

Moorcock, Michael. *Behold the Man*. 1969. London: Gollancz-Orion, 1999. Print. SF Masterworks.

Morris, William. *News from Nowhere and Other Writings*. London: Penguin, 2004. Print.

Nicholas, Jeffrey, ed. *Dune and Philosophy: Weirding Way of the Mentat*. Chicago: Open Court, 2011. Print. Popular Culture and Philosophy 56.

_____. "Facing the Gom Jabbar Test." Nicholas 3–12.

Nicholls, Peter. "Hard SF." Clute, Langford, Nicholls and Sleight, 28 Feb. 2013. Web. 3 Aug. 2015.

_____. "History of SF." Clute, Langford, Nicholls and Sleight, 2 Apr. 2015. Web. 13 May 2015.

_____. "Soft SF." Clute, Langford, Nicholls and Sleight, 20 Dec. 2011. Web. 13 Aug. 2015.

Nicholls, Peter, and John Clute. "Clarke, Arthur C." Clute, Langford, Nicholls and Sleight, 3 July 2014. Web. 11 Aug. 2014.

Nietzsche, Friedrich. *The Gay Science: With a Prelude in German Rhyme and an Appendix of Songs*. Trans. Josefine Nauckhoff and Adrian Del Caro. Ed. Bernard Williams. Cambridge: Cambridge University Press, 2001. Print.
_____. *Thus Spoke Zarathustra: A Book for Everyone and No One*. Trans. R. J. Hollingdale. London: Penguin, 1969. Print.
Oblivion. Dir. Joseph Kosinski. Universal Pictures, 2013. Film.
Olander, Joseph D., and Martin Harry Greenberg, eds. *Arthur C. Clarke*. New York: Taplinger, 1977. Print. Writers of the 21st Century Ser.
O'Reilly, Timothy. *Frank Herbert*. New York: Ungar, 1981. Print.
_____, ed. *The Maker of Dune: Insights of a Master of Science Fiction*. New York: Berkley, 1987. Print.
Orwell, George. *Nineteen Eighty-Four*. London: Penguin, 2000. Print.
Palmer, Christopher. "Philip K. Dick." Seed, *A Companion to Science Fiction* 389–97.
_____. "Postmodernism and the Birth of the Author in Philip K. Dick's *Valis*." *Science Fiction Studies* 18.3 (1991): 330–42. Print.
Palumbo, Donald. "Faith and Bad Faith in *Do Androids Dream of Electric Sheep?*" *The Journal of Popular Culture* 46.6 (2013): 1276–88. Print.
_____. "The Monomyth as Fractal Pattern in Frank Herbert's Dune Novels." *Science Fiction Studies* 25.3 (1998): 433–458. Print.
Parmenides. *The Fragments of Parmenides: A Critical Text with Introduction and Translation, The Ancient Testimonia and a Commentary*. Trans. A. H. Coxon and Richard McKirahan. Las Vegas: Parmenides, 2009. Print.
Parrinder, Patrick. *H. G. Wells*. Edinburgh: Oliver, 1970. Print.
_____, ed. *Science Fiction: A Critical Guide*. London: Longman, 1979. Print.
_____. *Shadows of the Future: H. G. Wells, Science Fiction and Prophecy*. Liverpool: Liverpool University Press, 1995. Print.
Parrinder, Patrick, and Christopher Rolfe, eds. *H. G. Wells Under Revision: Proceedings of the International H. G. Wells Symposium London, July 1986*. Selinsgrove: Susquehanna University Press; London: Associated University Press, 1990. Print.
Partington, John S. "The Death of the Static: H. G. Wells and the Kinetic Utopia." *Utopian Studies* 11.2 (200): 96–111. Print.
Pearson, Brook W.R. "Friedrich Nietzsche Goes to Space." Nicholas 189–205.
Philmus, Robert M., and David Y. Hughes, ed. *H. G. Wells: Early Writings in Science and Science Fiction*. Berkeley: University of California Press, 1975. Print.
Plato. *Plato's Cosmology: The Timaeus of Plato Translated with a Running Commentary*. Trans. and ed. Francis Macdonald Cornford. London: Routledge, 1966. Print. International Library of Psychology Philosophy and Scientific Method.
_____. *The Republic*. Trans. Desmond Lee. 2nd ed. London: Penguin, 2007. Print.
Rabkin, Eric S. *Arthur C. Clarke*. Washington: Starmont, 1980. Print. Starmont Reader's Guide 1.
_____. "Clarke, Arthur Charles." *Twentieth-Century Science-Fiction Writers*. 2nd ed. Chicago: St. James, 1986. 139–42. Print.
_____. "Genre Criticism: Science Fiction and the Fantastic." Rose 89–101.
_____. "Irrational Expectations; or, How Economics and the Post-Industrial World Failed Philip K. Dick." *Science Fiction Studies* 15.2 (1988): 161–72. Print.
Raglan, Lord. *The Hero: A Study in Tradition, Myth and Drama*. Mineola: Dover, 2003. Print.
Raknem, Ingvald. *H. G. Wells and His Critics*. Trondheim: Universitetsforlaget; Allen, 1962. Print.
Rank, Otto. *The Myth of the Birth of the Hero: A Psychological Interpretation of Mythology*. Trans. F. Robbins and Smith Ely Jelliffe. New York: Brunner, 1952. Print.
Reade, Winwood. *The Martyrdom of Man*. 1872. London: Watts, 1925. Print.
Reed, John R. *The Natural History of H. G. Wells*. Athens: Ohio University Press, 1982. Print.
_____. "The Vanity of Law in *The Island of Doctor Moreau*." Parrinder and Rolfe 134–44.
Roberts, Adam. "The Copernican Revolution." Bould, Butler, Roberts and Vint 3–12.
_____. "Frank [Patrick] Herbert (1920–86)." *Fifty Key Writers in Science Fiction*. Ed. Mark Bould, Andrew M. Butler, Adam Roberts and Sherryl Vint. London: Routledge, 2010. 101–06. Print.
_____. *The History of Science Fiction*. Houndsmills: Palgrave. 2006. Print.
Robinson, Kim Stanley. *Pacific Edge*. New York: St Martin's, 1995. Print.
Roos, David A. "Matthew Arnold and Thomas Henry Huxley: Two Speeches at the Royal Academy, 1881 and 1883." *Modern Philology* 74.3 (1977): 316–324. Print.
Rose, Mark, ed. *Science Fiction: A Collection of Critical Essays*. Englewood Cliffs: Prentice, 1976. Print.

Rossi, Umberto. "The Holy Family in Outer Space: Reconsidering Philip K. Dick's *The Divine Invasion*. *Extrapolation* 52.2 (2011): 153–73. Print.

———. "Illuminating Dick." Rev. of *Pink Beams of Light from the God in the Gutter: The Science Fictional Religion of Philip K. Dick*, by Gabriel McKee. *Science Fiction Studies* 31.3 (2004): 460–63. Print.

———. "Just a Bunch of Words: The Image of the Secluded Family and the Problem of λογοζ in P. K. Dick's *Time Out of Joint*." *Extrapolation* 37.3 (1996): 195–211. Print.

———. "The Shunts of the Tale: The Narrative Architecture of Philip K. Dick's *VALIS*." *Science Fiction Studies* 39.2 (2012): 243–61. Print.

Rousseau, Jean-Jacques. *The Social Contract*. Trans. Maurice Cranston. Harmondsworth: Penguin, 1969. Print.

Rudolf, Kurt. *Gnosis: The Nature and History of Gnosticism*. Trans. Robert McLachlan Wilson. San Francisco: Harper, 1987. Print.

Sammon, Paul M. *Future Noir: The Making of "Blade Runner."* New York: It Books, 1996. Print.

Samuelson, David N. "Hard SF." Bould, Butler, Roberts and Vint 494–99.

Schapiro, J. Salwyn. "Thomas Carlyle, Prophet of Fascism." *The Journal of Modern History*. 17.2 (1945): 97–115. Print.

Scheffer, Louis K. "Machine Intelligence, the Cost of Interstellar Travel and Fermi's Paradox." *Quarterly Journal of the Royal Astronomical Society* 35.2 (1994): 157–75. Print.

Schlossberg, Herbert. *Conflict and Crisis in the Religious Life of Late Victorian England*. New Brunswick: Transaction, 2009, Print.

Scholes, Robert. "The Roots of Science Fiction." Rose 46–56.

Scholes Robert, and Eric S. Rabkin. *Science Fiction: History, Science, Vision*. New York: Oxford University Press, 1977. Print.

Schulman, J. Neil. "Mondo Cult Presents Walter Cronkite Apollo 11 Interview with Robert A. Heinlein and Arthur C. Clarke." *YouTube*. Google, 16 Feb. 2015. Web. July 16, 2015. <https://www.youtube.com/watch?v=xMAmk5Rpltk&index=20&list=WL>.

Scigaj, Leonard M. "*Prana* and the Presbyterian Fixation: Ecology and Technology in Frank Herbert's *Dune* Tetralogy." *Extrapolation* 24.4 (1983): 340–355. Print.

Sears, Paul B. *Where There is Life*. New York: Dell, 1962. Print. Laurel Science Ser.

Seed, David. *A Companion to Science Fiction*. Malden: Blackwell, 2005. Print.

———. *Science Fiction: A Very Short Introduction*. Oxford: Oxford University Press, 2011. Print. Very Short Introductions.

Segal, Robert A. *Myth: A Very Short Introduction*. Oxford: Oxford University Press, 2004. Print. Very Short Introductions.

———. *Theorizing about Myth*. Boston: University of Massachusetts Press, 1999. Print.

Semler, Stephanie. "The Golden Path of Eugenics." Nicholas 13–26.

Shakespeare, William. *Hamlet*. Ed. Mike Gould. Hammersmith: Harper, 2012. Print. Collins Classics.

Shelley, Mary. *Frankenstein*. London: Penguin, 2006. Print. Red Classics.

Siegel, Mark. *Hugo Gernsback, Father of Modern Science Fiction: With Essays on Frank Herbert and Bram Stoker*. San Bernardino: Borgo, 1988. Print. Milford Ser. Popular Writers of Today 45.

Sims, Christopher A. "The Dangers of Individualism and the Human Relationship to Technology in Philip K. Dick's *Do Androids Dream of Electric Sheep?*" *Science Fiction Studies* 36.1 (2009): 67–76. Print.

Sless, David. "Arthur C. Clarke." *The Stellar Gauge: Essays on Science Fiction Writers*. Ed. Michael J. Tolley and Kirpal Singh Carlton: Norstrilia, 1980. 93–107. Print.

Slusser, George. "The Origins of Science Fiction." Seed, *A Companion to Science Fiction* 27–42.

Smith, David C. *H. G. Wells: Desperately Mortal: A Biography*. New Haven: Yale University Press, 1986. Print.

Source Code. Dir. Duncan Jones. Summit Entertainment, 2011. Film.

Spencer, Herbert. *First Principles*. 1862. London: Watts, 1937. Print. The Thinker's Library 62.

Spinrad, Norman. *Science Fiction and the Real World*. Carbondale: Southern Illinois University Press, 1990. Print.

Stableford, Brian M. "Proto SF." Clute, Langford, Nicholls and Sleight, 3 Apr. 2015. Web. 13 May 2015.

Stableford, Brian M., John Clute, and Peter Nicholls. "Definitions of SF." Clute, Langford, Nicholls and Sleight, 2 Apr. 2015. Web. 13 May 2015.

Stableford, Brian M., and David Langford. "Utopias." Clute, Langford, Nicholls and Sleight, 2 Feb. 2015. Web. 9 July 2015.

Stapledon, Olaf. *Last and First Men*. 1930. London: Gollancz-Orion, 1999. Print. SF Masterworks.

———. *Star Maker*. 1937. London: Gollancz-Orion, 1999. Print. SF Masterworks.

Star Wars Episode V: The Empire Strikes Back.

Dir. George Lucas. 20th Century Fox, 1980. Film.

Star Wars Episode IV: A New Hope. Dir. George Lucas. 20th Century Fox, 1977. Film.

Star Wars Episode I: The Phantom Menace. Dir. George Lucas. 20th Century Fox, 1999. Film.

Star Wars Episode VI: Return of the Jedi. Dir. George Lucas. 20th Century Fox, 1983. Film.

Star Wars Episode III: Revenge of the Sith. Dir. George Lucas. 20th Century Fox, 2005. Film.

Star Wars Episode II: Attack of the Clones. Dir. George Lucas. 20th Century Fox, 2002. Film.

Star Wars Rebels. Disney. 3 Oct. 2014–2 Mar. 2015. Television.

Steinmüller, Karlheinz. "Science Fiction and Science in the Twentieth Century." *Science in the Twentieth Century.* Ed. John Krige and Dominique Pestre. Amsterdam: Harwood Academic, 1997. Print.

Stilling, Roger J. "Mystical Healing: Reading Philip K. Dick's *VALIS* and *The Divine Invasion* as Metapsychoanalytic Novels." *South Atlantic Review* 56.2 (1991): 91–106. Print.

Stover, Leon. "Applied Natural History: Wells vs. Huxley." Parrinder and Rolfe 125–33.

Stratton, Susan. "The Messiah and the Greens: The Shape of Environmental Action in *Dune* and *Pacific Edge*." *Extrapolation* 42.4 (2001): 303–316. Print.

Sutin, Lawrence, ed. *The Shifting Realities of Philip K. Dick: Selected Literary and Philosophical Writings.* New York: Vintage-Random, 1995. Print.

Sutton, Thomas C., and Marilyn Sutton. "Science Fiction and Mythology." *Western Folklore* 28.4 (1969): 230–237. Print.

Suvin, Darko. Introduction. Suvin and Philmus 1–32.

———. *Metamorphoses of Science Fiction: On the Poetics and History of a Literary Genre.* New Haven: Yale University Press, 1979. Print.

———. "P. K. Dick's Opus: Artifice as Refuge and World View (Introductory Reflections)." *Science Fiction Studies* 2.1 (1975): 8–22. Print.

Suvin, Darko, and Robert M. Philmus, eds. *H. G. Wells and Modern Science Fiction.* Lewisberg: Bucknell University Press; London: Associated University Press, 1977. Print.

Szasz, Thomas S. *Ideology and Insanity: Essays on the Psychiatric Dehumanization of Man.* London: Calder, 1973. Print.

Touponce, William F. *Frank Herbert.* Boston: Twayne, 1988. Print. Twayne's United States Authors Series 532.

Turing, Alan. "Computing Machinery and Intelligence." 1950. Copeland 441–63.

———. "Intelligent Machinery." 1948. Copeland 410–32.

Ultimate Spider-Man. Disney. 1 Apr. 2012–4 Aug. 2015. Television.

Vernier, J. P. "Evolution as Literary Theme in H. G. Wells's Science Fiction." Suvin and Philmus 70–89.

Vint, Sherryl. "Animals and Animality from the Island of Doctor Moreau to the Uplift Universe." *The Yearbook of English Studies* Science Fiction. 37:2 (2007): 85–102. Print.

———. "Science Studies." Bould, Butler, Roberts and Vint 413–22.

Vogeler, Martha S. "Wells and Positivism." Parrinder and Rolfe 181–91.

Wagar, W. Warren. "Science and the World State: Education as Utopia in the Prophetic Vision of H. G. Wells." Parrinder and Rolfe 40–53.

Wallace, Alfred Russel. *The World of Life: A Manifestation of Creative Power, Directive Mind and Ultimate Purpose.* 5th ed. London: Chapman, 1911. Print.

Warren, James. *Presocratics: Natural Philosophers Before Socrates.* Berkeley: University California Press, 2007. Print.

Watts, Alan. *Myth and Ritual in Christianity.* 1954. London: Thames and Hudson, 1983. Print. Myth and Man.

Wells, H. G. *Anticipations of the Reactions of Mechanical and Scientific Progress upon Human Life and Thought.* London: Chapman, 1902. Print.

———. *Boon, The Mind of the Race, The Wild Asses of the Devil, and The Last Trump: Being a First Selection from the Literary Remains of George Boon, Appropriate to the Times.* London: Unwin, 1915. Print.

———. "The Contemporary Novel." 1914. James and Wells 131–56.

———. *Experiment in Autobiography: Discoveries and Conclusions of a Very Ordinary Brain (Since 1866).* 2 vols. London: Gollancz; Cresset, 1934. Print.

———. *The First Men in the Moon.* 1901. London: Gollancz-Orion, 2013. Print. SF Masterworks.

———. *The Food of the Gods.* 1904. London: Gollancz-Orion, 2010. Print. SF Masterworks.

———. *God the Invisible King.* 1917. Gloucester: Dodo, 2007. Print.

———. *H. G. Wells Classic Collection II: In The Days of the Comet, Men Like Gods, The Sleeper Awakes, The War in the Air*. London: Gollancz-Orion, 2011. Print.

———. "Human Evolution, An Artificial Process." Philmus and Hughes 211–19. Rpt. of "Human Evolution." *Fortnightly Review* ns 60(1896): 590–95.

———. *In the Days of the Comet*. 1906. Wells, *H. G. Wells Classic Collection* 1–202.

———. *The Invisible Man*. 1897. London: Gollancz-Orion. 2012. Print. SF Masterworks.

———. *The Island of Doctor Moreau*. 1896. London: Gollancz-Orion. Print. SF Masterworks.

———. *Joan and Peter: The Story of an Education*. New York: Macmillan, 1918. Print.

———. "The Limits of Individual Plasticity." 1895. Philmus and Hughes 36–39.

———. *Love and Mr. Lewisham*. London: Penguin, 2006. Print.

———. *Men Like Gods*. 1923. Wells, *H. G. Wells Classic Collection* 203–410.

———. *A Modern Utopia*. 1905. London: Penguin, 2005. Print.

———. "Morals and Civilisation." 1897. Philmus and Hughes 220–28.

———. *Mr. Britling Sees it Through*. New York: Macmillan, 1916. Print.

———. *The Outline of History: Being a Plain History of Life and Mankind*. Rev. ed. Vol. 2. London: Waverly, 1925. Print.

———. Preface. *God the Invisible King*. By Wells. 1917. Gloucester: Dodo, 2007. Print.

———. "The Province of Pain." 1894. Philmus and Hughes 194–99.

———. *The Sleeper Awakes*. Wells, *H. G. Wells Classic Collection* 411–603.

———. "The So-Called Science of Sociology." *An Englishman Looks at the World: Being a Series of Unrestrained Remarks Upon Contemporary Matters*. London: Cassell, 1916. Print.

———. *The Soul of a Bishop*. Toronto: Macmillan, 1917. Print.

———. *The Time Machine*. 1895. London: Gollancz-Orion, 2010. Print. SF Masterworks.

———. *The Undying Fire*. New York: Macmillan, 1919. Print.

———. *The War of the Worlds*. 1898. London: Gollancz-Orion, 2012. Print. SF Masterworks.

———. "Zoological Retrogression." 1891. Philmus and Hughes 158–68.

Wertheim, Margaret. *Pythagoras' Trousers: God, Physics and the Gender Wars*. 1995. New York: London, 1997. Print.

Westfahl, Gary. "Hard Science Fiction." Seed, *A Companion to Science Fiction* 187–210.

Wheen, Francis. Introduction. *A Modern Utopia*. By H. G. Wells. London: Penguin, 2005. xiii–xxvi. Print.

Wilson, Harris. *Arnold Bennett and H. G. Wells: A Record of a Personal and a Literary Friendship*. Urbana: University of Illinois Press, 1960. Print.

Woelfel, James. "Victorian Agnosticism and Liberal Theology: T. H. Huxley and Matthew Arnold." *American Journal of Theology and Philosophy*. 19.1 (1998): 61–76. Print.

Woodman, Tom. "Science Fiction, Religion and Transcendence." Parrinder, *Science* 110–130.

Woolf, Virginia. *Mr. Bennett and Mrs. Brown*. London: Hogarth, 1924. Print. The Hogarth Essays.

Wright, Peter. "Film and television, 1960–1980." Bould, Butler, Roberts and Vint 90–101.

Xenophanes. *Xenophanes of Colophon: Fragments: A Text and Translation with a Commentary*. Trans. J. H. Lesher. Toronto: Toronto University Press, 2001. Print.

Yinger, Milton J. *Countercultures: The Promises and the Peril of a World Turned Upside Down*. New York: Free, 1982. Print.

Young, Kenneth. *H. G. Wells*. Essex: Longman, 1974. Print. Writers and Their Works 233.

Zelazny, Roger. *Lord of Light*. London: Gollancz-Orion, 2010. Print. SF Masterworks.

Index

Aldiss, Brian 6, 8, 9–10, 159*n*2, 160*n*12, 160*n*15, 167*n*3, 168*n*10, 171*n*7, 172*n*8, 173*n*27, 174*n*3
Alexander, S. 54, 75–76
android 92, 94, 96–97, 102
Anticipations 24, 29, 34, 48
Arnold, Matthew 22, 24, 44, 45
Asimov, Isaac 5, 7, 159*n*1, 160*n*15, 160*n*16, 173*n*30, 174*n*4
atheism 50, 51, 54, 75, 79, 84, 90, 165*n*46, 166*n*5

Behold the Man 125
Benjamin, Walter 113
Bergson, Henri 53, 54, 62, 63, 166*n*12; *see also* vitalism
Bernal, J. D. 54, 65, 67, 68, 71, 163*n*29
Blade Runner 96, 155
Boon, The Mind of the Race, The Wild Asses of the Devil, and The Last Trump 26, 165*n*41

Campbell, John 139–40, 149
Campbell, Joseph 115, 173*n*24
capitalism 1, 16, 28, 30, 32, 52, 88, 89, 91–93, 97–98, 104, 105, 106, 107, 115, 154, 168*n*18; *see also* consumerism
Carlyle, Thomas 27, 38, 146–47
Chapterhouse: Dune 122, 125, 129–30, 140–41, 146–48, 150, 172*n*8, 173*n*23; *see also* *Dune* series
Chernyshova, Tatiana 10, 11, 14, 15, 161*n*1
Childhood's End 1, 16, 55, 56, 57, 62, 63, 64, 65–66, 69–70, 75–76, 77, 78, 82, 83, 154, 166*n*9, 171*n*52
Children of Dune 122, 129, 133, 134, 138–39, 140, 142–43, 146, 149, 152, 174*n*2; *see also* *Dune* series
Christianity 1, 15, 20, 21, 22, 27–28, 29, 31, 40, 43–45, 46–47, 49, 50–51, 71, 90, 110, 113, 115, 118, 125, 131, 154, 161*n*22, 162*n*7, 165*n*42, 167*n*20, 169*n*34, 170*n*35, 172*n*16, 173*n*21, 173*n*26; Catholic 19, 28, 90, 159*n*1, 161*n*2, 170*n*38; The Church 19, 22, 28, 43, 44–45, 46, 90, 141, 142, 161*n*2, 163*n*16, 165*n*39, 170*n*38, 173*n*26; Protestant 9, 141, 159*n*1; *see also* Protestant Reformation
The City and the Stars 16, 56, 57, 63, 66, 68, 70, 72, 73, 77, 163*n*29, 166*n*13, 166*n*18
Clarke, Arthur C. 1, 4, 5, 13, 15, 16, 17, 52, 53–85, 86, 90, 113, 140, 153, 154, 155, 157, 159*n*3, 159*n*4, 161*n*23, 163*n*29, 171*n*52; *Childhood's End* 1, 16, 55, 56, 57, 62, 63, 64, 65–66, 69–70, 75–76, 77, 78, 82, 83, 154, 166*n*9, 171*n*52; *The City and the Stars* 16, 56, 57, 63, 66, 68, 70, 72, 73, 77, 163*n*29; *The Fountains of Paradise* 56, 73–74, 78–79, 82–83, 167*n*25; *Greetings Carbon-Based Bipeds!* 56, 67, 72, 81–82, 83, 85, 153, 166*n*6, 166*n*7; "The Nine Billion Names of God" 166*n*18; *Space Odyssey* series 1, 16, 55, 57, 58, 59, 63, 68, 76–77, 78, 79–81, 82–83, 154, 166*n*10; *2001: A Space Odyssey* 16, 55, 56, 57, 60–61, 63–64, 66, 67, 68, 69, 70, 76, 78, 79–80, 82, 83, 84, 154, 166*n*9, 166*n*10; *2010: Odyssey Two* 56, 58, 60, 64, 69, 74, 80, 81, 82; *2061: Odyssey Three* 81; *3001: The Final Odyssey* 58, 59, 64, 73, 81, 83, 84–85
Comte, Auguste 45
consciousness 6, 10, 11, 53–54, 55–56, 57–60, 61, 63, 64, 67, 68–70, 80–81, 93, 100, 128, 139, 150, 166*n*12; *see also* mind
consumerism 16, 52, 88, 89, 91, 92–94, 97, 98, 104, 106, 113, 154, 168*n*18; *see also* capitalism
counterculture 86, 88, 89, 91; *see also* Marcuse, Herbert
Coupe, Laurence 13

Darwin, Charles 15, 19, 20, 27, 28–29, 30, 31, 32, 35, 39, 42, 45, 69–70, 161*n*2, 163*n*17, 163*n*19

187

Dasein 95–97, 99, 102, 106, 108, 124, 125, 126–28, 133–34, 135–36, 137, 138, 143–44, 145–52, 154, 171*n*5; Das Man 124, 142; *see also* Heidegger, Martin
DC 156–157
democracy 1, 38, 122–23, 125, 129, 141, 145–49, 150, 152, 154
Descartes, René 14, 54, 57, 61, 63, 161*n*21; *see also* materialism; mechanism; vitalism
Dick, Philip K. 1, 4, 5, 13, 16, 17, 52, 85, 86–120, 140, 150, 153, 154, 155, 157, 159*n*3, 160*n*10, 161*n*23; *Do Androids Dream of Electric Sheep?* 88, 91, 92, 93–97, 102–04, 105, 108, 109, 113, 115, 155; *Flow My Tears, the Policeman Said* 98; *A Maze of Death* 89, 91, 100, 101, 102, 103, 109, 110–12, 113, 114, 115, 116; *A Scanner Darkly* 107; *The Three Stigmata of Palmer Eldritch* 88, 90, 91, 92–93, 96, 102, 103–04, 106–08, 109, 113, 115; *Time Out of Joint* 168*n*11, 169*n*27; *The Transmigration of Timothy Archer* 169*n*34; *Ubik* 88, 89, 91, 100–02, 103, 109–13, 114, 116, 169*n*30, 169*n*35; *VALIS* 89, 90, 91, 98, 99, 102, 103, 107, 111, 113, 114–16, 117–20, 167*n*4, 167*n*6, 170*n*37
Do Androids Dream of Electric Sheep? 88, 91, 92, 93–97, 102–04, 105, 108, 109, 113, 115, 155
Doty, William G. 12, 13
The Dragon in the Sea/Under Pressure 172*n*15
Dune 122, 123, 125, 126, 131, 132, 134, 137, 137, 139–40, 141, 148, 155, 171*n*2, 172*n*13, 173*n*19; *see also Dune* series
Dune Messiah 122, 126, 127, 128–29, 137–38, 139–40, 142, 174*n*2; *see also Dune* series
Dune series 1, 17, 121–152, 154–55; *see also Chapterhouse: Dune*; *Children of Dune*; *Dune*; *Dune Messiah*; *God Emperor of Dune*; *Heretics of Dune*

education 28, 29, 32, 43, 45, 60–61, 66, 85, 91, 117–18, 125, 129–30, 132–33, 141, 147, 150, 160*n*16, 162*n*7, 163*n*16, 163*n*28
Eliade, Mircea 13, 105–06, 108
evolution 1, 9, 15, 16, 20, 21, 22, 28–29, 30, 31, 32–33, 34, 35, 36, 37–38, 40, 41, 42, 43, 45, 48, 49–50, 51, 52, 54, 56, 60, 62, 64–66, 67, 68–70, 71, 75, 76, 77, 78–79, 80, 82, 83, 84, 85, 107, 121, 125, 132, 133, 135, 138, 142–43, 146, 147, 148–49, 150, 152, 153, 154, 157, 161*n*2, 162*n*8, 163*n*17, 163*n*19, 167*n*20, 167*n*21, 167*n*28, 172*n*8, 173*n*30

fascism 97–98, 164*n*33; Nazi 96, 97
Feyerabend, Paul 14–15

The First Men in the Moon 163*n*25
Flow My Tears, the Policeman Said 98
The Food of the Gods 35, 39–40, 48, 51, 161*n*1, 162*n*13, 164*n*32
The Fountains of Paradise 56, 73–74, 78–79, 82–83, 167*n*25
Frazer, James George 50, 160*n*19
Freud, Sigmund 73–74

Gnosticism 16, 89–90, 109, 111–12, 114–15, 116, 117, 154, 167*n*6, 170*n*45, 170*n*49
God Emperor of Dune 122, 133, 134, 135–36, 142–145, 152, 174*n*2; *see also Dune* series
God the Invisible King 22, 41, 49–52, 165*n*41, 167*n*27
Greetings Carbon-Based Bipeds! 56, 67, 72, 81–82, 83, 85, 153, 166*n*6, 166*n*7

Haldane, J. B. S. 1, 53, 54, 55–56, 58, 63, 64, 65, 66, 68, 71, 72–73, 74–76, 78, 79, 84, 153–54, 163*n*29, 165*n*2; *see also* materialism; mechanism; vitalism
Haldane, J. S. 53, 61–62, 75, 83–84, 165*n*2
Heidegger, Martin 1, 16, 86, 91, 95–96, 99, 102, 106, 121, 122, 123, 124, 127–28, 131, 133–34, 143–44, 151, 154, 167*n*2; *see also* Dasein
Heinlein, Robert A. 5, 125, 166*n*15; *Stranger in a Strange Land* 125, 172*n*11
Henderson, Lawrence J. 14, 54, 63, 77, 153–54, 166*n*3
Heraclitus 89, 99, 102, 109–10, 112, 116, 117, 119, 168*n*9; *see also* Presocratics
Herbert, Frank 1, 4, 5, 16–17, 21, 52, 85, 121–52, 153, 154–55, 157, 159*n*3, 161*n*23; *Chapterhouse: Dune* 122, 125, 129–30, 140–41, 146–48, 150, 172*n*8, 173*n*23; *Children of Dune* 122, 129, 133, 134, 138–39, 140, 142–43, 146, 149, 152, 174*n*2; *The Dragon in the Sea/Under Pressure* 172*n*15; *Dune* 122, 123, 125, 126, 131, 132, 134, 137, 139–40, 141, 148, 155, 171*n*2, 172*n*13, 173*n*19; *Dune Messiah* 122, 126, 127, 128–29, 137–38, 139–40, 142, 174*n*2; *Dune* series 1, 17, 121–152, 154–55; *God Emperor of Dune* 122, 133, 134, 135–36, 142–145, 152, 174*n*2; *Heretics of Dune* 122, 125, 128, 130, 142, 143, 146, 147, 172*n*8; *The Santaroga Barrier* 122, 171*n*3
Heretics of Dune 122, 125, 128, 130, 142, 143, 146, 147, 172*n*8; *see also Dune* series
hero 17, 52, 121, 122–23, 125, 136, 138–40, 142–43, 144, 145, 146, 147, 148, 150, 154, 155–57, 166*n*9, 172*n*12, 173*n*25, 174*n*2; *see also* messiah; savior
Huntington, John 20, 21, 66, 69, 161*n*3, 164*n*32, 166*n*4, 166*n*8, 166*n*18, 167*n*3

Index

Hussey, Edward 99, 109, 116, 117, 119, 169n29, 169n31, 170n36, 170n39, 170n40, 170n42
Huxley, T. H. 16, 20, 21–22, 27–31, 33–34, 36–38, 39, 41–42, 44, 45, 46, 50, 161n2, 163n30

In the Days of the Comet 16, 21, 24, 27–28, 34, 35, 46, 47–48, 50, 51, 162n15, 165n39
The Invisible Man 161n1
The Island of Doctor Moreau 16, 19, 20, 21, 29–30, 35–36, 41–44, 51, 163n24, 164n37

James, Henry 23–26, 165n41
James, William 47
Jaspers, Karl 1, 121, 122, 123, 124, 126, 129, 131, 134–35, 138, 141, 142, 144–45, 147–49, 152, 171n5
Joan and Peter: The Story of an Education 165n45
Jung, C. G. 11, 20, 123, 166n9

Kant, Immanuel 88–89, 91, 100, 101
Kennedy, John F. 97, 137, 138
Korzybski, Alfred 121–22, 128, 129, 130–31, 132–33, 146, 151

language 12, 41–42, 84, 98, 119, 121–122, 128, 129, 150–51
Last and First Men 70, 163n29
Lewis, C. S. 166n16
Lord of Light 125
Love and Mr. Lewisham 24
Luckhurst, Roger 5–6, 8, 20, 21, 163n21, 163n24, 167n4, 169n26, 171n2, 171n3, 172n12
Lucretius 58, 60, 73; *see also* materialism; mechanism

Marcuse, Herbert 1, 16, 88–89, 91, 92, 93, 97–98, 100, 154; *see also* counterculture
Marvel 156–57
materialism 1, 3, 4, 7, 9, 10, 13, 14, 16, 52, 53, 54, 55–56, 57, 58–60, 61, 62–63, 64, 65, 70–71, 78, 79–81, 83, 84, 85, 119, 153–54, 155, 160n10; *see also* Descartes, René; Haldane, J. B. S.; Lucretius; mechanism; Turing, Alan
A Maze of Death 89, 91, 100, 101, 102, 103, 109, 110–12, 113, 114, 115, 116
Mckee, Gabriel 90, 159n6, 169n35, 170n48, 170n49
mechanism 53–54, 57, 58–60, 61–63, 64, 67; *see also* Descartes, Rene; Haldane, J. B. S.; Lucretius; materialism; Turing, Alan
Men Like Gods 46
messiah 1, 118, 121, 124–25, 135, 136, 137, 138–39, 140, 141, 142, 143, 145, 149, 150, 151, 155, 157, 171n6, 172n11, 173n21; *see also* hero; savior
mind 55–56, 57–60, 63–64, 67–68, 69, 70, 71, 79, 80–81, 151; *see also* consciousness
Mr. Britling Sees it Through 165n45
A Modern Utopia 16, 21, 22, 24, 25, 31, 34, 35, 37–39, 42, 44, 46–48, 51–52, 162n13, 164n31
Moorcock, Michael 125; *Behold the Man* 125
morality 12, 16, 19, 20, 21–22, 23, 25, 30–31, 32, 33, 36, 37, 40, 41, 42–44, 45–47, 49–50, 72, 75, 91, 92, 126, 148, 153, 165n40; immoral 95, 165n39
myth, definition 10–13

Nicholls, Peter 9, 53, 160n15, 165n1
Nietzsche, Friedrich 43, 146
"The Nine Billion Names of God" 166n18
Nixon, Richard 97, 98, 119, 138

Parmenides 100, 116–17; *see also* Presocratics
Plato 21, 31, 38–39, 40, 41, 46–47, 89, 99, 109, 114, 116–17, 143–44, 154, 162n5, 167n6
Presocratics 1, 2, 16, 52, 86, 89, 90, 91, 99, 100, 104, 109, 110, 111, 114, 116, 154, 168n8, 170n40; *see also* Heraclitus; Parmenides; Xenophanes
Protestant Reformation 9, 159n1; *see also* Christianity

reality 2, 3, 4, 10, 11, 13, 16, 19, 29, 30, 34, 35, 62–63, 73, 74, 75, 86, 88, 89, 90, 91, 92, 93, 94, 98, 99, 100–03, 104–05, 106, 107, 111, 113, 114, 116–117, 119, 124, 125, 127, 128, 129, 134, 136, 138, 139, 145, 146, 148–49, 151, 152, 153, 154, 157, 169n27, 171n52, 172n18, 173n26
religion, definition 13–15
Roberts, Adam 7, 9, 14, 17, 22, 54–55, 79–80, 155, 159n1, 159n6, 159n7, 160n12, 160n15, 164n33, 164n34, 164n37, 169n32, 169n33, 172n8, 172n11
Rousseau, Jean-Jacques 33

The Santaroga Barrier 122, 171n3
savior 17, 116, 118, 125, 137–38, 156; *see also* hero; messiah
A Scanner Darkly 107
science, definition 13–15
science fiction: definition 1, 4–10; hard SF 53, 54, 165n1; history 1, 8–10; soft SF 53, 165n1
The Sleeper Wakes 32, 40, 163n23, 164n38
social Darwinism 15, 21, 30, 31, 32, 33; *see also* Spencer, Herbert

The Soul of a Bishop 165n45
Space Odyssey series 1, 16, 55, 57, 58, 59, 63, 68, 76–77, 78, 79–81, 82–83, 154, 166n10; *see also 2001: A Space Odyssey*; *2010: Odyssey Two*; *2061: Odyssey Three*; *3001: The Final Odyssey*
Spencer, Herbert 21, 22, 30–31, 32, 33, 49, 165n40; *see also* social Darwinism
Stapledon, Olaf 70, 163n29; *Last and First Men* 70, 163n29; *Star Maker* 70
Star Maker 70
Star Wars 155–57
Stranger in a Strange Land 125, 172n11
Suvin, Darko 7, 88, 93, 160n10, 161n3, 162n5, 162n10, 167n6, 168n18, 169n25
Szasz, Thomas 128, 130, 135, 148

The Three Stigmata of Palmer Eldritch 88, 90, 91, 92–93, 96, 102, 103–04, 106–08, 109, 113, 115
3001: The Final Odyssey 58, 59, 64, 73, 81, 83, 84, 85; *see also Space Odyssey* series
The Time Machine 16, 20–21, 30, 32–33, 51, 66, 166n13
Time Out of Joint 168n11, 169n27
transcendence 47, 49, 54–55, 56, 63–65, 68, 69–70, 71, 75, 76, 77, 78–80, 81, 82–83, 84, 85, 104, 105, 106, 117, 124, 134–35, 136, 141, 146, 147, 150, 153, 154, 161n20, 165n1
The Transmigration of Timothy Archer 169n34
Turing, Alan 54, 59–60, 61; *see also* materialism; mechanism
2001: A Space Odyssey 16, 55, 56, 57, 60–61, 63–64, 66, 67, 68, 69, 70, 76, 78, 79–80, 82, 83, 84, 154, 166n9, 166n10; *see also Space Odyssey* series
2010: Odyssey Two 56, 58, 60, 64, 69, 74, 80, 81, 82; *see also Space Odyssey* series
2061: Odyssey Three 81; *see also Space Odyssey* series

Ubik 88, 89, 91, 100–02, 103, 109–13, 114, 116, 169n30, 169n35
The Undying Fire 165n45

VALIS 89, 90, 91, 98, 99, 102, 103, 107, 111, 113, 114–16, 117–20, 167n4, 167n6, 169n6, 170n37
vitalism 1, 16, 53–56, 57, 61–64, 69–71, 78–79, 153–54; *see also* Bergson, Henri; Descartes, René; Haldane, J. B. S

Wallace, Alfred Russel 14, 54, 77, 153–54, 161n2
The War of the Worlds 20, 164n38
Wells, H. G. 1, 4, 5, 8, 13, 15–17, 19–52, 65, 66, 72, 86, 90, 125, 140, 150, 153, 154, 155, 157, 159n3, 159n4, 160n10, 167n27, 168n12; *Anticipations* 24, 29, 34, 48; *Boon, The Mind of the Race, The Wild Asses of the Devil, and The Last Trump* 26, 165n41; *The First Men in the Moon* 163n25; *The Food of the Gods* 35, 39–40, 48, 51, 161n1, 162n13, 164n32; *God the Invisible King* 22, 41, 49–52, 165n41, 167n27; *In the Days of the Comet* 16, 21, 24, 27–28, 34, 35, 46, 47–48, 50, 51, 162n15, 165n39; *The Invisible Man* 161n1; *The Island of Doctor Moreau* 16, 19, 20, 21, 29–30, 35–36, 41–44, 51, 163n24, 164n37; *Joan and Peter; The Story of an Education* 165n45; *Love and Mr. Lewisham* 24; *Men Like Gods* 46; *A Modern Utopia* 16, 21, 22, 24, 25, 31, 34, 35, 37–39, 42, 44, 46–48, 51–52, 162n13, 164n31; *Mr. Britling Sees It Through* 165n45; *The Sleeper Wakes* 32, 40, 163n23, 164n38; *The Soul of a Bishop* 165n45; *The Time Machine* 16, 20–21, 30, 32–33, 51, 66, 166n13; *The Undying Fire* 165n45; *The War of the Worlds* 20, 164n38
Woolf, Virginia 24

Xenophanes 104, 109 *sees also* Presocratics

Zelazny, Roger 125; *Lord of Light* 125

www.ingramcontent.com/pod-product-compliance
Ingram Content Group UK Ltd.
Pitfield, Milton Keynes, MK11 3LW, UK
UKHW042011140426
5217IPUK00015B/1104